COMPUTERS AND READING

*Lessons from the Past
and the Technologies of the Future*

Ernest Balajthy

*State University of New York
at Geneseo*

Prentice Hall, Englewood Cliffs, New Jersey 07632

LIBRARY OF CONGRESS
Library of Congress Cataloging-in-Publication Data

Balajthy, Ernest.
    Computers and reading : lessons from the past and the technologies
 of the future / Ernest Balajthy.
        p.   cm.
    Bibliography: p.
    Includes index.
    ISBN 0-13-166562-6
    1. Language arts--Computer-assisted instruction. 2. Reading-
 -Computer-assisted instruction. 3. Language arts--Computer
 programs.   I. Title.
 LB1576.7.B35 1989
 428.4'07'8--dc19   88-4129
                                                            CIP

To the Reading Program Faculty at the
Rutgers University Graduate School of Education,
1974-1982:

Martin Kling, my valued mentor
Edward B. Fry
Josephine S. Goldsmith
Joseph Zelnick

Cover design: Photo Plus Art
Manufacturing buyer: Margaret Rizzi/Peter Havens

Printed in the United States of America

10 9 8 7 6 5 4 3 2 1

ISBN 0-13-166562-6

Prentice-Hall International (UK) Limited, *London*
Prentice-Hall of Australia Pty. Limited, *Sydney*
Prentice-Hall Canada Inc., *Toronto*
Prentice-Hall Hispanoamericana, S.A., *Mexico*
Prentice-Hall of India Private Limited, *New Delhi*
Prentice-Hall of Japan, Inc., *Tokyo*
Simon & Schuster Asia Pte. Ltd., *Singapore*
Editora Prentice-Hall do Brasil, Ltda., *Rio de Janeiro*

CONTENTS

PART IV—*Artificial Intelligence and Reading*

PREFACE

Karen Blixen, in her memoirs of the colonial days in British East Africa, *Out of Africa* (1980), recounts the story of an acquaintance, a Swedish professor who was enamored of the new anthropological theories. He was determined to investigate the relationship of man and monkey. He proposed to do so by shooting 1,500 Colobus monkeys at Mount Elgon on the Uganda-Kenya border, in order to investigate the thumb development of their fetuses.

Without comment, Blixen noted that the colonial government's response to the anthropologist's proposals was to raise his hunting quota from four monkeys to six. She went on to describe a conversation with the anthropologist, who was a skeptic, as were many of the natural scientists of his day.

> In the course of our debates about the monkeys he enlightened me upon various facts and developed many of his ideas to me. One day he said: "I will tell you of a highly interesting experience of mine. Up at Mount Elgon, I found it possible to believe for a moment in the existence of God, what do you think of that?"

Here Blixen could not refrain from describing her reaction to the professor's egocentric perspective:

> I said that it was interesting, but I thought: There is another interesting question which is: Has it been possible to God, at Mount Elgon, to believe for a moment in the existence of Professor Landgreen? (p. 237)

As with poor Professor Landgreen, we educators get ourselves into trouble when we lose our sense of perspective. We spend far too much time looking for the answers to our problems. We react to the problems that beset us. We let those problems set our agendas.

Instead, we need to sit back and consider. Where do we want to go? What are our ultimate objectives? What kind of children do we want our children to be, and what kind of teachers do we want to be? These questions are often asked, but the answers are almost invariably clichéd, shallow, ill-considered. We need to set aside more time to contemplate the ultimate concerns of our philosophies before we go charging off to implement the latest educational methodologies.

Sproul (1986) tells the story of attending a parent-teacher night at his youngster's preschool. The superintendent explained in detail how each minute aspect of the school's curriculum had been developed in order to achieve specific objectives. Yes, children played with puzzles in school—but that activity was not "simple" play. It had measurable objectives for perception, fine motor coordination, and so forth.

Finally, after a comprehensive overview of the curriculum, the superintendent asked the parents if there were any questions. Their first reaction was awestruck silence. No one could think of any questions after such a thorough and professional presentation.

Then Sproul raised his hand. "I am impressed with your curriculum," he complimented the superintendent. "You and your teachers have been thorough in planning the details of my child's schooling. But I'd like to ask one thing: How does all this fit into your ultimate goals? What kind of children do you want to graduate from your school?"

The superintendent thought for a bit, then admitted that he had never been asked the question before, and that he was unprepared to give an answer.

Before we can begin to use computers effectively to achieve our goals, we will need to know what those goals are. One of my purposes in writing this book was to investigate some of the ways in which computer-based education's cart has been assigned a place in front of reading/language arts education's horse. Yet neither computers nor literacy is an ultimate goal in the search for what humankind should be: We teachers must spend more time thinking about our place—and our children's place—in the cosmos.

A second purpose in writing this book—and I hope in your reading it—was to think about the relationship of computer-based methods to reading/language arts education. A surprising number of people outside the teaching profession have accepted as fact that computer-based education is better than traditional methods. They are shocked when I disagree. After all, they've heard it from journalists on TV and in the newspapers—it must be true, mustn't it?

Well, as you will find in this book, the answer is not quite so simple. Few answers in education or psychology are simple—a phenomenon that constantly perplexes and sometimes discourages the undergraduate and graduate education majors with whom I work. Computers are still new to educational applications. Research in computer-based instruction is still in its infancy. We are far from final answers. In fact, we are still looking for the correct questions to ask!

My third purpose in writing this book has to do with the impact of cognitive psychology and the newer technologies on future prospects of reading instruction. The issues involved in this field cut to the heart of human concerns: Who am I? What am I? How does my mind work? What is the relation of mind to soul and consciousness? How do I learn? How does what I learn change me?

Computer modeling of cognitive operations such as reading and writing—use of natural language—has begun to give us some answers to these questions. The answers are tentative, and even now many of the firm conclusions drawn in the early days of cognitive science (that is, ten years ago) have been challenged and rejected. No doubt the same fate awaits most psychological findings of the past decade.

Yet there is the excitement of the hunt, even if final answers evade our generation of psychological researchers and theorists. Today it is only the tiniest bits and pieces of research findings that fit together to form a tentative answer to our inner cognitive puzzles. Still, one can feel some part of Johannes Kepler's (1571–1630) enthusiasm when, after years of searching, he finally determined the laws of planetary movements:

> I give myself over to my rapture. The die is cast. Nothing I have ever felt before is like this. I tremble, my blood leaps. God has waited six thousand years for a looker-on to his work. His wisdom is infinite, that of which we are ignorant is contained in him, as well as the little that we know.

Yet how much greater in complexity is the human mind than the planetary cycles? And, as Huey (1908) suggested in the early days of reading research, when we understand reading, we will understand the human mind.

My fourth reason for writing stems from a concern that my earlier Prentice Hall textbook, *Microcomputers in Reading and Language Arts* (1986a), an introduction to the topic, left much unsaid. This earlier text provided an up-to-date introduction to computer applications in the major skill and concept areas in reading and writing. I was not able to include more advanced topics of interest to many teachers, such as those in Chapters 1 through 4 of the present volume. I was also unable to discuss the "cutting edge" topics of interest to serious students of educational computer applications, such as artificial intelligence and its implications for the classroom. This present text provides a vehicle for presenting information about these critical topics.

1

USING COMPUTERS TO INTEGRATE READING AND WRITING

In recent years, teachers have increasingly realized the importance of a holistic, integrative approach to the language arts. While integrative language arts methods received attention in the past (Allen 1976; F. Smith 1978), recently they have attracted even more widespread attention among reading teachers. Many reading teachers now commonly include significant amounts of in-class writing, often in response to readings, instead of focusing solely on reading skills.

The importance of integrating instruction in reading and writing lies primarily in the message such integration communicates to students: Instruction in the basic language skills has the common purpose of improving meaningful communication among human beings. Rather than segmenting the various language skills into discrete lessons, comtemporary research suggests that the four basic skills of reading, writing, listening, and speaking merit increased integration within the classroom. Athey (1983) noted that all four skills share a common foundation: "The common root, and hence the reason for the interdependence among the four aspects of language, lies in the search for meaning" (p. 197).

The purpose of this chapter is to describe one particular type of software and its implications for reading-writing integration. Story-creation software provides structured experiences in which children can creatively share meaningful communications with others. Children work cooperatively to develop stories using the software. To complete the writing process cycle, the "published" versions of the students' stories are made available in the classroom library for reading by other children.

PRACTICAL PROBLEMS FOR LANGUAGE ARTS INTEGRATION

A key method for achieving reading-writing integration in the classroom has to do with encouraging students to act as an audience, rather than simply as authors. That is, the teacher establishes the meaningfulness of student writing by creating an audience within the class for composition. Writings may be published in a classroom newspaper, for instance, or bound in cardboard covers as additions to the classroom library. Peer response groups are often formed to give feedback on style and content of written work.

Experience in observing a variety of classroom settings in which peer involvement in reading compositions and creative writings is encouraged by the teachers has indicated what seems to be a universal problem: Motivation on the part of students for reading their peers' creations is lacking. Few students are at all interested in reading the stories of other students. Classroom teachers recognize this problem, and as a result they often avoid even experimenting with the method.

Teachers can take a number of steps toward solution of the problem. First, they themselves must be convinced of the possibilities inherent in the method. Their enthusiasm in encouraging students to interact will in turn convince the students of the importance of peer responses. A variety of researchers have drawn attention to the realization that language is first and foremost a social event (Vygotskii 1978; Harste, Woodward, & Burke 1984). Teacher guidance is crucial in reestablishing the interactive, social nature of writing.

Second, teachers should realize that this method involves a long-term attitudinal change on the part of students. Most children have been trained to believe that the teacher is the only appropriate audience for their written work. A change to the recognition of the importance of peer evaluation cannot be made in a day—it will more likely take months for the readjustment to occur.

Third, if student writing is to attract an enthusiastic peer audience, care must be taken to choose topics and discourse types that are interesting and involving. Sonnets motivate few students; concrete poetry or limericks may succeed. Essays will not provoke as positive a response as horror or mystery stories. Teachers can initiate an emphasis on peer response with high-interest activities and gradually build toward greater sophistication.

A fourth and final suggestion is that students should be held accountable for their work in providing responses to their peers. They should be given guidance as to what kinds of responses are helpful, and positive behaviors should be rewarded. Teacher modeling of feedback and use of stylistic checklists (Calkins 1986) to aid student analysis are both essential.

THE COMPUTER AS A SOLUTION

Reading and Writing Integration via Computer

Using computers to teach reading will not change the basic way children find success in learning to read. The most important principle of learning to read is simple. It does not require teachers with years of experience. It does not require reading specialists for tutorial instruction. It does not require expensive sets of instructional materials.

The basic principle of learning to read can be summed up in the phrase: Spend a lot of time reading.

It's as simple as that. Of course, well-trained and dedicated teachers are vitally important. Excellence in reading materials is motivational and a key factor. A well-constructed foundation of word-recognition skill development is crucial. The most important thing you can do for children in furthering their reading ability, however, is to encourage them to spend time reading.

Teachers and parents are often tempted to pass this off as obvious. Of course, they say, that's true, but let's get on to the really important things about teaching our children to read.

This is the really important thing. Anything one can do on the computer that encourages a child to spend time reading will be important. Children today read little. Adolescents read even less. Largely as a result, test scores across the country have been falling. If all teachers motivated their children to read just a half-hour a day in their spare time, reading ability test scores would skyrocket (Leinhardt, Zigmond, & Cooley 1981).

One more general principle of reading instruction is important to mention at this point. Reading ability is related to the child's general ability in dealing with language. Children who write well tend to read well, and vice versa. As much as possible, reading activities should include some writing (Bereiter & Scardamalia 1984).

How can these two key principles be put together as children work on the computer? Teachers can pay special attention to software that meets the demands of both. Schools should choose programs that involve interesting reading-related activities and that have the child both read and write (Anderson-Inman 1987).

The importance of constructing a meaningful, language-rich environment in the classroom using computers is sometimes described in terms of creating a "functional learning environment." In such an environment, the meaningful function involved in children's activities dominates the academic objectives. For example, writing activities have the stated academic objective of improving writing ability. Writing drills focused on this academic objective dominate instruction in many classrooms.

In schools that use the *QUILL* microcomputer writing system or *The Newsroom*, however, children are engaged in writing a classroom newspaper using the word-processing, planning, and electronic mail functions of the program. In such an environment, the meaningful project involved in constructing the newspaper dominates the activities and gives children a sense of purpose (L. Miller in press; Rubin & Bruce 1984). The basic academic objectives are achieved, but they are achieved in a setting that communicates the real purpose of writing-communication.

A variety of techniques are being used to provide this sense of purpose to microcomputer reading-writing activities. These activities offer teachers the ability to carry out reading-writing lessons based on a holistic, language-experience approach to development of language skills.

Word-Processing Technology

One of the most exciting innovations in microcomputer applications in education has been the use of word-processing software to encourage and facilitate children's writing (Balajthy 1986a; Daiute 1986; Miller 1985). Word processors such as *Bank Street Writer* and *The Milliken Word Processor* pioneered efforts to provide text-editing technology appropriate for use with children. Today, a wide variety of programs are satisfactory for use with intermediate grade—and sometimes even younger—children.

The microcomputer serves as a unique solution to the problem of student interest in peer-constructed writings. Students today react positively to almost any microcomputer activity, perhaps linking the activity in their minds with electronic video games. This advantage can be put to use in enhancing the reading-writing connection, rather than simply using the microcomputer as an expensive (albeit motivational and effective) replacement for a drill book. Using microcomputers in this important language arts context also helps illustrate to students the important role of computers as communication devices.

The basis of reading-writing integration in the classroom is the word processor. Word-processing software enables microcomputers to work like typewriters, with some important extra functions. Writers can enter text into the computer and use the DELETE key for simple corrections. Text can be edited at any time, using sequences of keyboard commands for inserting new words, deleting old words, or moving paragraphs from one section to another. The written product can be stored in electromagnetic form on an inexpensive plastic diskette, to be retrieved at any time for editing or printing on paper.

Despite the relatively recent appearance of word processors in the classroom, an impressive body of research has already been carried out on their effectiveness:

- Students are motivated to produce greater amounts of text than by using pen and paper (Daiute 1982, 1986; Piper 1983; Simon 1984).
- Students revise more when using a word processor (Daiute 1983). A

later study (Daiute 1986) found that students may follow different strategies in revising when using a word processor than when recopying in pen and ink.

- Students edit more carefully when using word processors, resulting in fewer errors (Daiute 1986).

- While simple use of the word processor may not automatically improve writing ability (Hansen & Wilcox 1984), its use in conjunction with prompting, instruction, and feedback can (Collier 1983; Daiute 1986). As Scholes and Comley (1981) have warned, "The way to write better is to write more—but not alone, not aimlessly, not without guidance and encouragement" (p. vii.).

- The limited amount of text allowable on a monitor screen may create visual/spatial problems that hinder writers from getting an overall view of their compositions. Teachers may want to encourage students to use hard copy for some revising tasks (Haas & Hayes 1986).

- Teacher enthusiasm for the use of word processors is largely based on increased student motivation for writing (Piper 1983; Rodriguez 1984), ease of revision (Bean 1983), and its career-educational importance, as word processors are becoming standard equipment in business offices.

Adventure Story Creation

More recently, software packages have been published that incorporate word-processing technology into story-creation programs. These packages allow children to create their own stories and reports. The end result of such activities is the development of a classroom disk library of stories that can be read and reread for years to come.

One new program that capitalizes on the key principles of motivating reading and encouraging reading-writing integration is called *Story Tree*. *Story Tree* is based on the choose-your-ending type of story that has been popular with children for the past several years. In a choose-your-ending story, the child reads a page, then is presented with a variety of options. For example, in a story about pirates, the page might end with the following:

```
Suddenly, a voice cried out, "Ship ahoy! She's fly-
     ing the skull-and-crossbones!"
```

Readers are then presented with several options. For each option, they are directed to turn to a different page that will describe the outcome of the choice.

```
What should the captain do next?
```

1. Raise more sail and try to run away. (Turn to page 50.)
2. Turn about and arm the cannons. (Turn to page 51.)

3. Raise the white flag to surrender. (Turn to page 52.)

On these pages, different options are again presented. Children usually look through each of the options as they read the book, exploring the variety of possible outcomes. Quite a few choose-your-ending books are available in bookstores. If the children are not familiar with the style of such books, it would be helpful to buy some for the classroom library before using *Story Tree*. Purchasing a number of such books for your classroom library would be an important elaborative activity for following up on using *Story Tree*.

Story Tree allows youngsters to create their own choose-your-ending stories with the help of the computer. The package comes with several sample stories included. All stories created by the children can be stored on formatted disks and read as often as desired. Children love to read their own writing. Story disks created by children can be shared by all in the classroom, so the *Story Tree* activities combine both reading and writing. In addition, children should be encouraged to expand upon stories they've already created, adding new plot elements and characters in an ongoing project.

Adventure story creation programs such as *Story Tree* are complex. A child cannot be expected to be able to turn the computer on and figure out how to work it. Close attention to the printed directions is required. Ten- or 11-year-olds will need an adult to teach them how to use the program for an hour or two before they are able to work on their own. Younger children will need a constant adult presence in order to use the program. The best idea with young children is to have them dictate their stories as an adult types. Students in junior high school ought to be able to study the documentation and learn to use *Story Tree* independently.

While the commands are slightly complicated, the function of the program is fairly easy to describe. The top of the screen display is allotted to the story. The bottom of the screen page describes the options.

As the morning wore on, the wind picked up, filling the sails and increasing our speed westward. The crew went about its daily routine, scrubbing decks and making the dozens of necessary small repairs to sails and woodwork. The captain strolled about the deck, inspecting the boat and its crew.

Suddenly a voice cried out, "Ship ahoy! She's flying the skull-and-crossbones!"

What should the captain do next?
1. Raise more sail and try to run away.
2. Turn about and arm the cannons.
3. Raise the white flag to surrender.

Story writers build their stories in screen pages. Each page contains some text. Most also contain options. The writers are able to direct the program from each option choice to specific screen pages. That is, when the reader chooses option 1, the program moves to a specific screen page that will describe what happens if the ship tries to sail away from the pirates. If the reader chooses option 2, another screen page is displayed and the story moves in a different direction.

Story Tree lends itself to creative reading-writing integration. It is particularly effective in teaching students story structure. It requires a real time commitment on the part of the teacher, but the benefits in terms of making the important connection between reading and writing can be great.

That's My Story is structured much like *Story Tree*. Readers move through a series of frames that present story parts. At the end of each frame, the reader is presented two choices as to how she or he would like the story to proceed. *That's My Story* is more structured than *Story Tree*, in that the latter allows a great deal more flexibility. In *Story Tree*, not all frames end in choices, the computer can be ordered to make certain choices, and more than two choices can be made. With the decrease in flexibility in *That's My Story* comes increased ease of story creation, however. A computer user experienced in word processing can figure out most of the directions without referring to the user's manual. As a result, *That's My Story* is appropriate for younger children and requires less teacher monitoring than *Story Tree*.

In *That's My Story*, stories may be stored on formatted disks. Another component of the program that will help younger children is the "story starters" included. These are short introductory passages that start the young writers off on a story. They are provided the beginning of the story, then construct their own events for the rest of the story. The program comes with 40 story starters, and more can be added by the teacher or students if desired.

The *PlayWriter* series consists of four disks, purchased separately, entitled *Adventures in Space, Tales of Me, Mystery!*, and *Castles & Creatures*. Each involves students in story creation. The title is a bit misleading, as the final product is a story, not a play. The *Mystery!* disk, for example, offers students a choice of four stories to create.

The story creation process involves a high amount of structure. Much of the work is done by choosing options from a multiple-choice listing. For example, after originating a character's name (Sam Sneed), the student is offered the following screen page:

```
Your story opens with Sam Sneed arriving at the
    detective agency feeling:

  1. As sharp as a tack.
  2. Bored and wishing a good case would come up.
  3. Exhausted from a wild night on the town.
  4. Other.
```

If the student chooses 1, 2, or 3, that phrase would simply be added to the prior part of the story. Choosing option 4 allows the student to write his or her own phrase to fit the end of the sentence.

Similar situations and options are presented, one following the other. At some points in the story, students are presented the option of writing some paragraphs to, for instance, describe one of the characters.

At the end of the session, the computer organizes all the inputs, both those chosen by multiple choice and those written by the student, into a cohesive story and allows the story to be printed out in hard copy.

The Writing Adventure is based on use of a word processor that is similar to typical word processors such as *AppleWorks* and *The Milliken Word Processor*. The other program components in *The Writing Adventure* serve to complement the word processor by providing a series of structured activities to engage students in the writing process by creating an adventure story. These components are particularly effective when dealing with students who have difficulty developing ideas for their stories.

The program consists of two major components. The *Story Starter* component provides a series of illustrated adventures for characters chosen by the student and thought-provoking questions. These ideas are then used as the basis for *Story Writer*, the word processor, with which students write their own adventure story. Only one basic story line is included in *Story Starter*, but it involves many option choices, like a choose-your-ending story, so that it can provide the foundation for many writing experiences if desired.

Story Starter serves as a prewriting experience in which students are presented ideas and make initial plans for writing. In *Story Starter*, students choose a character on whom the adventure will be centered. This character is placed in a variety of situations, each of which is illustrated by a high-resolution graphic and a short description. The student must then take some notes on the situation in preparation for writing. If necessary, the student can request a series of questions for help in taking the notes. The notes are typed onto the screen, using a simple word processor, and stored on disk for future reference. They can be printed in hard copy if desired.

For example, the story might start with a picture of a cave and the following sentences:

```
Elrond discovers the entrance to a cave. He enters
    the cave hoping to find adventure and excite-
    ment.
```

Students are then asked questions:

```
Where is this cave located?

What was Elrond doing when he discovered the cave?

What did Elrond expect to find inside the cave?
```

They write answers in the form of notes. These notes are available to them as they write the first draft of their story, using the word processor on the *Story Writer* disk.

Story Writer contains one of the first grammar- and style-checking programs developed for use in the classroom. These programs (see Balajthy 1986a, in press a, for a detailed description) analyze word processor text files for possible errors. In *Story Writer*, for example, the student's composition is analyzed for style, commonly misused words, troublesome verbs, adjectives, adverbs, and pronouns, and punctuation. Checkers such as this are not actually able to spot errors—they simply indicate possible trouble spots.

For example, the overuse of "to be" verbs in compositions is a frequent stylistic weakness (or this sentence might be better written, "Students frequently overuse *to be* verbs). The style checker component of *Story Starter* indicates to the writers each use of a *to be* verb in their stories, offers the rule ("*Be* verbs are weak verbs even when used as helpers with action verbs. Can you think of a more descriptive verb to use than *was*?"), and gives some examples. The writers then have the opportunity to reconsider their use of the verb *was* and to rewrite the sentences.

Student-created stories are stored on formatted blank disks. Students may reenter the story creation program at any point in time, as all results are saved on disk.

Illustrated Stories

Several programs are now available that allow students to create stories using the computer screen for display, then illustrate the stories by using high-resolution graphics.

Scholastic's *Story Maker: A Fact and Fiction Tool Kit* is one of these programs designed to encourage the integration of reading and writing activities. Students are able to construct illustrated screen pages of text that can be displayed in sequence on the computer monitor to form stories or essays. One important advantage of this particular program is that students need not draw their own pictures. High-resolution graphics are stored on picture disks that accompany the program. These can be automatically placed in any position desired on the students' screen pages. The use of these predrawn pictures can save a great deal of student time in constructing illustrations to accompany their stories. They also offer a solution to the problem of those students who want to use graphics but lack artistic ability.

Students will find creation of the story pages fairly easy. The background may be colored by choosing a color from one of the picture disks. Three disks of high-resolution pictures accompany Scholastic's *Story Maker*: a general topics disk, a science fiction disk, and a fantasy disk. Picture items are chosen from a menu page. For example, if the student wants to draw a forest scene, he or she uses the joystick to position the cursor over the picture of the forest on the menu page. Clicking the cursor button transfers the monitor screen to the picture page on which the student is creating the illustration. By using the joystick, he or she can position the cursor at any point on the page and click the button to automatically "stamp" the forest scene onto the picture page at that position.

After completing the graphics in this fashion, students type the words of their story onto the picture page. They position the cursor at the spot where they want to begin typing, press the cursor button, then type normally. The program has a limited built-in word processor that makes typing simple. Many editing functions typical of more sophisticated word processors are missing, however, and corrections are awkward to make once the text has been typed.

The documentation notes that the program allows students "to share their writing with others and to write for others with great security. By becoming 'published' authors, they also become more sensitive and appreciative toward professional authors" (p. 25). Certainly this program is ideal for encouraging student writers to develop a sense of audience, a vital realization that gives students a purpose for writing. Stories are stored on formatted blank disks. As many data disks of stories as desired may be created and stored in a classroom library or traded with other classes.

A variety of existing story creation programs allow students to draw their own high-resolution pictures to illustrate their stories, including Sierra On-Line's *Story Maker* and *Bank Street Story Book*. Scholastic's *Story Maker* also has a drawing option to complement its disk library of predrawn pictures. The graphics creation packages in these programs are primitive in comparison with most computer drawing programs. Students use their joysticks to draw lines by moving a cursor on the monitor screen. But, as anyone who has used this outmoded technique can attest, most would-be artists can create only the crudest of drawings with a joystick. Using an electronic drawing pad allows for faster and better artwork.

Suggestions for Use of Story Creation Software

1. Encourage team creation of stories for increased peer feedback and interaction. Allowing students to cooperate also results in students working together to solve low-level "how-to-do-it" problems.
2. Facilitate the reading-writing connection by having students read each other's creations. Keep a class library of story diskettes and make this reading part of the regular classroom program.
3. Have students make additions to stories created by other students. By chaining together story disks (for example, including directions at points within the story to go on to other disks that continue the story), teachers can make the creation of a superlarge story into a month-long project.
4. Present the program's operational directions to the entire class in a demonstration. Wagner, O'Toole, and Kazelskis (1985) found that instructor demonstration of word-processing program operation to classes resulted in more writing and better motivation than either independent study of the manual or a simple lecture by the instructor.
5. Pretrain student assistants or teacher aides to provide help as students begin working on the program. These can handle the frequent low-level questions about program operation.

6. Allow those students who develop deep interest to continue using the program indefinitely—in place of other projects or for extra credit. Teachers may well find that the excitement about writing and the practice in the skill will result in better achievement than turning students' attention back to grammar and spelling drills.

7. Copy the file disks that contain student-created stories, and trade with other classes and other schools through the mail. Some files may even be traded, using modems and electronic mail systems. Most programs produced to date, however, do not handle the story files in a way that would be amenable to sending through electronic mail.

8. Assign your students to create stories for younger children. Then set aside a day in which your students read their stories to the younger ones.

9. If computer time is scarce due to lack of facilities in your classroom, have students write out the stories in longhand first, then enter them into the computer. This helps avoid confusing students by overloading them with demands for typing ability, knowledge of the word processor commands, and creativity all at the same time.

10. Be careful about confusing your students by using more than one of these programs. Unfortunately, different command systems for each program can be bothersome. Software publishers have not worked out a standardized system in which, for example, the same commands would be used in the publisher's word processor as in the story creation programs.

11. Some of the programs require far more time to draw computer graphics than will be used in the more productive writing work. Any program in which children spend 5 minutes writing for every 45 minutes of drawing shapes on the computer screen must be critically examined.

12. Do not assume that simple use of word processors or word-processing story creation programs will automatically improve language skills. The teacher's critique and constant monitoring of production remain vital. Graves's (1976) work with the development of the writing process has shown that adults must work with students during writing rather than waiting until after the writing is finished.

Story Creation for Younger Readers

The limited vocabulary of beginning readers allows software designers greater freedom in terms of programming the software to understand and respond appropriately to story writing. In this software, such as the *Story Machine* program (described in detail in Ch. 11, "Natural Language for Reading Instructional Software," and in Balajthy 1986a), children type sentences into the computer to form stories. As words are typed, characters appear on the screen and act out the actions. In *Story Machine*, for example, the sentence THE BOY WALKS TO THE HOUSE produces high-resolution figures of a boy and a house. The boy then is animated to walk across the screen to the house.

Another program that functions in similar fashion is *Kermit's Electronic Storymaker*. In this program, the actions are acted out by characters from "The Muppets" TV show.

This program is designed to allow prereaders or beginning readers to have fun creating their own animated stories. The program is for the purpose of story creation and reading. It does not provide direct instruction. Rather, it is designed to provide children with exposure to words and sentences, illustrating their meanings, by using popular Muppet characters and easily recognizable situations and actions.

A series of blanks are provided at the top of the monitor screen. The child moves the cursor to the first blank, using a joystick or the keyboard. The child can fill in the blank by pressing the RETURN key to see a variety of words or phrases. Each is illustrated, and some have sound accompaniment. When the choice is made, the child goes on to the second blank, and so forth. All choices are grammatically correct, though many are silly ("delightfully absurd," in the words of the accompanying manual).

Children do not use the keyboard to type words. All appear automatically as the RETURN key is pressed. A variety of sentence forms are available, from simple three-part sentences (such as THE MONSTER SWIMS IN SPACE) to more complex constructions (such as IN THE DESERT, FOZZIE WALKS, THE CLOCK RINGS).

Tinker Tales provides a more structured approach to story creation by children. Its format is much like the choose-your-own-ending stories described above. Several story outlines are provided from which to choose. At crucial points in the story, children can choose from several branches. Stories can be re-created over and over, with a wide variety of possible routes through the story tree. As with *Story Machine* and *Kermit's Electronic Storymaker*, the characters and actions in the stories are animated on the monitor screen.

READING AS MICRO COMPOSITION

Tierney and Pearson (1983) have written an article entitled "Toward a Composing Model of Reading" in which they suggest that the reading process is much like the composition process. Reading is not passive. Participants in both reading and writing actively construct personal meaning. For the writer, that meaning is constructed for the purpose of communication and/or self-expression. For the reader, that meaning is constructed for the purpose of understanding and/or learning.

As software developers have considered moving beyond limited programmed computer-assisted instruction (CAI) software, they have begun to see the possibilities in encouraging this active construction process among readers. While the story creation programs described earlier certainly can evoke active reading, a variety of programs have been developed to target specific types of creation-thinking among readers. Some require students to complete computer-monitored cloze exercises to enhance sentence-level construction. Others require students to make guesses as to upcoming events in a story, similar to the activities carried out in Stauffer's (1969) popular Directed Reading-Thinking Activity lesson plan format.

The Puzzler is designed to deal with the important reading skill of predict-ing outcomes and confirming strategies. Goodman (1967) called reading a "psycholinguistic guessing game," an ongoing process of making inferences as to relationships and upcoming material. *The Puzzler* attempts to suggest to students the importance of carrying on this conversation with the text.

What kinds of reading exercises most accurately suggest to the student just how reading and learning from text take place? Do multiple-choice recall drills communicate the essence of the mature reading process to our students? Is reading comprehension, in other words, simply a rote process of memoriz-ing facts? Or is reading comprehension far more complex, an interaction of many subprocesses, unified by the mind of the mature reader into an intricate pattern involving access to background knowledge, identification of the rela-tive importance of ideas within text, prediction of upcoming information, inferential relating of concepts within and without the text, and so forth?

Certainly the reading field advocates the latter definition of the reading comprehension process. Rumelhart (1977; Rumelhart, McClelland, & the PDP Research Group 1986), for example, proposed such "interactive" theories of reading. Wittrock (1974) described learning from text as "generative" in nature. That is, readers generate their own meaning structures from what they read, based upon such factors as their background knowledge, their purpose in reading, and the content and organization of the text.

If this is so, it behooves reading teachers to search out methods that encourage "active reading" (Singer 1978) among their students. Readers must learn to actively seek out meaning, rather than passively sitting back as they read, hoping that something will sink in. If the construction of meaning is a function of what happens *during* reading, however, merely testing recall of information *after* reading may be insufficient for real learning about the com-prehension process to occur. In addition, since this construction of meaning is a truly personal process, one that will inevitably vary between individuals, whole-class instruction may not be the most effective method.

The microcomputer offers a unique opportunity to encourage students to view the reading comprehension process as an active search for meaning. In some ways, microcomputers are limited. A computer cannot truly *understand* inputs. As a result, its responses are highly limited (Balajthy 1985, in press b). But computers offer the possibility of providing students with truly individu-alized instruction, within these constraints. The student can be one-on-one with the computer as it responds to personal meaning-constructions based on reading the text.

Several microcomputer programs have become available that are designed to give students experiences in active involvement in reading and constructing meaning from text. The interactive nature of microcomputer instruction—the ability of the micro to respond to student inputs—makes this medium superior to traditional textbooks and drill books in this regard. While certainly a trained human tutor would provide more effective interaction, the microcomputer can serve an important limited function when the software is appropriately designed (Miller & Burnett 1986a).

The creators of *The Puzzler* suggest that their program fosters readers' ability to use three related strategies during reading: predicting, confirming, and integrating. Based on their reading and on their prior background knowledge, mature readers predict words, sentences, and concepts, thereby making the reading process more fluent. These predictions are either confirmed or disconfirmed as reading proceeds. Once confirmed, they are integrated into the reader's knowledge store.

In order to foster these skills, *The Puzzler* presents a story, page by page. After each page, the student is asked an inference question, the answer to which has not been explicitly provided. She or he types in the response and it is recorded on the monitor screen for future reference. The on-disk instructions warn students that there are no single correct answers: "There are many good answers to every puzzle. You can have fun talking about your answers with your friends." As succeeding pages of the story appear, the student is given more clues to the answer. After reading each page, the student is allowed to make more guesses (up to six) as to the correct answer to the inference question and to delete former guesses that have been disconfirmed by new information.

In the story "The Unusual Friend," one of five on the disk, the opening page offers a few clues to the inference question "Who is Fred?"

> It's here! Karla rushed into the house waving a white envelope with a colorful Canadian stamp. This was the big moment!
>
> Tearing open the envelope, her thoughts centered on Fred. Had anything happened to Fred since she left last August? For five summers Fred had been there when she arrived to visit her grandparents. It had been fun watching Fred grow but more exciting having such an unusual friend.

A guess that Fred is a squirrel might, for example, be disconfirmed later in the story when it is found that Fred lives in a marshy area. By the end of the story, the reader has accumulated quite a few facts as to Fred's identity, but the program's authors avoid the temptation to provide any final answer. It is left up to the students to discuss their predictions with one another. While both students and teachers often find the lack of a final answer somewhat frustrating, the message is clearly conveyed that predicting is not an exact process. Different readers take different interpretations away from the text they read.

SOURCES OF INFORMATION

Careful consideration of the theoretical underpinnings of reading and language arts instruction is often lacking in contemporary considerations of computer-based instruction. Each of the following sources on computer-based instruction includes a discussion of the importance of language skill integration in meaningful contexts.

BALAJTHY, ERNEST. 1986. *Microcomputers in Reading and Language Arts.* Englewood Cliffs, NJ: Prentice Hall.
Chapter 8 ("Software: Reading Comprehension") presents a comparative listing of evaluative criteria for two types of software: integrated, holistic, language-based programs and subskill programs. Three key points are included to help teachers choose appropriately between holistic and subskill applications:
1. Use meaningful, natural-language activities unless the situation suggests otherwise.
2. Interweave subskill instruction with holistic activities.
3. Monitor student progress in subskill areas.
Chapter 12 is titled "Activities for Reading and Writing."

MILLER, LARRY, AND J. DALE BURNETT. 1986. "Theoretical Considerations in Selecting Language Arts Software." *Computing Education* 10, no. 1: 159-165.
Two of the developers of *The Puzzler* advocate that teachers closely examine their theoretical beliefs before choosing software. They suggest that many teachers have holistic theories and "see language as a socio-psycholinguistic process with linguistic systems operating interactively rather than linearly" (p. 162). But sometimes these same teachers use linear subskill software exclusively because they have not closely examined the implications of their theories for practice.

RUBIN, ANDEE, AND BERTRAM BRUCE. 1984. "Quill: Reading and Writing with a Microcomputer." Reading Education Report no. 48. Urbana: Center for the Study of Reading, University of Illinois.
Rubin and Bruce, who were involved in the development and field-testing of the Quill microcomputer-based writing system, discuss the theoretical implications of a classroom communication environment based on microcomputer technology. Among the goals of a properly administered Quill classroom are the following:
1. Development of planning and critical thinking skills
2. Integration of reading and writing
3. Support for meaningful communication with real audiences
4. Encouragement of writing with and for peers
5. Facilitation of revision.

SOFTWARE REFERENCES

Bank Street Story Book
Mindscape
3444 Dundee Rd.
Northbrook, IL 60062
Apple II series, IBM-PC, Commodore 64

Kermit's Electronic Story Maker
Simon & Schuster Computer Software Division
1230 Ave. of the Americas
New York, NY 10020
Apple II series, Commodore 64

The Newsroom
    Scholastic
    PO Box 7502
    2931 E. McCarty St.
    Jefferson City, MO 65102
    Apple II series

PlayWriter Series
    Woodbury Software
    127 White Oak La. CN 1001
    Old Bridge, NJ 08857
    Commodore 64, Apple series, IBM-PC
    Separate disks for *Adventures in Space, Tales of Me, Mystery!,* and *Castles and Creatures*

Puzzler
    Sunburst Communications
    39 Washington Ave.
    Pleasantville, NY 10570
    Apple II series, IBM-PC, Commodore 64

Quill
    D. C. Heath
    125 Spring St.
    Lexington, MA 02173
    Apple II series

Story Machine
    Spinnaker Software
    215 First St.
    Cambridge, MA 02139
    Apple II series, IBM-PC

Story Maker
    Sierra On-Line
    Coarsegold, CA 93614
    Apple II series

Story Maker: A Fact and Fiction Tool Kit
    Scholastic
    Apple II series

Story Tree
    Scholastic
    Apple II series, IBM-PC, Commodore 64

That's My Story
    Learning Well
    200 South Service Rd.
    Roslyn Heights, NY 11577
    Apple II series

Tinker Tales
    Compu-Teach
    240 Bradley St.
    New Haven, CT 06510
    IBM-PC

The Writing Adventure
    DLM Educational Software
    One DLM Park
    Allen, TX 75002
    Apple II series

2

SECONDARY AND COLLEGE INSTRUCTION

The purpose of this chapter is to suggest ways in which microcomputers can be used to improve instruction in reading, study, and language skills at the secondary and college levels. This chapter first surveys the curriculum of instructional topics that are of importance at this level, including comprehension, general vocabulary development, specialized vocabulary development, study aids, preparation for standardized tests, speed reading, integration of reading and writing, and motivation of students.

The second major section of the chapter deals with training students to use the computer as a tool for the intellect, a device to enhance thinking and learning. Again, a variety of topics are surveyed, including study aids, word processing, composition heuristic programs, and data retrieval and management.

Microcomputer-using reading teachers at the secondary school and college levels are facing the same software shortages encountered by elementary teachers in the early 1980s. Teachers of high schoolers needing remedial instruction can make do with the now abundant software designed for younger students, but there is precious little for older average or advanced readers. Alexander, in her survey of computer use at the developmental college level, was forced to conclude, "In my own view and the views of most of my colleagues, there is not much software currently available" for use by older readers (1984, p. 29).

These shortages result from the lack of two particular types of software: (1) tutorials, which provide direct instruction and offer closely monitored practice with detailed feedback; (2) drill-and-practice programs, which provide for reinforcement and automatic performance. Alexander's (1984) research indicated virtually nothing on the market to provide such instruction to older learners in comprehension and learning-from-text skills.

Even a cursory examination of computer software for older students indicates that traditional study skills and reading textbooks are often of superior quality. The low-level "skill-and-drill" approach used in most of the existing software simply does not prepare students for the analysis and synthesis needed to deal with content-area texts, especially at the college level, nor does it teach effective learning strategies.

Instructors must consider ways that microcomputers can be used today to improve—not simply replace—traditional reading instruction for learners at the secondary and college levels. Rather than waiting for software publishers to develop "reading for the main idea" drills at the twelfth-grade level to replace existing workbooks, instructors ought to take the opportunities provided by developments in the newer electronic learning media to reevaluate their pedagogical philosophies and methods. There is no need to wait for future developments in computer-based learning. Computers already can provide possibilities for helping teachers to meet objectives that are difficult to attain with traditional media.

A key theme running throughout this chapter involves the use of the microcomputer as a tool for learning—what some have called an "intellectual prosthesis." Whether as an aid in organizing study of terminology or of facts and concepts, or as a tool for production of text, the computer serves best in its capacity to act as a device that can cooperate with the human mind to enhance intellectual productivity.

DIRECT INSTRUCTION

Individualized Skill Development

Soll (1984) has noted that there is no agreement on a theoretical base for college developmental curricula, nor is there a close match between what developmental educators profess and what they do. This confusion about the basis of reading instruction for older learners exists at the secondary level as well.

Two valuable principles of reading and writing instruction for older students are the following:

1. The curriculum should stress the process and tools of learning rather than subskill rules about reading and writing.
2. The reading/writing/study skills curriculum must closely match and augment students' content curricula.

Language skills courses at the secondary and college levels in which all students perform the same routine of meaningless subskill drills are burdensome and alienating. As a result, these courses are often seen as irrelevant by both students and administrators.

Sadly, with rapidly expanding availability of subskill drill software, many educators will be tempted to use computers primarily as electronic workbooks. Classes will be assigned isolated drill work that is based on outdated comprehension and writing theories from more than 20 years ago (Anderson, Osborn, & Tierney 1984).

In terms of direct instruction, the real advantage of the computer is its ability to provide for individualization of instruction. Rather than assigning whole classes to particular tutorials or drills that have doubtful transfer value to either real-life or academic reading and writing, educators must rethink the structure of their courses in order to use the capabilities of computers effectively.

Skills teaching required by entire classes is probably best handled in typical teacher-led lectures and discussions. Tutorial and drill software should be chosen for the purpose of individualized, independent work. If a student's compositions indicate a need for subject-verb agreement instruction, then perhaps a tutorial and drill on that skill is called for. If a student has problems reading charts and tables in sociology class, then a tutorial on that skill is appropriate. It is in these individual cases, where a software disk with self-contained instruction can be pulled from the shelf and assigned by the instructor, that the power of the computer to deliver individually targeted instruction and practice is effectively put to use.

Another consideration when dealing with direct instruction by computer at the secondary and college levels has to do with availability of software. Developmental educators have a huge choice of books for the teaching of skills, many of which have been written by experts who have years of experience and study in the field. Superior software designed for older developmental students, on the other hand, is in short supply. A comprehensive survey of college reading software availability carried out by Alexander (1984) indicated that virtually nothing is on the market except for some vocabulary drills. Doyle noted, "There are few software programs which retain the dignity and wholeness of the reading and writing process, and enhance the learning necessary to master this process" (1983, p. 144). The next few years, however, will inevitably see more and more quality software available as developmental education experts turn their attention to its design and as publishers realize the potential market.

Comprehension

The difficulties involved in constructing programs of greater sophistication than the typical multiple-choice drill are discussed in Chapter 11 of this volume. The key problem involves language—the computer's inability to deal effectively with standard language patterns. A computer cannot comprehend, nor can it react intelligently to student comprehension or failure to comprehend.

As a result, most computer materials written to develop comprehension of older students are "page-turner" programs that do little more than place textual material on the screen and provide comprehension tests with immediate feedback on answers. While these "electronic tutors" do not have anything like the sophistication of a human tutor, this questioning is valuable in its own right. It focuses attention on important aspects of reading material and improves comprehension and retention (Anderson & Biddle 1975). If this questioning process can be internalized so that students learn to generate their own questions as they read, active participation in the reading process is enhanced (Singer 1978) and comprehension will continue to improve even without teacher-provided questions (Singer & Donlan 1982; Wong 1985; Balajthy 1986c).

Vocabulary Development

General vocabulary development.   Microcomputer applications for the teaching of vocabulary must be considered critically. While a well-planned sequence of vocabulary development is essential for secondary readers, reading/study skills programs in college also often include a time-consuming vocabulary component. Most such courses do not last long enough for any substantive vocabulary improvement. "The deficiencies accumulated over twelve or more years of elementary and secondary schooling [cannot] be corrected in a single semester" (Richardson, Fisk, & Okun 1983, p. 164).

In addition, except for immediate feedback and motivation, vocabulary software offers few advantages over traditional drill books. Well-designed vocabulary activities that, for instance, teach words in meaningful categories by using techniques similar to semantic mapping or semantic feature analysis can be far superior to today's microcomputer software.

For those instructors who insist on a general vocabulary development component in their course, several programs are available that deal with advanced vocabulary. Most actually drill rather than teach. That is, they offer multiple-choice exercises on the computer screen that require students to match words and definitions. Instruction is not organized according to any meaningful categories. Reinforcement and review are insufficient. The usefulness of such programs for substantial vocabulary gains is as doubtful as playing Trivial Pursuit is for improvement of general background knowledge. When well contructed, however, these programs can be motivating.

For example, *Vocabulary Baseball* is a high-resolution video game. Students compete against each other. Each decides whether to try for a single, double, or triple. Depending on the choice, an easier or more difficult word is given, accompanied by four possible definitions. A correct choice yields a hit.

An incorrect choice gives the batter an out, and the correct definition is displayed. No real teaching is carried out, no organized reviews are offered, and it is doubtful that students will learn much from the unorganized presentation of randomly chosen words, but the game is motivational.

Content-area vocabulary development. One key problem in dealing with older developmental students is that, simultaneously with taking a reading/study skills course, they are struggling for survival in their content-area courses. Most of those courses are introductory in nature, consisting largely of memorizing key names, vocabulary, and concepts. Introductory courses in psychology, for example, deal with many technical terms used by psychologists.

Developmental educators should deal with the vocabulary words students must learn for their content classes. If a student is studying geology, he or she should study geology terminology. If another student needs to memorize the names and characteristics of dozens of trees for a forestry class, she or he should do that. The developmental educator ought to be most interested in teaching the techniques of vocabulary development (and, importantly, supplying the motivation for applying those techniques) rather than specific lists of words. By teaching such techniques through use of vocabulary that the student is required to learn in order to succeed in content-area courses, developmental studies take on new meaning for students and can be motivational.

It is with this kind of vocabulary development—individualized to meet the specific needs of particular students—that computers can be helpful. With traditional forms of instruction, it is difficult and time-consuming to individualize in this manner. The computer can do it effectively, using what is called teacher utility software.

A teacher utility is a special program, or part of a program, that allows teachers (or students) to type their own lists of vocabulary words into the computer. Does a student need to learn a list of 50 terms in behavioral psychology? A teacher utility allows her or him to type those terms and their definitions into the computer program and save them on disk so that they can be used at any time. When ready to study, the student simply loads the vocabulary drill program into the computer, and the program presents the terms necessary to pass behavioral psychology.

Quizit is one such vocabulary drill-game that can be used with older students. The game is based on the general idea behind the TV show "Name That Tune". A contextual sentence is offered:

```
Pavlov's dogs were trained using _____  ___
    conditioning.
```

The student is given the opportunity to select any number of the target word's initial letters to be revealed by the computer. The more letters requested, the easier the word will be to guess, but the fewer the points that will be won.

While the *Quizit* disk contains several built-in lists of words and contextual sentences, the real function of the program is to use lists provided by the computer user, whether it be the teacher or student. A simple command allows entry into the teacher utility subprogram. The user is requested to type the target word, its definition, then a sentence using the word in context. These words and sentences are stored on a diskette. As many files of words and sentences as desired can be created for use with *Quizit*, on an innumerable variety of topics. Words and sentences may be edited and changed at any time.

One effective strategy for using utility programs like *Quizit* is to poll students as to courses in which they are encountering large numbers of technical terms. Students might then be grouped according to course, with all students studying behavioral psychology in one group and all students studying medieval history in another, for example. Their biweekly assignment would be to use the teacher utility in *Quizit* to create a 20-question computer quiz based on the past weeks' terminology. Each member of the group would be required to take all the quizzes constructed by the other members and to provide feedback to the quiz makers on the quality of the questions. This technique is teacher-time effective, as the teacher is not required to spend long hours preparing individualized vocabulary work. It is also highly motivational, for the students see the importance of the vocabulary study and are learning effective techniques for future vocabulary development.

Test Preparation

A common function of secondary and college reading teachers is to provide preparation for standardized tests, such as state basic skills tests, the Scholastic Aptitude Test, or the Graduate Record Examination. Many microcomputer programs designed to teach test-taking skills for the various standardized tests are on the market. Webster (1984) and Mullins (1985) provide comparative listings of available SAT-preparation microcomputer programs.

The chief advantage of such programs is the high motivational power of multiple-choice items presented by the computer, as opposed to presentation in one of the huge, forbidding SAT or GRE preparation books. Few students are motivated to spend much time practicing in such books. Even if the items are simply multiple-choice questions transferred from some book to the computer screen, the computer presentation is more interesting.

Well-designed test-preparation programs will do more than simply give exposure to the types of questions presented on standardized tests. Instruction in analytical techniques for analogies, for example, is a valuable inclusion. Feedback to students must be specific and detailed. Poorly designed programs usually state only the correct answer. They do not explain why it is correct, or else the explanation is sketchy.

The bulk of material in test-preparation programs is often devoted to simple vocabulary drills supposedly designed to improve vocabulary in preparation for the verbal components of the tests. As experienced instructors in

SAT and GRE courses realize, these drills are perhaps the least effective method of teaching vocabulary. Vocabulary improvement is a long-term project. The likelihood is that not a single word studied in the drills will appear on the actual test.

Instruction in test-taking techniques is still best carried out by human instructors who are knowledgeable about the test-taking research. Computer software functions best in administering the tedious drill work necessary for test-taking improvement. As the test date approaches, however, students should use printed books containing practice tests that closely match conditions in the actual examination (Bracey 1985).

Speed-Reading Programs

Everyone wants to learn to speed-read, and these programs are often best-sellers. Earlier programs did little more than flash words and phrases on the computer screen at varying speeds, then administer a multiple-choice comprehension test. Traditional reading machines with accompanying workbooks can perform much the same tasks at a fraction of the price of a computer. Improved speed-reading development programs are now beginning to appear on the market, however (Balajthy 1986a, ch. 9).

MicroSpeedRead, for instance, teaches some basic concepts of speed-reading, such as idea clustering by separating phrase units and Z and S hand-movement patterns. Practice exercises with accompanying comprehension tests are included for speed-reading, skimming, and scanning.

The most valuable of the speed-reading programs are equipped with a utility to allow users to type in their own passages to be read in speed drills. A reading teacher could survey the school's social studies and science textbooks for key passages that could then easily be typed into the computer and permanently stored on disk for future use. Assigning students to do the typing would save a good deal of teacher time.

Integrating Reading and Writing

For some time, some language theorists have suggested that both reading and writing are derived from the same underlying cognitive structures based on oral language development (Goodman 1976; Moffet & Wagner 1983; F. Smith 1975). Educators have more and more begun to recognize the importance of integrating reading and writing instruction (Kennedy 1980; Martin, Martin, & O'Brien 1984; see also Ch. 1 of this volume). Collins (1984), for example, has published an innovative textbook for high-risk college freshmen called *Read, Write, Reflect,* in which the integration of reading, writing, and thinking is encouraged for improved college performance.

Reading teachers, however, may often be ill prepared to capitalize on the benefits of such integration and unaware of integrative methods that are effective in developing the two skills (Nist & Sabol 1984). The increased availability of microcomputers in classrooms can be useful in helping reading teachers to achieve this integration. Increased writing in reading classes can be aided by computer tools in several ways, including use of word-processing software and of direct instructional programs in writing skills.

Word Processing.   Use of word-processing software is the most important application of microcomputers for developmental secondary and college students (Daiute 1983). The word processor enables microcomputers to be used as typewriters, but with important extras. Papers typed into the computer can be saved on disk for later additions and revisions. Typing errors can be spotted on the computer screen and corrected instantly. Spelling-checker software designed to accompany the word processor, such as *Sensible Speller* or *Bank Street Speller*, can be used to check automatically for spelling errors.

Word processors are not simply fancy typewriters, however. Teachers who use word processors with children find that the ease of text entry and correction encourages a qualitatively different attitude toward writing than that achieved with handwritten or typewritten composition work. With these traditional methods, correction of errors is a laborious chore that students avoid. With a word processor, correction of errors on the computer screen is no work at all. Writers become far more willing to engage in the revising and editing processes so important to clear communication and effective writing, and they develop more positive attitudes toward writing (Piper 1983; Rodriguez 1984).

This is not to say, however, that simply making word processors available to students will automatically improve their writing. There has been a tendency in some classes, both at the college level and in grade schools, for writing instruction to be replaced by instruction in the mechanics of word processing—which keys to press to adjust margins or to print double-spaced, for example. There is a clear failing in such instruction. Word processing must supplement writing instruction, not replace it. Teachers must still pay close attention to teaching the writing process, to guiding students and providing feedback. Word processors are simply tools that facilitate student output and encourage students to experiment with language.

This experimentation with language, an approach to written text as fluid rather than as final product, is the key concept that instructors must communicate to their students. When word processors were first introduced into classrooms, many teachers believed that children would naturally carry out such experimentation. After all, they reasoned, it is easy to change a sentence or paragraph to see what an alternative construction might look like. It is easy to move paragraphs to see what a different organizational pattern might do for the composition. Won't all students do this?

After several years of trying out word processing in the classroom, teachers have found that students do *not* automatically engage in such in-depth experimentation (Hansen & Wilcox 1984). While researchers do report a statistically significantly greater amount of writing and revisions by children using word processors than by children using handwriting (Daiute 1982; Piper 1983; Simon 1984), this improvement is often so small as to be of little educational significance. Instead of thoughtful analysis and revision of composition structure, students using word processing often limit their changes to superficial, mechanical alterations.

As a result, "The instructor cannot remain passive and let the students figure out for themselves how they will write on the machines" (Hansen & Wilcox 1984, p. 3). Teachers must target their attention to two factors: modeling the revising process and monitoring student revisions (Balajthy, McKeveny, & Lacitignola 1986, 1986–1987).

First, we shall consider modeling revision. Teachers have long known the importance of modeling the thought processes involved in improving text by revising (Norton 1985). For example, class discussion may focus on the revisions of professional authors, that is, the changes that have been made from the first draft of their manuscripts to published versions of short stories or poems. Other techniques involve projecting student compositions on a screen, using an opaque projector, so the teacher can talk through the thought processes involved in improving early drafts.

Use of a word processor and monitor screens large enough to be visible to all students greatly enhances such instruction. Changes can be made in the text as desired, and the modified text will be readable and neatly printed within seconds. Sections of the text can be easily moved from one part of the composition to another. New paragraphs can be added as quickly as they can be typed into the computer.

Teachers may carry out such modeling in whole-class situations. Compositions to be discussed can be printed out on ditto masters and duplicated for prior reading so that informed discussion takes place and so that students have immediate access to the entire composition rather than being limited to the small portion displayed on the computer monitor screen. Students can also be assigned to work in small peer groups to provide feedback to one another as they gather around a computer and read their compositions. In individual conferences, students can bring their disks so that change can be made instantly on the computer as instructors or tutors provide feedback.

Second is monitoring revision. Feedback is central to successful use of word processors. Secondary students and high-risk college students often lack the language and conceptual sophistication to choose correctly from written alternatives. If the students cannot tell which is the most effective way of making a statement, then they certainly cannot be expected to experiment effectively with language. Simply using the word processor will not suddenly confer linguistic or conceptual knowledge. The teacher's critique and constant monitoring of production remain vital. Graves's (1976) work with the development of the writing process has shown that adults must work with students *during* writing rather than after it has been finished.

Teachers seeking ideas for exercises that employ word-processing revision capabilities can check the manuals that accompany word processors specifically designed for use in the classroom, such as *Milliken's Word Processor* and *Bank Street Writer*. Richards's (1984) book on word-processing activities for the classroom offers many ideas that can be adapted to the secondary and college levels, as does the *Activity Book for the Bank Street Writer*, a workbook (Scholastic 1984).

Third is direct instruction in writing. Some tutorial and drill software is available for dealing with writing needs of secondary and college students. *Sentence Combining*, for example, is an interesting tutorial-drill combination containing a variety of ideas for increasing sentence structure and comprehension sophistication based on research-validated (Piper 1983; Stotsky 1975) techniques for combining shorter sentences into more complex ones. Students choose from lessons dealing with compound subjects and predicates, possessives, relative pronouns, restrictive and nonrestrictive clauses, infinitive phrases, and so forth. The advantage of the sentence-combining technique is that students do not simply study the theory behind parts of speech and of sentences. They are actively involved in using the theory and rules to construct sentences.

For those instructors who wish to use workbook-like subskill tutorial software for individualized teaching of grammar and usage, a variety of comprehensive programs are available. *English Achievement I-V* (Microcomputer Workshops) is designed specifically to prepare students for the College Entrance Examination Board's Achievement Test in English Composition, but it can be used for general composition skill work. A variety of topics are included, such as sentence fragments, parallel structure, wordiness, pronoun antecedents, and awkward constructions.

Content-Area Supplemental Software

In their analysis of developmental programs in community colleges, Richardson, Fisk, and Okun (1983) pointed to the desperate need for "more full-time instructors who are trained to teach basic skills and who know how they can be taught in tandem with required content" (p. 169). Since the major purpose of a developmental program is to enable its high-risk students to succeed in their content courses, the availability of special tutorial software designed to supplement instruction in those courses is helpful. Such tutorials can be of great benefit if they are well designed and if they simultaneously deal with the content of the target courses and develop language skills.

In order to make decisions as to software purchases, the cooperation of the content faculty is crucial. The selection process can be helpful in promoting a working partnership between the developmental programs and content-area departments. Developmental educators must convince other faculty members that the developmental curriculum is ultimately designed to increase student achievement in their content courses.

While content faculty may on occasion be aware of helpful computer software, the burden of responsibility for researching the availability of software will often rest on the developmental teachers. One important source of information on this software is the professional journals for each content area. Another efficient method of previewing software is to attend national professional conferences to view publishers' products.

English-as-a-Second-Language Instruction

Many older developmental students have limited backgrounds in the English language. They require specialized instruction in English as a second language (ESL) or English as a foreign language (EFL). Surprisingly, few developmental educators are aware of the excellent resources available for microcomputer instruction in this area.

Soon after the Apple computer was developed, the American Language Academy (ALA), a private educational organization with campuses scattered across the United States, made a strong commitment to computer-assisted instruction to supplement teacher-led instruction for training of college-age foreign students in English-language skills. Over the years the ALA has developed an extensive collection of Apple II-compatible computer software designed specifically for ESL and EFL students.

These materials are now published by the Regents/ALA Company. Their two major series of tutorial and drill programs are called *Vocabulary Mastery* and *Grammar Mastery*. Regents/ALA also publishes some microcomputer vocabulary word games and *Essential Idioms in English* for practice with the idiomatic expressions so puzzling to ESL and EFL students.

Motivating Independent Reading

Smith (1978) has noted that students learn to read by reading. The encouragement of independent reading is a key factor in the success of any developmental reading program. Some microcomputer programs have been designed to accompany particular books as study devices. These consist largely of multiple-choice comprehension tests on the books. While there are many methods for encouraging enjoyment of reading, one that has generated considerable success for some teachers is the integration of adventure games with reading (Dickson & Raymond 1984).

These programs place computer users in fictional or historical settings and allow them to make choices as to course of action. Interactive fiction software spans the popular literary genres, from detective stories and fantasies to historical adventures. It can be exciting and motivational. Some basic skills instructors have reported favorably on its use as a motivational device and have suggested that the problem-solving strategies involved in playing the games might develop thinking skills of use in secondary school and college. The programs lend themselves to a wide variety of writing assignments as well.

Unfortunately the reading involved in such programs is often limited in extent. Also, it does not match the expository reading typically required of secondary and college students for content course-work. For motivational purposes, however, the advantages of such software are obvious (Balajthy 1986a, Ch. 9). Imaginative teachers can tie in book and short story reading with adventure games of the same genre (Jarchow & Montgomery 1985). For example, the popular *Zork* series would fit in well with fantasy novels such as Anne McCaffrey's *Dragonriders of Pern* series (Del Rey/Ballantine Books) or J. R. R. Tolkien's *Lord of the Rings* trilogy (Houghton Mifflin). *Deadline*, an interactive mystery investigation, might match an Agatha Christie mystery novel or a Sherlock Holmes short story.

Several software publishing houses have begun to produce adventure games that deal directly with specific books. For example, Arthur C. Clarke's science fiction book *Rendezvous with Rama* has an interactive counterpart. Douglas Adams's *The Hitchhiker's Guide to the Galaxy* is another science fiction novel/adventure game pair.

INTELLECTUAL TOOLS

Study Aids

The development of effective study habits is one of the major goals of reading/study skills courses. Indeed, many teachers find that motivated reading-deficient students with effective study strategies outperform most "normal" students.

Microcomputers can be effective for motivating and developing study strategies. For example, computerized "flash card" programs are designed to help students learn. These programs come by their name because they function much like flash cards. A question or statement is placed on the computer screen. The student must then give the answer. The computer checks the answer for accuracy and keeps a record of how well the student responds.

As with the teacher utility vocabulary programs discussed above, flash card programs are designed for the input of students' or teachers' own questions and answers. In one program, questions are typed into the computer and stored in files on a blank disk. Students may create as many files as desired; for History 100, for French 205, or for units within those courses. After each question is typed, the computer asks for the answer, which is typed and stored on disk also.

The questions can be displayed in two modes. In the first, a flash card mode, the question is presented and the student thinks of an answer. She or he presses a key, and the correct answer to the question appears on the computer screen. If the student sees that the answer she or he had thought of was correct, she or he presses a "C" for correct. If she or he was wrong, she or he presses a "W." Questions answered incorrectly will be repeated later in the exercise for reinforcement. This flash card mode is most suitable when answers are too complex or too long to be typed.

The second mode, a type-in response mode, is best suited to short-answer questions such as vocabulary terminology or multiple-choice formats. A question is displayed, and the answer must be typed. The computer checks the response against the correct answer stored in its memory. Again, incorrectly answered questions are repeated later on.

As with the teacher utility vocabulary programs described earlier, students can easily set up their own disk files of questions for content-area courses. Reading instructors should team up students who are in the same course to take turns making up question files. Disk files may be saved from year to year for the various courses, so that future students will have ready-made study aids for their own use.

Another useful application of flash card programs involves the development of a personalized writing drill. As students do their composition work, whether for developmental or for content courses, certain patterns of errors appear. Perhaps a particular student is unaware of the rules regarding split infinitives or dangling participles. There may be words that the student needs to learn to spell. A file can be specially created to cover these personal learning needs. The process of creating the file by typing the questions and rules can provide valuable learning, and an occasional review will help make the learning permanent.

Word Processing

While word-processing programs have been described in an earlier section as useful for improving writing skills by encouraging students to write and revise, their chief function is as tools for writing. Fewer and fewer professional writers use pen and ink or typewriters. Word-processing software enables writers to write more fluidly, decreasing physical and psychological constraints (Daiute 1983) and freeing them for increased thinking.

Prewriting Planning Programs

Composition starter programs pioneered by Burns's (1984a) INVENT software do not actually involve direct instruction. Instead, they model the prewriting process for students, leading them through the thinking and planning steps necessary for production of well-organized, complete composition. Basically, composition starters consist of questions such as "Can you think of three arguments in support of your opinion?" or "Give two examples of your topic." The student's typed responses are saved and later printed out in hard copy for referral during writing of the first draft.

As advances are made in the study of artificial intelligence, computers will be better able to respond to written compositions and provide on-line feedback to writers. Burns (1984b) suggests that the ultimate goal of such software is to produce "an intelligent computer-assisted tutor of rhetoric—an electronic Socrates" (p. 181). Hashimoto (1985), however, has criticized these highly structured heuristic approaches, suggesting that they give students an oversimplified view of the thinking and composing processes. He argues that teachers should see the limitations in the methods and should use less formal procedures.

Write a Narrative and *Write a Character Sketch* are two composition starters designed for the specific types of writing mentioned in their titles. *The Writing Workshop: Prewriting* is designed for grades 3–10. It leads students through brainstorming by free association and planning by branching (a more flexible form of outlining), and it provides a series of incomplete sentences to start students off in their choice of five writing types (persuasive, explanatory, descriptive, story, or letter). *Quill* also includes a program to help students plan and organize written work.

A variety of other programs have been field-tested by researchers interested in this process-based approach to composition computer-based instruction. *Wordsworth II* (Selfe 1984) is an interactive program developed at Michigan Technological University for the Terak 8510A computer. Each of its eight modules deals with "planning" and "polishing" drafts of typical college writing assignments. The eight topics are description, narration, personal writing, classification, evaluation, persuasion, comparison-contrast, and literary analysis.

Another experimental program designed for interactive rhetorical invention includes RICHARD (Aronis & Katz 1984), which has limited ability to react to natural language. PREWRITE deals specifically with planning college-level compositions. Southwell (1984) provides a well-researched annotated list of writing software for older students.

Word-Processing Supplements

Several useful types of programs supplement use of word processors in developmental classes. Spelling checkers, for example, analyze compositions and spot many possible misspellings. Each word in the composition is compared against a dictionary within the software. Any word that does not have a match in the dictionary is identified as possibly misspelled. The writer must then go through the list of identified words to check which ones are actually misspelled.

Several "thesaurus" programs are available that offer synonyms for almost any word typed. Since these programs are cumbersome, time-consuming, and less thorough than printed thesauruses, they are of little value.

If students will be using spreadsheet software to perform mathematical or financial computations, or using data-base management software to handle information electronically, an "integrated" software package is a good choice. Integrated packages allow word processors, spreadsheets, and data-base management programs to interface (that is, work together easily). A file of addresses from the data base can be automatically inserted in a standardized form letter constructed by the word processor, for example. Integrated packages such as the PFS series and *AppleWorks* are designed to make such interfacing easy to carry out.

Finally, expect to see greater availability of grammar checkers. Computers can be programmed to spot certain types of grammar or stylistic errors fairly easily. *Sensible Grammar*, for example, is able to identify redundancies such as "join together" and to deal with errors such as use of "must of" instead of "must have." Several such programs are being used experimentally in some college writing programs to provide automatic feedback to students (Schwartz 1984).

Perhaps one of the most sophisticated of such program systems is Bell Labs experimental *The Writer's Workbench*, which can check spelling, punctuation, wordiness, split infinitives, and commonly misused word pairs (such as affect-effect) (Frase et al. 1981; Frase & Diel 1986). This mainframe program also computes readabilities, calculates percentages of passive verbs, and identifies -*ize* verbs. IBM's experimental mainframe program, EPISTLE (Jensen & Heidorn 1984), is a more sophisticated effort still under development. It is capable of detecting some subject/verb agreement errors, non-parallel forms, and faulty pronoun reference.

Data-Base Management Software

Secondary and college students will benefit from training in organization of research information using data-base management programs such as *Bank Street Filer* or the more sophisticated *PFS File* and *AppleWorks*. These programs function as electronic filing cabinets, handling and sorting information of all types (Balajthy 1986a, Ch. 20).

Data-base management software is excellent for teachers and administrators of developmental programs to aid in handling the burdensome managerial tasks of correspondence, student scheduling, grading, and testing information. Its use offers some problems to secondary and college students, however. The information used in research papers (and even most doctoral dissertations) is simply not repetitive enough or comprehensive enough to warrant using the computer as a filing system. Ordinary index cards or file folders might serve just as well, if not better, Students who are trained to use such software tools will be prepared for the future, however, as data-base management becomes more important in government and industry, as well as in academia.

Computerized Remote Information Retrieval

A wide variety of computerized data bases have been established to aid researchers in reviewing relevant prior research. A psychologist, for example, can use a computer connected by modem and phone line to a remote (that is, located in a different place) data base of psychological research, such as the American Psychological Association's PsycINFO. By using descriptors—carefully chosen words that describe the particular combination of topics desired—the computer can provide references and short descriptions of related research. Other data bases include Magazine Index and Newsearch, which covers 1,700 magazines and journals as well as the *New York Times*.

These retrieval systems are invaluable for detailed research. The present chapter, for example, was researched in ERIC, an educational research data base, using descriptors *secondary schools, college, reading, writing,* and *computers*. The problem, however, is one of information overload. Most secondary and undergraduate research papers deal with relatively wide topics. A data-base search might locate hundreds of references to the topic chosen. The student would be bogged down in a morass of information.

Students need careful teacher guidance in limiting topics for computerized searches if data bases are to be used effectively. Many research papers would be written far more effectively by using traditional methods rather than the computer data-base searches. Students ought to start off with a few good references on their chosen topics, perhaps books recommended by their teachers or professors. These texts can then direct lines of research to important and worthwhile articles or other books on the topics. Since it is difficult for secondary students and undergraduates to sort out what is important from what is unimportant in the information spouted out from a data base, training in this particular use of the microcomputer is more for the sake of future preparation than for present usefulness. Data bases do, however, become far more important to students at the graduate level, due to the students' increased background knowledge in the research topics. See Chapter 10 of this volume for more information on data bases and networking.

SOURCES OF INFORMATION

ALEXANDER, CLARA. 1984. *Microcomputers and Teaching Reading in College*. Research Monograph Series, Report no. 8. New York: Instructional Resource Center, Office of Academic Affairs, City University of New York.
    A comprehensive survey of computer applications for the teaching of reading to developmental college students, concentrating especially on efforts within the CUNY system. Can be obtained from the center listed above, at 535 E. 80th St., New York, NY 10021.

DAIUTE, COLETTE A. 1983. "The Computer as Stylus and Audience." *College Composition and Communication* 34, no. 2 (May): 134-145.
    An informed and thoughtful analysis of the role of the computer and of word processing in writing instruction. The author discusses physical and psychological constraints on writers, then describes how computers can help alleviate these constraints.

RUDE, ROBERT. 1986. *Teaching Reading Using Microcomputers*. Englewood Cliffs, NJ: Prentice Hall.
    Contains additional information on topics such as word processing, spelling checkers, electronic thesauruses, and speed-reading.

SCHWARTZ, HELEN J. 1984. "Teaching Writing with Computer Aids." *College English* 46, no. 3 (March): 239-247.
    Deals specifically with software available today for use in teaching and analyzing components of the writing process. The components include invention, organization, and revision.

SINGER, HARRY, MARIAM JEAN DREHER, AND MICHAEL KAMIL. 1982. "Computer Literacy." In *Secondary School Reading*, ed. Allen Berger and H. Alan Robinson, pp. 173-192. Urbana, IL: National Council of Teachers of English.

Provides background information on research on computers in education, including a short history of the field. Special attention is is paid to secondary school instruction, the concept of computer literacy, and training of teachers to use computers in classrooms.

SOUTHWELL, MICHAEL G. 1984. "Computer Assistance for Teaching Writing: A Review of Existing Programs." *Collegiate Microcomputer* 2, no. 3 (August): 193-206.

A comprehensive annotated listing of computer writing programs designed for older students. Topics include tutorial instruction, practice and testing, simulations, instruction in heuristics (pre-writing and during-writing planning programs), text analysis, miscellaneous support programs, and using computers to manage classroom activities.

COMMERCIAL SOFTWARE

AppleWorks
Apple Computer, Inc.
10260 Bandley Dr.
Cupertino, CA 95014
Apple II series

Bank Street Filer
Scholastic, Inc.
PO Box 7501
2931 E. McCarty St.
Jefferson City, MO 65102
Apple II series, Commodore

Bank Street Speller
Scholastic, Inc.
Apple II series

Bank Street Writer
Scholastic, Inc.
Apple II series, IBM-PC, Commodore, Atari

Deadline
Infocom
125 Cambridge Park Dr.
Cambridge, MA 02140
Apple II series, Macintosh, Atari, Commodore, IBM-PC, TRS-80, and others

English Achievement
Microcomputer Workshops
225 Westchester Ave.
Port Chester, NY 10573
Apple, Commodore, IBM-PC, TRS-80

Essential Idioms in English
Regents/ALA
2 Park Ave.
New York, NY 10016
Apple II series

Grammar Mastery
Regents/ALA
Apple II series

Hitchhiker's Guide to the Galaxy
Infocom
Apple II series, Macintosh, Atari, Commodore, IBM-PC, TRS-80, and others

MicroSpeedRead
CBS Software
1 Fawcett Pl.
Greenwich, CT 06836
Apple, Commodore, IBM-PC

Milliken's Word Processor
Milliken Publishing Co.
1100 Research Blvd.
St. Louis, MO 63132
Apple II series

Milliken's PreWrite
Milliken Publishing Co.
Apple II series

PFS File
Scholastic, Inc.
Apple II series, IBM-PC

Quizit
Regents/ALA
Apple II series

Sentence Combining
Milliken Publishing Co.
Apple II series

Sensible Grammar
Sensible Software
210 S. Woodward, Suite 229
Birmingham, MI 48011
Apple II series

Sensible Speller
Sensible Software
Apple II series

Vocabulary Baseball
J&S Software
14 Vanderventer Ave.
Port Washington, NY 11050
Apple II series

Vocabulary Mastery
Regents/ALA
Apple II series

Write a Character Sketch
Minnesota Educational Computing Corp. (MECC)
2520 Broadway Dr.
St. Paul, MN 55113
Apple II series

Write a Narrative
  Minnesota Educational Computing
    Corporation (MECC)
  Apple II series

Zork
  Infocom
  Apple II series, Macintosh, Atari,
    Commodore, IBM-PC, TRS-80,
    and others

3

INTEGRATED READING CURRICULA

The major trend in use of computers in reading education has been the use of microcomputer software as a supplement to the traditional classroom curriculum. Some schools have chosen to purchase one of a wide variety of large-scale computer curriculum systems. This chapter will first discuss integrated learning systems (ILSs), which are classroom computer networks. The remainder of the chapter will discuss other efforts to design comprehensive developmental reading curricula based at least in part on computer software.

WHAT IS AN INTEGRATED LEARNING SYSTEM?

An ILS is a computer-based instructional system of hardware and software. It differs from the typical classroom microcomputer primarily in that its component work stations are terminals connected to a central computer or memory storage device. Instructional software is supplied by the publisher. ILSs offer some important advantages over microcomputers, though there are serious disadvantages as well. ILSs are called by a variety of different labels, such as professional learning systems.

Not every networking system is an ILS. A variety of manufacturers supply hardware and software to link computers into a network, but these networks often are designed specifically for businesses rather than for education. Copyright laws and copy protection programming (this "protects" a program from being copied) applicable to most educational software make it difficult, if not impossible, for a school system to construct its own software system using networking hardware and choosing published commercial software. Some manufacturers do cooperate closely with school districts in this effort (see Ch. 10 of this volume and Balajthy 1986a, Ch. 13).

ILS instructional software is typically traditional computer-assisted instruction (CAI), a combination of tutorial presentations and drill-and-practice exercises. Most of the software is targeted to the teaching of basic skills such as mathematics and reading, and it includes a comprehensive management system for tracking student progress. In recent years, some vendors have recognized the increased interest in using computers as tools and have developed word-processing and data-base software for their systems.

The systems are usually designed to provide students with some specified amount of time each day for practicing the targeted basic skills, perhaps 15 minutes or so. Many school systems find ILSs particularly appropriate for supplying underachieving students with additional drill-and-practice work (Reinhold 1986). ILS software typically has been developed specifically for the ILS system and is not available commercially for use on ordinary classroom microcomputers.

Two types of ILSs are available. The first type, the minicomputer-based system, usually follows in the path of traditional CAI in using a minicomputer as a central device to which "dumb" terminals are connected as student work stations. Minicomputers have much greater memory capabilities than microcomputers. They can deal with many students at one time. A "dumb" terminal has little memory storage of its own. In contrast with microcomputers, the program remains in the central minicomputer. The terminal simply presents a monitor display derived from the software program in the central minicomputer and allows students to input information to the minicomputer by way of a keyboard.

The second type of ILS is the microcomputer-based network. These systems take advantage of contemporary microcomputer technology by using microcomputers as work stations. Each microcomputer is connected to a central memory storage device, a hard disk capable of storing large numbers of programs, and can access that memory as required. The use of a microcomputer as work station has the added advantage of being able to employ the microcomputer's disk drives to access software not specifically designed for the ILS. The central device in these systems, however, does not have the computing power of a minicomputer, and the management and record-keeping capabilities are limited.

MINICOMPUTER-BASED SYSTEMS

The computing power of the minicomputer is far greater than that of a standard microcomputer, allowing for increased flexibility, complexity of programming, and extensive management and record keeping. The minicomputer is typically connected to a hard-disk storage device that allows it to access a wide variety of programs instantly and to store large amounts of student records. The operating system allows "multitasking"—that is, different students can have access to different parts of the software at the same time. Some students might be working on letter recognition, others on comprehension development, and still others on arithmetic drills. All are working at their own work stations, which in turn are simultaneously accessing the central minicomputer.

Some systems, such as Computer Curriculum Corporation and PLATO, have recently begun to use self-functioning microcomputers as terminals. These work stations ordinarily are directly connected to the minicomputer, but they can be disconnected for independently operated software on diskettes.

Different systems have differing capabilities in terms of number of terminals acceptable, ranging from 5 to over 100. When evaluating systems, schools that foresee the possibility of someday approaching the maximum number of terminals acceptable should carefully check response speed under those conditions. Overloading a minicomputer system with too many work stations will result in dramatically slower responses to student input from the computer.

Many of the systems include utility software in addition to the instructional programs. Most have an authoring program that allows teachers and schools to construct their own CAI software. The *WICAT System 300* series, for instance, also has administrative software, a spreadsheet calculator, and a word processor.

An Example of A Minicomputer-Based System in the Schools

The Ridge School District (a composite of several actual districts) has developed a highly subskill-oriented reading program for its compensatory education students. All students are administered a series of locally developed paper-and-pencil criterion-referenced tests. Each school's reading specialist uses the test results to assign subskill tutorials and practice exercises to be completed during morning reading periods. All compensatory students receive 30 minutes of reading lab instruction per day in addition to their regular classroom reading period.

Each school's reading laboratory is equipped with about five Apple II series microcomputers and five terminals that access an ILS minicomputer. Two aides provide most of the supervision and instruction on the basis of the specialist's assignments. The reading specialist's duties are primarily consultative, as she must also supervise classroom teachers in their implementation of the school's developmental reading program.

Children in the reading lab typically are assigned 2 to 3 15-minute sessions using the microcomputers each week. In addition, they complete 3 15-minute ILS lessons per week. Each computer-based instruction (CBI) session is geared toward development of a specific skill identified as a weakness by the district's criterion-referenced testing.

The Ridge District's response to the use of CBI is enthusiastic. Reading scores have "noticeably improved." The paper-and-pencil testing, though cumbersome and time-consuming, is viewed as a crucial component of the reading program. The ILS lesson pretests are used as well. If a child passes the ILS pretest, he or she does not need to complete the related skill lesson.

Despite the overall positive reaction, teachers do have some complaints, many of which identify characteristic problems with ILSs. Only one lesson is available per skill. If a child fails the lesson posttest, he or she is simply recycled back into the same lesson. Ridge teachers typically move such students on to workbook or microcomputer drills on the same subskill rather than subjecting them to another run through a lesson that had failed to teach them the first time.

In addition, student attention span is limited due to the unvarying format of the ILS lessons. The district reports have had at one time assigned students to 30-minute ILS sessions. Students were unable to maintain attention for that length of time, however. The teachers report that educational microcomputer games are most motivational. The ILS comes in second, and workbook-based exercises third.

A minimum of teacher training is necessary to use the ILS, less than is required for use of the microcomputers. Supervision responsibilities appear to be minimal as well. Children seem well able to function independently.

The district office reports that classroom teachers can consult the ILS management system for feedback on student progress. Few or no teachers take time to do this, however. The reading specialist serves as the direct source of diagnostic information to the classroom teachers.

WICAT System 300

The *WICAT System 300* is a minicomputer-based ILS that accepts up to 30 student work stations. The system has audio capability that is particularly useful with beginning readers, and it can use Apple II series or IBM-PC microcomputers as work stations. These allow students to work with both the *System 300* software and standard diskette-based programs. Schools can also choose to use WICAT's own work station equipment that features touch-sensitive screens. *System 300* includes software for primary reading, reading comprehension, writing, language arts (with language arts skills, spelling, and sentence-combining components), English as a second language, and other academic subjects.

The Primary Reading curriculum is based on 13 types of activities (see Figure 3-1). These 13 types of activities are used to form 1,010 activities in 285 lessons. Forty lessons are at the kindergarten level, 75 at the first grade, 90 at

1. Letter matching discrimination

2. Picture story sequencing

3. Letter identification

4. Consonant sounds

5. Sight word identification

6. Sound patterns I

7. Sight word practice in context

8. Sentence comprehension

9. Paragraph comprehension

10. Sound Patterns II

11. Word identification through context

12. Multiple word meanings

13. Word meanings through context

FIGURE 3-1.   Activities in the WICAT Primary Reading Curriculum

the second grade, and 80 at the third grade. Each activity takes several minutes to complete, and consists of a short tutorial followed by a practice exercise.

The Reading Comprehension curriculum is composed of 565 lessons, each of which is presented as a newspaper article or story. For each lesson, students work on one of four types of activities. In one activity, a portion of the story is displayed and students are presented with a question about it. In another activity, students must remove irrelevant sentences from a passage. The third type of activity involves interpretation of graphs, tables, or maps. The final type of activity involves an evaluation of an editorial, in which students must answer questions as to the author's point of view and evaluate the acceptability of the arguments used in the editorial.

Douglas and Bryant (1985) reported on use of the system in a Texas school system. Teachers and students seemed pleased with results of the lessons, which averaged 20 minutes per day. Reading gains of 9 percent in the third grade and 6 percent in the fifth grade were reported, but these statistics were not based on comparison with a control group, so they are of dubious validity.

Computer Curriculum Corporation

Patrick Suppes, director of the pioneering Stanford University CAI project in mathematics (see Ch. 5 of this volume), founded Computer Curriculum

Corporation (CCC) in 1967. The corporation's MICROHOST system, based on the Stanford software, is the most financially successful system on the market today (Bork 1985). While other companies may dispute this assertion, there is no doubt that CCC brings a wealth of experience to computer-based instruction.

MICROHOST is based on a central minicomputer using the well-known UNIX operating system for increased flexibility. Atari ST microcomputers serve as student work stations. Each has built-in disk drives for using diskette-based software independently of the MICROHOST system. MICROHOST can also use the IBM-PC and Apple II series as work stations, but software is limited for these models. MICROHOST provides a speech system for voice synthesis of some lessons. Up to 128 work stations can be run on the system, though its speed slows considerably if that number is being used at the same time.

The MICROHOST curriculum includes mathematics, reading, language arts, and computer literacy, from grade 1 through adult. Figure 3-2 illustrates the teacher report function. The Gains Report indicates the reading comprehension gain over the student's prior 20 sessions, as well as the total gain for the academic year and the student's present grade equivalent standing. It gives exact measures, up to 0.01 of a grade level, though these distinctions cannot be accepted as valid. Reading performance cannot be measured so accurately.

Computer Curriculum Corporation's Audio Reading component is designed for grades 1 and 2. The system provides two years of daily 12-minute sessions on letter identification, phonics, sight words, meaning vocabulary, and sentence and passage comprehension. A digitized voice synthesizer gives instructions, poses problems, and offers feedback. In the phonics lessons, for example, the synthesizer reads a word or word part on the monitor screen and asks students to repeat it. The students then type a letter or word to fit the pattern.

Houghton Mifflin Dolphin Curriculum

Houghton Mifflin's *Dolphin* curriculum is designed to supplement teacher-directed instruction with computer-assisted instruction in hundreds of reading and language arts skills. The system operates on the Digital Equipment Corporation's PDP-11 minicomputers.

FIGURE 3-2. MICROHOST Student Reports. Used by permission of Computer Curriculum Corporation, Palo Alto, CA.

Gains Report	Gain Last Period (20 sessions)	Time Last Period	Total Gains (% Grade Year)	Total Time (hrs.)	Course Average (grade level)
Tony Garcia	.20	3:21	.36	4:52	4:76

The *Dolphin* reading component is designed to provide daily 15-minute lessons for children in grades 3 to 8. The entire component consists of 354 lessons, including word attack, comprehension, vocabulary, and study skills (see Figure 3-3).

Each lesson follows the same basic format: pretest, practice, posttest, and referral. Five multiple-choice items are presented to students in the pretest. If four of the five are answered correctly, the students are moved on to the next

FIGURE 3-3. Houghton Mifflin *Dolphin* Curriculum, Grade 6: Vocabulary and Comprehension Skill List (from Houghton Mifflin, 1981).

Skill Code	Number of Practice Questions	Skill
631	10	Unknown Words (words in context)
632	12	Synonyms/Antonyms
633	15	Homonyms
634	12	Multi-Meaning Words
635	12	Oral Emphasis (context strategies)
636	12	Verb Tense
637	11	Pronoun Referents
638	10	Visualizing
639	12	Details
640	7	Main Idea
641	12	Tone
642	8	Draw Conclusions
643	12	Figurative Language
644	10	Necessary Sequence (Cause/Effect)
645	12	Sequence (Setting/Events)
646	10	Compare/Contrast
647	8	Predict Outcomes
649	12	Fact/Opinion
650	12	Authors. Qualifications
651	12	Authors. Biases
652	10	Authors. Motives

skill. If students do not meet the criterion score, they receive a short tutorial and some practice exercises. The practice exercises are concluded with a short summary of the principles learned.

Students then take a posttest with the same format as the pretest. If they pass, they move on to the next skill. If they do not, they are referred elsewhere for help. Teachers can design their own referral messages to appear on the monitor screen. For example, if a child fails a posttest on finding main ideas, a teacher might command the following message to appear:

Please complete Problems 1-10 in the *Understanding Main Ideas* booklet, Mark.

The *Dolphin* curricula have been used since the late 1970s. The U.S. Office of Education included this sytem in its National Diffusion Network of exemplary educational projects, and the system has been reviewed positively (Dudley 1983). Houghton Mifflin also has evaluated the system extensively (Palmer 1979; Lindsay & Rogers 1982; Harris, Sandacca, & Hunter 1985), with generally favorable results.

TOAM Computer-Aided Instruction System

DEGEM Systems' TOAM Computer-Aided Instruction System was developed by Israel's Center for Educational Technology for mathematics and multiple-choice drill instruction. The system's designers planned for use of a 20-key terminal, excluding all alphabetic characters. Newer software oriented to language use requires addition of a full keyboard to the student work station.

TOAM lessons are designed for 20-minute periods. As students achieve satisfactory levels of proficiency, they are moved on to higher-level lessons. If they do not show progress, they are kept at the same level or moved to an easier level.

MICROCOMPUTER-BASED NETWORKS

Local PLATO Delivery System

PLATO provides a microcomputer-based system called the *Local PLATO Delivery System* (*LPDS*). Student work stations consist of IBM-PC-compatible microcomputers with a touch-screen monitor that allows students to input information by touching the screen instead of using the keyboard. All work stations are connected to a central hard disk that stores the software. Courseware is designed for older students. The Remediation Package includes a basic skills component in third-to-eighth-grade remedial reading and arithmetic, a GED (General Educational Development) examination preparation component, and a survival skills module. There is also an Advanced Placement

Package for college-bound students in science, mathematics, and computer programming.

Lessons typically follow a pretest/lesson/posttest pattern. If students pass the pretest, they move immediately to the next lesson. If not, the lesson is presented, followed by a posttest. If the posttest is failed, students are recycled through the lesson.

Houghton Mifflin Microcourse

Houghton Mifflin, the publisher of the *Dolphin* minicomputer-based system described above, also publishes a microcomputer version of its subskill-oriented reading lessons. This system, called *Houghton Mifflin Microcourse*, contains much the same lesson formats as in the *Dolphin* system. The microcomputer version does not have as sophisticated a management system, however.

Tandy ESTC

The Tandy ESTC system is designed to run on Tandy's IBM-PC clones. Each microcomputer is equipped with a mouse, a Votrax phonemic synthesizer board, and earphones. A 300-megabyte hard drive contains the software. Up to 32 stations can be connected to the hard drive.

ESTC has 1,500 20-minute lessons in its reading component, for grades K through 6. A typical lesson from the Story Comprehension component begins with the story's title:

```
"Rap! Rap! Rap!"
```

Students are asked, "What do you think this story will be about?" and are offered three choices. Then the short story is presented, accompanied by high-resolution graphics and followed by comprehension questions, including both literal level and higher levels:

```
"Do you think the old man laughed at his joke?"
Student response: "No."
"Really? I think he did, Greg."
```

Tandy has taken advantage of recent developments in sound and graphics to provide motivational enhancements in its software. Comprehension lessons also reflect more of a concern for developing higher-level skills than in older learning systems.

ADVANTAGES AND DISADVANTAGES

The most obvious advantage of an Integrated Learning System is implied by the term itself. These systems are integrated for ease of use. Teachers need not be as concerned with the mechanics of operation of a variety of separate microcomputer systems. The management system is automated to the point that monitoring of student progress by the teacher is exact and simple. Teachers need not be concerned with keeping track of student work on a variety of separate disks. The central reporting system allows easy access to management files on students so that the teacher's burden is lightened considerably in comparison with the situation when using microcomputers.

The ease of management function is a special advantage to school systems that are concerned about close tracking of student achievement and early identification of possible academic problems. While schools have long recognized the advantages in maintaining detailed records of student achievement, the paperwork burdens of such tasks are impossible for teachers to handle when they are imposed on top of their more important instructional responsibilities. Computers can handle much of the paperwork involved in such record keeping, keeping a close watch on daily, weekly, monthly, and annual progress and identifying students who may be having trouble. The computers can also respond easily to advanced students who may have no need for particular lessons and drill work. Such students could be directed to more challenging assignments, whether on- or off-line.

Another important advantage of an integrated system is the ability to branch instruction. In early research on CAI, this capability was hailed as one of the important contributions of computers to education. When a computer's software recognized that students were having difficulty (or, on the other hand, that they were finding the work too easy), the students could be branched to a part of the program that was more applicable to their needs. The limited memory capabilities of microcomputers, combined with too-hasty production of software and the storage limitations of the 5.25-inch diskette format, severely limited branching in microcomputer-based instructional software. The greater computing power of minicomputers gives much more freedom to instructional designers to allow for this vital component of computer-based instruction.

Among the useful management functions an ILS can offer is the ability to instantly print out on the monitor screen or in hard copy up-to-date student achievement records. The computer can tabulate, average, and analyze student work. Typical student reports include the level at which each student is working and the number of questions answered correctly and incorrectly. The report may also include a time-on-task analysis. In a comprehension reading exercise, for instance, the report may indicate student success on a variety of subskills, as well as the overall success rate. Some systems, such as Computer Curriculum Corporation's MICROHOST, may also group students for instruction in subskill areas diagnosed as weaknesses.

In addition, the integration and organization of an ILS remove much of the managerial burden from supervisory personnel. Highly trained teachers need not spend their time running from one terminal to another to solve mechanical problems or answer low-level "How do I get this thing to work?"-type questions. They need not use their time keeping track of dozens of diskettes of software. Ideally, an ILS laboratory could be run by a teacher's aide, though the overall administration of a comprehensive ILS would require training and commitment of time on the part of the school's professional staff. Resta and Ross (1986) field-tested four ILSs in the Albuquerque public schools. They noted that the Computer Curriculum Corporation's system was designed to function without an operator's presence and that WICAT's *System 300* and Houghton Mifflin's *Dolphin* systems required operators. Their final conclusions, however, suggested that a full-time operator is necessary no matter what the system.

Computer-based instruction is only as good as the software used. The ILS seriously limits the range of software accessible by students. For the most part, only software designed by the ILS vendor can be used with the system. This presents no problem if the vendor supplies excellent software and is capable of updating programs and staying current with the needs of educators. The expense of updating courseware makes this difficult for publishers, however. Schools considering purchase of an ILS are making a serious, long-term commitment to the software available. There is far less flexibility of applications than that typical with most educational use of microcomputers.

For example, the advent of microcomputers, with their glitzy graphics and gamelike approaches to drill and practice, presented a serious problem to ILS publishers who had already invested enormous amounts of money in the technology of an earlier day. Computer Curriculum Corporation, for example, defended its drab text presentations by claiming that graphics misrepresent the serious nature of the lessons and distract students from the important tasks involved in learning. Loss of potential customers who demanded enhanced graphics for motivation of students later forced the corporation to begin development of more sophisticated screen presentations. This development did not occur until several years after such sophistication was readily available in microcomputer software, however.

Many systems offer special, add-on programs that expand their versatility. PLATO, for example, allows schools to add a word processor to its system. An authoring program allows teachers to create their own software for the system. Computer Curriculum Corporation's software also includes an electronic mail function for students and teachers to send messages to one another.

Another crucial problem affecting software development is also related to its cost. Basal reading series publishers spend millions of dollars for development of their publications. Great efforts are expended to develop a variety of high-interest workbook practice exercises, for example. Stories included in the basals are often chosen from best-selling children's trade books. ILS publishers simply do not have the financing or the potential market to develop materials with such care. As a result, practice exercise formats are repeated over and over. Stories presented for reading comprehension exercises are third-rate, at best.

In addition, since systems are designed to augment classroom reading instruction rather than to replace it, schools must be aware of the need for integrating the computerized materials with teacher-directed instruction. The school's reading curriculum and the ILS curriculum should be closely matched for compatibility of content and philosophy (Resta & Ross 1986). Isolated computer instruction, in which students see no relation to classroom or real-life reading tasks, will simply waste time and money. In addition, teachers ought to be provided extensive training in how to use the ILS to supplement instruction and how to use the management system to provide increased individualized attention to student needs. An obvious need that is often neglected by schools is the issue of compensating teachers for the time necessary to work through the system's software themselves.

The cost of an ILS can be formidable. The more complex systems may run over $100,000 for initial installation. The more complex the software system and the greater the number of students to be served, the more expensive the ILS will be. Schools must also consider hidden costs, such as training and salaries of supervisory personnel, training of teachers so that the computer-based instruction can be integrated smoothly into the classroom curriculum, cost of the laboratory rooms to be used (including any necessary electrical connections), and future software purchases. Schools must prepare for maintenance costs as well.

MIXED-MEDIA DEVELOPMENTAL READING CURRICULA

An increasing number of efforts are being made to formally incorporate microcomputer instruction into comprehensive developmental reading programs. Developers have taken several different routes in their planning. Some, such as IBM, have designed curricula from scratch. Others are supplying software designed to supplement existing traditional curricula.

Writing to Read

In 1984 IBM released a curriculum package developed under the guidance of John Henry Martin, a former principal. The package included a complete curriculum for beginning reading instruction, including texts, materials, software, and hardware.

The *Writing to Read* curriculum was originally developed for IBM's PC-Jr., but it is also compatible with the PC. All software runs on microcomputers without need for a central storage device. The curriculum is designed for beginning readers and presents an eclectic combination of holistic reading/writing integration and subskill approaches. In *Writing to Read*, however, the computer software plays only one role in instruction. Children also write, use tape recorders for drills and reading stories, and type on typewriters. Much classroom time is spent in small groups, where students and teachers discuss things they have read or written.

The computer software consists primarily of word-recognition and synthetic-phonics drill work. A picture of a fish appears on the computer screen. "This is a fish." Children wear headphones to listen to a voice synthesizer pronounce the word. "Say the word *fish*." The children are supposed to repeat the word aloud, though the computer is not capable of monitoring pronunciation. Then the computer goes on to present a short synthetic phonics lesson on the word, emphasizing letter sounds in isolation: "Say *f-f-f-f*. Say *i-i-i-i*. Say *sh-sh-sh-sh*." The children finally type the word *fish* into the computer.

Writing to Read has received a great deal of attention due to a major publicity campaign by its publisher. An evaluation carried out by Educational Testing Service yielded generally positive results as to effectiveness (Educational Testing Service 1984). While some within the field of reading have applauded the approach used by *Writing to Read* (for example, Mason 1986), others have condemned the program as too expensive, too limited in imagination, and too heavily synthetic-phonics-based (Rotenberg 1984; G. Modla 1986).

Reactions to *Writing to Read* from outside the field of reading have been generally enthusiastic. Jackson and Deal (1985), for example, have noted that the package is a well-considered example of harmonious interaction among pieces of the curriculum and different methods.

SOURCES OF INFORMATION

The best policy for investigating the varied learning systems described in this chapter is to check directly with publishers listed below. Little substantive research has been carried out to compare the different systems, except for superficial characteristics such as number of teaching modules, hardware characteristics, and cost.

REINHOLD, FRAN. 1986. "Buying a Hardware Software System." *Electronic Learning* 5, no. 4 (February): 42–47, 67. This article briefly describes a number of integrated learning systems, both minicomputer- and microcomputer-based. A comparison chart of information is included.

Publishers

Computer Curriculum Corporation
    1070 Arastradero Rd.,
    PO Box 10080
    Palo Alto, CA 94303

DEGEM-SOLCOOR
    2 Park Ave.
    New York, NY 10016-5635

Houghton Mifflin Co.
    Educational Software Division
    PO Box 683,
    Hanover, NH 03755

International Business Machines Corp.
    4111 Northside Parkway
    Atlanta, GA 30327
PLATO
    8800 Queen Ave. S.
    Minneapolis, MN 55431
Tandy Corp.
    400 Atrium,
    One Tandy Center
    Fort Worth, TX 76102
WICAT Systems
    1875 S. State St.
    Orem, UT 84058

4

DIAGNOSIS AND PRESCRIPTION

One of the more important advantages computers have to offer reading teachers is the capability of aiding in the diagnostic/prescriptive process. The first part of this chapter introduces the concept of computer-based testing of reading achievement. After this, the power of the computer for making decisions about diagnosis and prescription is discussed, and several software systems are described.

Some computer-based decision-making systems are already available, most of which are traditionally programmed and designed for research use only. The recent development of expert systems that use artificial intelligence concepts as their foundation of operation offers tremendous potential for the future. The chapter concludes with discussions of the relationship of the medical model of diagnosis to reading diagnosis and of use of computers in the training of reading clinicians.

While educators anxiously await substantive developments in artificial-intelligence (AI) natural-language programming, the expert system subcategories of AI research have begun to offer practical benefits that will be of more immediate importance to the field of reading. Several software publishers are now making available expert system shells (see Ch. 14 of this volume), software tools that can be adapted for reading diagnosis. They offer immense promise for identification, diagnosis, and prescription pertaining to reading disabilities.

While the future is hard to predict, there seems to be little to impede the design of expert systems that can take over a large variety of diagnostic tasks ordinarily performed by reading specialists. Expert systems can even be designed to deliver certain aspects of the prescribed instruction, drawing on a computer-based instructional subprogram system. Among the possible applications are the following:

Normed and criterion-referenced testing

Diagnostic analysis of both formal and informal test results

Maintenance of student records

Automatic formation and printing of reports such as individual educational profiles (IEPs)

Prescription of assignments and teaching methods

Grouping decisions

Scheduling of teacher responsibilities, small group work, and individualized instruction.

Freedom from these low-level responsibilities will allow reading teachers to devote their valuable time to vital tasks that cannot be performed by computers as well as they can be by humans:

Instructional delivery of higher-level concepts

Feedback on learning

Counseling

Partnership with students in the reading/writing process

Discussion of readings

LIMITATIONS OF COMPUTER DIAGNOSIS AND PRESCRIPTION

Will expert systems do away with the diagnostic responsibilities of reading teachers? Certainly not, as much of the input to the expert system must be based on human observation, insight, and discernment. A computer, for example, cannot itself directly obtain information about the student's general appearance or facial expressions, nor can a computer satisfactorily explain to students its diagnostic decisions and resulting prescribed instruction.

Teachers will be asked by the expert system to use their training to identify a variety of problems. Many of these problems are noticed by teachers as a matter of course during regular classroom instruction.

Similarly, properly designed expert systems will consult the teacher about decision making in the prescription process. The teacher may be asked on which basal series the prescription is to be based, or the expert system may give a choice between holistic and subskill prescriptions, or provide both.

Dreyfus and Dreyfus (1984, 1986) have argued that the crucial aspects of expert professional decision making go beyond a programmed step-by-step paradigm to a more holistic foundation based on years of experience. A novice reading specialist may make diagnostic decisions based on the simplified set of instructions specified in reading textbooks and graduate programs. The expert goes beyond these simplifications to base decisions on experiential knowledge that may well prove too intuitive and subtle for computers to mimic (see Ch. 11 of this volume for a more complete discussion).

COMPUTER-BASED TESTING

Computer-Scored Testing

While this chapter deals primarily with tests directly administered by computers, the procedure of using computers to correct test answer sheets and report on results has been in existence for some time. Almost every standardized test publisher offers a computerized scoring service. Many now also offer microcomputer software for the purpose, employing a card-reader peripheral device to scan answer sheets (see Balajthy 1986a, Ch. 20). Hsu (1986) listed a wide variety of publishers who offer software for computing class and school test profiles and statistics. Such programs allow teachers to score tests immediately after administration and provide them with the kinds of computer-managed class reports traditionally available only from remote scoring services.

Computer-Administered Standardized Testing

A wide variety of studies have found that results of traditional paper-and-pencil tests are closely equivalent to results of computer-administered tests (Blanchard 1987; Vicino & Hardwicke 1984; McBride & Martin 1983; McKinley & Reckase 1984; Calvert & Westfall 1982; Hoffman & Lundberg 1976; Olsen, Maynes, Slawson, & Ho 1986).

Occasional findings that students score higher on computer-administered tests apparently reflect an increased ease and speed of test taking. Computer-administered tests take a significantly shorter time for students to complete. Olsen, Maynes, Slawson, and Ho (1986), for example, used the same mathematics items from the California Assessment Program to test third and sixth graders via both the traditional paper-administered method and the computer-administered method. They found that the computer-administered tests took third graders half as long and sixth graders three-quarters as long as paper-administered tests. Considering the amount of time students spend on testing during the typical school year, such cutbacks in testing time could result in important gains in time for actual instruction.

Computerized Adaptive Tests

Another significant advantage of computer-based testing programs involves the development of adaptive testing. This form of testing is not familiar at present to most teachers. It is, however, a well-researched format and offers tremendous improvements over traditional testing methods, both paper- and computer-based.

In traditional testing, every student is administered the same test items. In order to suit a wide range of student abilities and simultaneously maintain a reasonable test length, test publishers design tests to be more accurate with students of average ability than students with above- or below-average ability (Lord 1980; Hambleton & Swaminathan 1985). Diagnostic tests are exceptions to this general case. Such tests are designed to be accurate with below-average students and less accurate with average and above-average students.

In adaptive testing (Lord 1980; Weiss 1979, 1983), the computer administers only items it chooses to suit the individual student being tested. Properly designed, an adaptive testing program decreases the amount of time spent on the test and actually increases the accuracy of the test across the spectrum of student abilities.

In a computerized adaptive test, the student is given an item of average difficulty. If this first question is answered correctly, the student is given a harder question. If the first question is answered incorrectly, the student is given an easier question. After each response, the computer revises its estimate of student ability and chooses an item at the new estimated ability level. Testing is continued until the computer calculates that a sufficiently high accuracy of results (that is, reliability) has been achieved.

Needless to say, the construction of an adaptive test requires a great deal of field-testing and statistical analysis of each item stored in the test bank. But results are worthwhile. In a mathematics testing study, Olsen, Maynes, Slawson, and Ho (1986) found that both third and sixth grade students who were administered an adaptive test took one-fourth the time necessary for paper-administered tests.

Placement Tests

Several reading instructional software systems have placement pretests, to be carried out either on-line or with paper and pencil prior to beginning the lessons. The purpose of these tests is to determine the reading level of students so as to place them at the appropriate level of instruction.

Each of the comprehensive ILSs (see Ch. 3 of this volume) incorporates a series of criterion-referenced pretests as part of its course work. Students typically are tested on each skill included in the system and then assigned to instruction and practice exercises with the skill or passed on to a more advanced skill, depending on the results.

Informal Testing

A limited number of commercial reading testing programs are available for use with computers. These programs are for the most part informal tests and inventories. They have not been normed by administration to large sample populations. As such, their results must be considered tentative at best. One of the important advantages of many nonelectronic informal tests is the teacher-pupil contact, during which the teacher can make important observations of pupil responses and attitudes. Since computer-based tests are administered independently of the teacher, this crucial characteristic of informal tests is lacking.

Another serious disadvantage of computer-based informal tests lies in the possibility that results may be given too much weight by teachers, parents, and students who are impressed by the fact that the test was administered on a computer. Computer printouts, for example, often carry a good deal of clout. People forget that a poorly constructed test is invalid whether it is administered via paper and pencil or via the computer.

An important component of any computer-administered test is the resulting diagnostic report. Since the results can be automatically analyzed, a well-designed system will yield a specific and detailed report of the results of each student. Some existing systems also include a limited amount of prescriptive information.

Reading Style Inventory.   The *Reading Style Inventory* (RSI) is a microcomputer software diagnostic device for determining students' "reading styles" and for matching students with appropriate instructional strategies based on those reading styles. The concepts of learning and reading styles have been advocated by Dunn and Dunn (1978) and their associate Carbo, who developed the RSI test. The RSI may be administered and graded at the microcomputer, or students may fill out answer sheets and the publisher will score the tests.

The usefulness of the RSI will depend largely on whether one accepts the premises involved with the concept of reading styles. The reliability of such diagnoses, which depend partially on differentiation of readers into auditory, visual, tactile, and kinesthetic categories, has been seriously called into question. Such classification has been consistently shown to be unreliable (Pikulski 1985).

Perhaps the most useful approach to using the RSI is to view it as a detailed study skills, interest, and attitude inventory. As such, it provides a wide variety of information, answering questions such as:

How often do I complete my reading assignments?
In what kind of chair do I like to read?
Do I like to listen to music while I read?
Do I like to read at night?

On the other hand, a number of questions are of dubious value: "When I look at words, I often mix up letters like b and d" or "I always remember the sounds letters make." Few students will be able to accurately diagnose their own ability on such issues. Self-report data are notoriously unreliable.

The diagnostic report is well-designed and informative. Diagnoses are reported on perceptual strengths and preferences, preferred reading environment, emotional profile, sociological preferences, and physical preferences. Each diagnosis is accompanied by a variety of suggested strategies for instruction and by a listing of suggested commercial materials.

The test provides some interesting and useful insights into the perceived desires and needs of learners. A detailed report can be printed out in hard copy of each learner (see Figure 4-1 for a small sample section). Group profiles, which allow the teacher to obtain the test results in more easily manageable form, are a real necessity for classroom administrations of the test. The *Reading Styles Inventory* can be a valuable tool for adjusting instruction to meeting individual interests and to making reading a more pleasant, attractive activity for students.

Computer-Based Reading Assessment. This is a silent informal reading inventory based on Johns's (1981) *Advanced Reading Inventory*. It consists of seven graded reading passages, from grade 7 through college. Each passage is presented on the monitor screen and is followed by nine multiple-choice comprehension questions. Student answers are graded by the computer and stored on disk for later retrieval.

When answering questions, the student can refer back to the story at any point. After each selection's questions are finished, the computer prints out correct and incorrect answers and allows the students to review the questions.

The teacher may reference the student file at any time to print out reports on the screen or in hard copy. The student files include overall score per passage, identification of types of questions asked (main idea, fact, vocabulary, inference, and sequence), and number of times the student referred to the text during questioning (see Figure 4-2).

Computer-Based Reading Assessment Instrument. This is an informal reading inventory based on passages and word lists developed by Blanchard (1985). A Spanish version is also available. The inventory includes two forms of eight passages each, from the first through the eighth grade levels. Each passage is followed by questions at both the literal and the inferential levels.

FIGURE 4-1. Partial sample of *Reading Styles Inventory* diagnostic report. Used by permission of Learning Research Associates, Roslyn Heights, NY.

```
HIGHLY RECOMMENDED
------------------
  THE LANGUAGE-EXPERIENCE METHD IS HIGHLY RECOMMENDED W/THE FOLLOWING MODFCATIONS
  -PRVIDE QUIET WRITG/READG AREA         -CHECK WORK IMMEDIATELY
  -DONT SCHDULE TO READ W/PEERS OFTEN    -DONT SCHDULE READ W/1 PEER OFTEN

  THE INDIVIDUALIZED METHD IS HIGHLY RECOMMENDED W/THE FOLLOWING MODFCATIONS:
  -CHECK WORK IMMEDIATELY                -TCHR SHOULD CHECK STDNT'S WORK
  -DONT SCHDULE READ W/1 PEER OFTEN

  THE CARBO RECORDED-BOOK METHD(PP.54-5 RSI MANUAL),IS HIGHLY RECOMMENDED IF STDN
  IS IN ELEMENTARY GRD AND/OR READG BELOW GRD LEVEL.MAKE THESE MODFCATIONS:
  -PRMIT MANY CHOICES RECORDED BOOKS    -HAV READ IMMDTLY AFTR LISTENG TAPE
```

```
---------------------------------------------
STUDENT'S NAME: GIBBONS   ESTHER
PASSAGE 1: GRADE 7


STUDENT RESULTS

  1   2   3   4   5   6   7   8   9   QUESTION #

  M   F   V   F   F   F   V   I   S   TYPE

  D   C   B   D   B   A   C   D   B   RESPONSES

  D   C   B   D   B   A   C   D   B   ANSWER KEY




COMPREHENSION: 100%
NUMBER OF TIMES RETURNED TO TEXT: 0
---------------------------------------------
STUDENT'S NAME: GIBBONS   ESTHER
PASSAGE 2: GRADE 8


STUDENT RESULTS

  1   2   3   4   5   6   7   8   9   QUESTION #

  M   F   V   F   F   F   V   I   S   TYPE

  A   B   C   D   A   C   B   B   D   RESPONSES

  A   B   C   A   C   D   B   A   B   ANSWER KEY

          *   *   *       *   *


COMPREHENSION: 44.4444445%
NUMBER OF TIMES RETURNED TO TEXT: 1
```

FIGURE 4-2. Student profile from John's *Computer-Based Advanced Reading Inventory.* Used by permission of Jerry L. Johns, Northern Illinois University Reading Clinic, De Kalb, IL.

There are also two types of word lists. The content-specific lists contain words chosen from the passages and questions included in the test. The nonspecific lists contain words chosen from graded word lists. The word lists are administered with a teacher's help. The child reads the word aloud from the screen and the teacher determines whether it was pronounced appropriately.

COMPUTER-ASSISTED REMEDIATION

Computer instruction lends itself to remedial work for many of the same reasons it is effective in developmental instruction. The novelty provides motivational appeal. Immediate reinforcement strengthens learning. Branching can allow for increased individualization. Student learning can proceed at individual rates.

As with developmental instruction, however, computer-based learning is no panacea. In an observational study of students at a college reading clinic,

Dreyer, Boehm, and Sandberg (1984) noted that close supervision of remedial youngsters is an essential part of the process, since the software available for microcomputers today does not support independent learning with these children. In fact, in their study, tutors were working one-on-one with youngsters at the microcomputers.

DIAGNOSIS AND PRESCRIPTION: TRADITIONAL PROGRAMMING TECHNIQUES

Some of the most exciting possibilities for future diagnostic and remedial work involve use of artificial intelligence programming. Most work to date, however, has been based on more traditional programming techniques for decision making. This involves a technique called hard programming, in which commands identify specific diagnostic circumstances and relate them to specific prescriptive outcomes.

Hard programming can be simple, as when a student receives a low vocabulary score and a high comprehension score on an achievement test. The program can be designed to identify such a discrepancy (for example, in a command to subtract the vocabulary score from the comprehension score and identify whether the result is greater than a given number of points) and print out instructions to the teacher to concentrate on vocabulary instruction.

Most reading diagnostic programs are hard-programmed. For example, program commands might indicate that if a student's score on a pretest is lower than 70 percent, the student should be assigned to an intermediate-level lesson. If the score is between 70 percent and 95 percent, the advanced level might be assigned. If the score is lower than 40 percent or above 95 percent, the teacher might be informed that the instructional lessons associated with the pretest are inappropriate for the student. In a study skills inventory, if a student responds to the statement "I take effective notes in class" with a NO or SOMETIMES, the program may automatically print out a diagnosis involving extra work on note-taking skills.

More complex hard-programmed diagnostic analyses, such as that of the *Computer Assisted Diagnostic Prescriptive Program* described by Roberson and Glowinski (1986), would involve an increased number of variables. A variety of subskill scores would be reviewed by the program, for instance, with an increased number of possible outcome prescriptions. These hard-coded systems are sometimes called categorical (Szolovits & Pauker 1978), as students are placed in discrete, clearly identified categories on the basis of diagnostic data.

Example Diagnostic/Prescriptive Reading Programs

TRILOG. Several prototype systems have been developed to aid teachers in interpretation of diagnostic results. Wagner (1984) used an Apple II series program named TRILOG to aid teachers in diagnostic data collection.

The system administered tests, such as the Slosson Oral Reading Test or Gray Oral Reading Test, with teacher guidance. It also accepted simple data entry. The system maintained a disk-based record of student scores. The program is not available commercially.

CARA.   McKenna (1986a) has developed a program titled CARA (Computer Assisted Reading Achievement) that analyzes a variety of general information about students' backgrounds, perceptual development, home environment, learning modalities, and so forth (see Figure 4-3 for a listing of components). Teachers fill out test and observational data on a coding form to facilitate entry of data into the computer. Actual entry of data into the computer takes only a short time.

A particular strength of the CARA program is its ability to carry out the detailed analysis necessary for interpretation of informal reading inventory (IRI) results. An informal reading inventory consists of sequenced, graded reading passages, each of which is followed by comprehension questions. Some passages are read silently by the student, while for others the student listens to the teacher read. A third type of passage, the oral reading selection, is read aloud by the student while the teacher records miscues—oral readings that do not correspond with the printed target passage.

The CARA program manual (McKenna 1986b) explains the various types of miscues and gives teachers instructions for classifying them into the categories of insertion, repetition, omission, reversal, teacher prompt, and substitution. Once an IRI has been administered, the miscues categorized, and the resulting raw data entered on the coding sheet, the information is input to

FIGURE 4-3.   Categories of General Information on the
Computer Assisted Reading Assessment
(CARA)

Language Background

Support from the Home

Sibling Background

Student's Attendance Pattern

Graded Materials

Intelligence Test Results

Vision and Hearing

Attitude and Behavior

Word Recognition Skills

Learning Style

CARA, which then analyzes the data and reports the child's independent, instructional, frustration, and hearing comprehension levels. Any IRI may be used, and the program analyzes the data according to the standard scoring procedures established by Betts (1946).

CARA prints its diagnostic report in hard copy or on the monitor screen. All information is saved on disk, so that teachers can add to or amend data for revised or enlarged diagnoses.

McKenna (1986b) notes that CARA is not a replacement for the insight of an experienced reading clinician. It is especially useful for inexperienced teachers as a consultative aid. Experienced reading specialists will find it useful in preventing oversights. Balajthy (in press a) has reported on successful use of CARA in a graduate education course. Reading clinicians-in-training found CARA a valuable tool for simulation in analyzing case-study results as they compared their own analyses with the CARA findings. Other students in the course who had little background in reading education found the program important for providing a preliminary understanding of the reading diagnostic process. All students reported an increased appreciation for such programs as tools for helping the classroom teacher think about students' reading problems in analytical terms.

Problems with Traditional Techniques

Early researchers in computer-based decision making focused on medical diagnosis for three reasons (Barr & Feigenbaum 1982): (1) the obvious benefits to society from an increase in reliability of medical diagnostic work; (2) the existence of a body of prior research knowledge about the cognitive processes involved with clinical medicine; (3) the highly organized knowledge base for certain aspects of medical diagnosis.

Continued work on computer-based decision making indicated serious flaws in traditional systems and in early artificial intelligence systems. One method of solving problems, called a state-space search, has the computer develop an optimum path from a specified initial state to an objective, a final state. The state-space search might be used to make decisions on moves in a game of chess, for example. In medical diagnosis, the initial state would be the patient's initial condition. The final state would be a healthy patient. The computer would search for the optimum operators—drugs, physical therapies, and surgical procedures—to attain the desired final state.

The difficulties in applying this problem-solving method to medical diagnosis involve the uncertainty factor. The exact initial state—the complete picture of the patient's problems—is often unclear. In addition, application of operators—treatments—does not guarantee consistent results.

Reading diagnosis and medical diagnosis have much in common. Neither is an exact science. Yet medical diagnostic expert systems such as CASNET and MYCIN have been rated as performing at human-expert levels (Yu et al. 1979a; Yu et al. 1979b).

In order to contend with these difficulties, researchers in artificial intelligence developed methods of dealing with inexact knowledge, sometimes called fuzzy knowledge. One such method involves the use of confidence ratings to estimate accuracy of information input to the system. Another method involves a threshold level based on confidence ratings of decisions. Above a certain threshold level, the system determines that a possible decision is plausible. Below that level, the possible decision is rejected as implausible. These methods are built into contemporary expert system programs. Such systems are sometimes called probabilistic, as they are designed to estimate the probability that a decision is accurate (Szolovits & Pauker 1978).

EXPERT SYSTEMS FOR READING DIAGNOSIS

Chapter 14 contains a description of an expert system, as well as a discussion of the advantages and disadvantages of such systems. Chapter 15 details the construction of a system based on an expert system shell, a utility program that makes the construction process easier. Both chapters use a prototype experimental system as an example. The discussion below focuses on the major concerns that face the reading field as it considers construction of these systems for diagnosis and prescription.

Past experience with development of large-scale computer-based instructional reading systems has shown that such projects are often based more on the preconceptions of computer programmers about reading instruction than on the consensus of the field of reading. Hundreds of thousands of research dollars have been spent on putting together software systems that will not be used by anyone with a clear understanding of what reading instruction is all about.

Unless reading teachers begin to deal with the challenges of expert systems now, grant monies for their development will be spent on projects without a sound basis in reading diagnosis and instruction. Perhaps even worse, once large-scale diagnostic systems have been developed, they will almost certainly be imposed upon teachers in the field by institutional administrations. If the diagnoses and prescriptions are not based on sound understandings of reading, this could have a profound negative impact on the next generation of children.

Jones (1984) described an expert system developed for assessment of reading problems. The system is based on a model consisting of three levels of diagnostic intensity: basic educational skills, problems with which will lead to a prescription of a corrective program; psychoeducational correlates, problems with which will lead to a prescription of remediation in necessary auditory, visual, or language skills; and noneducational factors, such as medical and social factors, problems with which will lead to a prescription for therapy in the necessary area.

Jones's expert system begins by questioning the user about the child's physical, mental, emotional, social, and academic histories. Results of educational tests and tests designed to analyze intellectual, visual, auditory, and language skills are also requested. The system finally pinpoints specific skills and abilities that appear to be the child's primary weaknesses. A prescription is then printed.

The system is programmed in LISP. Jones reports that it has been evaluated by comparing its diagnoses with the findings of human diagnosticians and that "In general, the results of the comparison are encouraging" (1984, p. 60), especially in terms of the extensive qualities of the system's diagnoses.

IS THE MEDICAL MODEL APPROPORIATE FOR READING DIAGNOSIS?

Wagner (1984) noted that the medical approach to diagnostic decision making has some important differences from the approach used in the reading profession. Perhaps most important is the reading specialist's task of administering treatment to more than one student at the same time. Wagner suggested that despite these differences, the diagnostic work of the two professions has much in common:

1. Interaction with a person who has a problem
2. Collection of data about the case
3. Determination of diagnostic classification
4. Selection and application of treatment
5. Monitoring of results.

Critics of the medical model of reading diagnosis often charge that medical diagnosis is an exact science, whereas reading diagnosis is not. Yet, while it is certainly true that the facts about reading difficulties and treatment are far from exact, so are the facts about medical diagnosis. The medical model involves a process of informed decision making, not exact, mechanical, step-by-step precision. Just as within the reading field two specialistis often reach different conclusions based on the same facts (Gil, Huffmeyer, vanRoekel, & Weinshank 1979; Weisberg 1984), so two medical professionals can prescribe different treatments for the same patient characteristics.

In discussing expert system development in fields about which there is no firm consensus, Basden (1984) has warned against pessimism, suggesting that research may open up avenues that are not now apparent. In fact, Kolodner (1984) reported innovative attempts to deal with the field of psychiatric decision making, in an expert system called SHRINK. Kolodner's efforts began with diagnostic paradigms described in the American Psychiatraic Association's (1980) *Diagnostic and Statistical Manual of Mental Disorders*. SHRINK was designed to intergrate new cases into its memory as it processed them, and to make generalizations about similarities with past cases. It used an analytic structure based on an adaptation of Schank's (1980, 1982a) approaches to episodic memory—memory for experiences—that records and organizes individual episodes or events in a person's life.

Vinsonhaler, Weinshank, Polin, and Wagner (Reinking in press) suggested that reliability of reading diagnosis can be improved by increased training of reading specialists. They observed that medical training is based on hundreds of real and simulated patient cases, with feedback from expert clinicians. Reading specialist training consists of diagnosis and remediation of only one or two cases.

The study of diagnosis and prescription within the medical field can serve as a key reference point for analysis of the problems facing a reading diagnostician who wishes to design an expert system. A variety of issues must be studied before appropriate computer-based decision-making systems can be designed. Among these issues are assessment standardization, assessment adequacy, and evaluation of clinical models.

Assessment Standardization

The medical field has developed a considerable degree of mutual consent on measurement standards. The analysis of blood content, for example, is fairly standard across the profession. As a result, physicians can understand communications about these measurements with precision.

In reading, the measurement vocabulary is less precise and less standardized. Comprehension assessment, for example, can be carried out using any one of a variety of techniques, including informal reading inventories, normed tests based on multiple-choice or cloze questions, and informal cloze tests. Devices vary wildly in quality of construction, and resulting validity and reliability. Assessment of comprehension ability may even be carried out indirectly, with diagnosis based on an oral word list or a vocabulary test. Outcomes may likewise be reported using a variety of different grading systems, including percentiles, normal curve equivalents, grade levels, and stanines.

The different possible inputs create great difficulties in the construction of a system that will have wide applicability across the profession. Different teachers and school systems would have different assessment results available for input, and the expert system would have to be able to deal with them.

The lack of standardization in assessment also has led to a problem in that results of treatments cannot be easily compared across the practices of reading professionals (Wagner 1984). Will a treatment that results in growth on an informal reading inventory also result in growth on a specific norm-referenced test? Such an assumption is unwarranted.

Assessment Adequacy

The reading process is highly complex. It is influenced by background knowledge that in turn involves aptitudes, and by values and motivations based on prior experience and training, and socioeconomic status. It is also influenced by a variety of underlying language and perceptual factors. Comprehension itself is not unitary (Davis 1972), but is based on an undetermined number of interacting subskills, including vocabulary knowledge.

All of these factors play a direct role in influencing success in reading. Can appropriate diagnosis, therefore, be carried out without a fairly exhaustive understanding of the learner? In addition, in building the comprehensive, organized structure of research knowledge about diagnosis and treatment necessary as the knowledge base of an expert system, can research treatments in which the subjects are incompletely described be helpful?

The answer in both cases appears to be a qualified "No." A comprehension treatment may, for example, be effective with readers of slightly below-average ability but ineffective with those who are severely remedial (Balajthy 1982, 1986c). Another treatment might work well with high internal locus of control (having a feeling of power over one's destiny and environment) students but not with high-externals. Research in which the treatment groups are not closely analyzed into levels of ability or measured for locus of control might very well be misleading.

It is clearly impossible under present circumstances, with funding shortages and the practical limitations of research with human subjects, to exhaustively assess every group of research subjects for every possible factor related to reading. Indeed, even the medical field does not test for every possible factor related to health. Yet, there must be some consensus on the relevant factors that are to be tested, or else the body of reading research on remedial treatments will remain as uninterpretable as it is at present.

Evaluation of Clinical Models

Reading is a complex, covert activity. Component processes are not directly observable. As a result, research on reading depends critically on design of theoretical models of the internal processes involved. The medical field has developed fairly precise models of anatomical and physiological processes that allow physicians to make substantially accurate decisions. Within the reading field, a wide variety of models have been proposed, ranging from psycholinguistic to information-processing to developmental and others (Davis 1971; Singer & Ruddell 1985).

Historically in the sciences, models involve specification of the workings of a system. These workings are usually portrayed physically, diagrammatically, or verbally. The relationships of variables proposed in the model are thought by the modeler to be suitably analogous to the system.

The purpose of such a theoretical model is to enable an organized, systematic study of its components. By manipulating the variables and observing the consequences, inferences can be made about the actual system upon which the model is based. "A model in this sense is merely the indication of a simpler and more accurately determinable state of affairs, with the intention of facilitating deduction of further consequences that can then be tentatively reapplied to the more complex and elusive real system" (Gellner 1964, p. 435). Models are meant to be tested empirically, then to be accepted, refined, or rejected on the basis of experimental data.

Two complementary approaches to this traditional modeling process have been apparent. Newell (1973), for example, criticized the lack of general principles arising from the mass of research carried out in cognitive psychology. His solution, and the solution of others who followed him, was to develop complex models of the human mind using information-processing paradigms based on computer simulations. These complex models were designed to synthesize a wide variety of psychological processes, including reading.

Posner and McLeod (1982) contrasted this synthesis approach to modeling with an analytic approach. They surveyed research in which modelers had analyzed psychological processes into elementary operations that appeared to yield specific performances, constructing comparatively simple models of those operations for experimental study. A proposed model of letter and letter-string recognition, for example, might be tested with a matching or detection task.

Beaugrande (1981) has argued that these traditional views of the scientific modeling process—views based on a theory of scientific thinking that is derived from Enlightenment philosophers such as John Locke (1632–1704) and has recently been called into question (Polanyi 1962; Gunton 1985)—have not been substantiated in the realities of the scientific endeavor.

For example, Kuhn's (1962) survey and analysis of scientific "revolutions" suggested that the history of science shows that scientists reject theories for reasons other than that of contrary evidence. Stegmuller (1976), in his analytical treatment of theorizing, argued that the interrelationships of theory and evidence are so intricately entwined that the two cannot be separated. All data gathering is influenced by theory. Facts cannot be completely separable from theory. A researcher's expectations or bias must influence results, for example. Research is often aimed at proving a point rather than at determining truth, whatever truth may be. This may be especially true in the social sciences. Certainly the field of reading is replete with a grand variety of theories and models for which extensive testing has never been carried out (Balajthy 1984a).

Operational definition must involve construction of a set of competencies for reading specialists. A competency, in this sense, is the ability to perform certain behaviors when presented with a specific set of conditions. Construction of a comprehensive expert system in a field requires prior construction of a comprehensive set of competencies. Scanlan (1978) has given an example of a typical competency-based simulation problem, based on a list of competencies provided by the American Association for Respiratory Therapy:

> You are a respiratory therapist working nights in the Regional Newborn Unit of a 400-bed medical center. The nurse has just called to your attention a 2000-gram neonate being managed for RDS Type I by IMV at a rate of 20, FIO_2 of 0.6, and a PEEP level of +10 cm H_2O via a 3.0 mm orotracheal tube. The infant's skin color has deteriorated rapidly over the last 10 minutes, the heart rate has dropped to below 80/minute, and the infant's spontaneous breathing rate has increased to 70/minute. The umbilical artery catheter is not patent, and the staff neonatologist is unavailable.
>
> You would now (choose only one):
> 1. Extubate the infant and bag with mask and high FIO_2
> 2. Increase the PEEP level to +15 cm H_2O
> 3. Increase the FIO_2 to 0.80
> 4. Quickly try to gather more pertinent information

The construction of an expert system demands this kind of precise specification of relationships between diagnosed conditions and treatments. Such precise predictions should be verified by research. Unfortunately, many extant reading models are not operationally defined, cannot be verified, and lead to increased confusion in the field rather than clarification.

HOW CAN COMPUTER-BASED DIAGNOSIS AID IN CLINICIAN TRAINING?

Use of computers as aids for reading diagnosis can be helpful in several ways. In medical diagnosis, for example, most of the errors made by physicians are errors of omission. In attempting to identify a disease, physicians may overlook possibilities. The computer-based diagnostic system, whether in medicine or in reading, exhaustively surveys and considers each possibility.

For less experienced teachers, the system may structure data collection so as to aid in decision making. It may stress the importance of monitoring student behaviors during class, for instance, or identify particular areas of concern.

Another important advantage of a computer-based diagnostic system would be the ability to readily access prescriptive information. For given identified prescriptions, the actual page numbers of relevant exercises and tutorials in textbooks might be stated, and descriptions of techniques might be available. On-line data files of remedial activities and worksheets could be immediately available to the teacher.

An educational computer simulation is, by definition, a simplification of a reality. The reading field may not be capable at present of fielding a full-blown diagnostic system, but a variety of researchers have developed programs designed to simulate the reading diagnostic process. The purpose of these simulations is to train reading specialists and teachers. Most systems developed to date, such as the TRILOG and CARA programs described earlier, have been used primarily in teacher training rather than in direct diagnostic applications.

A variety of studies have indicated the need for improved training of reading specialists in diagnostic and prescriptive work. Weisberg (1984), for example, found little consistency in diagnosis by reading specialists based on informal reading inventory results when those specialists were trained in different colleges and universities. She suggested that consistency and depth of training are necessary for increased reliability. Vinsonhaler, Weinshank, Wagner, and Polin (1983) reported a series of six studies of diagnostic procedures carried out in simulation by reading and learning disabilities specialists and classroom teachers. They found almost no common diagnostic conclusions. The mean diagnostic agreement between clinicians was about .10, and diagnostic agreement on the same case by the same clinician was also low, about .20.

Computer-based clinical simulations may offer one solution to this training problem. Scanlan (1978) has suggested that simulations have several key advantages in the training of clinicians:

1. The participants are convinced of the relevance of the problem to their own professional needs.
2. Evaluation of the clinical tasks can be standardized.
3. Primary elements of skill applications can be emphasized and irrelevant complexities avoided.
4. Objective ratings of performance can be obtained in a short time.
5. No adverse effects can be caused to clients, as might happen if clinicians practice in real-life situations.
6. Realistic feedback can be provided.

No other method—whether it be written tasks, oral exams, self-reports, or peer observations—provides participants with as much hands-on experience in judgment and decision making (Reinecker 1985). Jones and Keith (1983), in a study of the effectiveness of computer simulations in health sciences, found that students acquire better decision-making skills than when they are trained by traditional noncomputer tasks.

Alvermann (1985) used a microcomputer interface with a videocassette player to provide teacher training in use of informal reading inventories. Traditional computer-assisted instructional information and questions are presented in conjunction with videotaped scenes from staged IRI administrations. In one scene, for example, the reading specialist who administered the IRI confers with the classroom teacher on video. The specialist suggests that the teacher administer instruction in vowel digraphs and diphthongs. Students using the program are then presented with a text screen with the following frame:

```
Which of the following worksheet examples best
    reflects an attempt to give April practice in
    recognizing common vowel digraphs and diph-
    thongs?

a. Matching:  rain bead
              toy  stain
              read boy

b. Define the term vowel digraph. Then write a sen-
   tence using the term vowel digraph.

c. The b___ was far away from the girl. He had to
   sh___t, ''M___t me on the pl___ygr___nd.''

d. Unscrambling words:

houst droa lmae
```

The correct answer, c, serves as an example of appropriate digraph/diphthong practice.

Vinsonhaler, Weinshank, Polin, and Wagner (Reinking in press) have developed a series of ten programs to provide a computer-based internship for reading specialists. Each program provides a wide variety of information on the computer "patient," such as school records, vision and auditory test results, standardized diagnostic test results, teacher comments, and so forth.

In *Meeting Stephen*, for example, clinicians-in-training are introduced to a simulated remedial reader for whom extensive diagnostic testing has been carried out. The clinician can obtain this information by making selections from menu pages. The main menu offers the following choices:

```
Initial information on reader
    Sight vocabulary
    Decoding ability
    Vocabulary
    Oral reading
    Silent reading
    Listening comprehension
    Motivation/attention
    Other (that is, biographical, health, family,
    and classroom behavior information)
```

The silent reading option above provides scores on the Gates-MacGinitie Comprehension Subtest and the Durrell Analysis of Reading Difficulty Silent Reading Subtest. The sight vocabulary option provides Dolch Sight Word and Slosson Oral Reading Test results.

Once the data have been obtained, clinicians are asked to provide simple diagnoses on a wide variety of subskill categories. The input of a *P* indicates that the student has a problem in the category, an *N* indicates no problem, and a *U* indicates that the clinician is unable to decide. At the completion of the diagnosis, the computer prints out a comparison of the clinician's decisions with a diagnosis prepared by the program's authors. Disagreements are flagged and a final score is given, indicating the percentage of agreement on diagnosis.

Graduate students in the study were provided 30 hours of instruction, in which they interacted with the computer cases, preparing a written diagnosis based on the information provided by the computer. The students were supervised and provided feedback by an instructor experienced in clinical diagnostic and remedial work. Final posttesting indicated significant improvement in consistency and reliability of diagnoses.

CHALLENGES FOR THE READING PROFESSION

In conclusion, the reading profession must meet a variety of challenges as it faces the task of integrating computerized diagnostic/prescriptive systems. At present, most of these challenges must be met in schools of education at colleges and universities. A great deal more model building and researching is needed for development of effective computer systems, and a great deal of teacher training is needed for effective implementation of those systems. Five critical research tasks are discussed below.

1. Construction of Systematized Diagnostic/Prescriptive Models

Researchers must reformulate the vague, ill-defined processes of reading remediation into concrete, exactly specified models. These models may be flexible, in the sense that alternative methods can be used for achieving the same goals. But the goals and their relationships to the methods must be specified so as to be verified empirically.

Wagner (1983) has suggested several questions for researchers to consider as they construct these models:

1. For a given diagnostic profile, what treatments (instruction) are available?
2. For a given diagnostic profile, what treatment is most effective? What are the expected outcomes?

3. For a given diagnostic profile and a particular treatment being administered, when and how can the instructor determine if the gain is going as expected?
4. For a particular outcome achieved by a student with profile X given treatment Y, how should this outcome have an impact on future instruction for similar entering profiles?

The last question is targeted to collection of data on effectiveness of treatment as an ongoing part of the reading professional's responsibilities.

2. Programming and Field-Testing of Systems

The next step into further specificity involves the actual construction of diagnostic/prescriptive programs and field-testing of those programs in classroom settings. Such field-testing will inevitably result in major modifications that must be carried out under the direction of both computer and reading experts. Unless models are specified so precisely as to be programmable, they should be rejected as vague and unworkable.

3. Integration of Differing Models into a Unified General System

Requirements of specificity need not rule out the possibility that differing diagnostic/prescriptive models may be equally effective under the same circumstances. In such cases, the system should be designed to offer as many possibilities as may seem helpful to the system users.

4. Integration of Adjunct Subsystems

Once the basic format for entry of diagnostic data, storage and analysis of those data, and formation of diagnostic/prescriptive reports has been designed, additional subsystems may be added to the program body for increased ease and sophistication of information delivery. Such subsystems might include on-line testing of students, teacher training modules for instruction in use of the system and in the general principles of diagnosis and prescription applied by the system, and instructional delivery programs for remediation of students.

5. Investigation of New Teacher Roles and Retraining

As reading specialists and teachers are relieved of certain responsibilities by diagnostic/prescriptive computer applications, the reading field must investigate what new roles teachers can assume to improve education. With decrease in emphasis on testing, perhaps, teachers may find that they are able to devote more time to holistic, natural language instructional tasks, or to counseling of students with problems, or to any of a wide variety of challenging needs that, in today's classroom, remain largely unmet.

SOURCES OF INFORMATION

ROID, GALE H. 1986. "Computer Technology in Testing." In *The Future of Testing*, ed. Barbara S. Plake and Joseph C. Witt, pp. 29-69. Hillsdale, NJ: Lawrence Erlbaum.
This chapter serves as a research-based introduction to the many applications of computers for testing purposes in general education. It includes sections on test administration, scoring, and interpretation.

HSU, TSE-CHI, AND ANTHONY J. NITKO. 1983. "Microcomputer Testing Software Teachers Can Use." *Educational Measurement: Issues and Practice* 2, no. 3 (Winter): 15-30.
This article surveys a wide variety of microcomputer programs that are applicable to testing purposes, including item-analysis programs, test-item data banks, grade book programs, test-result analysis programs, and on-line testing software. The article has been updated by a paper by Hsu presented at the April 1986 American Educational Research Association conference in San Francisco: "Developments in Microcomputer Applications to Testing."

SOFTWARE

Computer-Assisted Reading Assessment
(CARA)
    Southern Micro Systems
    PO Box 2097
    Burlington, NC
    800-334-5521
    Apple II series

Computer-Based Advanced Reading
Inventory
    c/o Dr. Jerry L. Johns
    Northern Illinois University
    Reading Clinic, 119 Graham
    De Kalb, IL 60115
    Apple II series, TRS-80 Model 4

Computer-Based Reading Assessment
Instrument
    Kendall/Hunt Publishing Co.
    2460 Kerper Blvd.
    PO Box 539
    Dubuque, IA 52001
    319-588-1451
    Apple II series, IBM-PC
Reading Style Inventory
    Learning Research Associates, Inc.
    PO Box 39
    Roslyn Heights, NY 11577
    800-331-3117, 516-248-8002
    Apple II series, TRS-80 Model 3 and 4,
        Commodore 64, IBM-PC

5

AN OVERVIEW OF RESEARCH ON
COMPUTERS AND READING

While most teachers have felt the impact of computer-based learning on reading instruction only since the early 1980s, research on this topic has been carried out since the 1960s. The purpose of this chapter is, first, to examine the crucial research questions educators must ask about computer-based instruction and, second, to provide an overview of the major summative compilations of research on the topic. In conjunction with a critical evaluation of this research, the chapter provides some thoughts on the limitations that educational researchers face when designing evaluative projects. Finally, the chapter examines two large-scale computer-based reading projects that were highly influential for early developments in computer-based learning, the Stanford and PLATO projects.

THE IMPORTANT RESEARCH QUESTIONS

Is Computer-Based Instruction Effective?

Yes. There is no doubt at all that computer instruction is effective. A host of individual research studies, meta-analyses (statistic-based compilations of individual research studies), and research reviews (summaries and conclusions based on evaluations of individual research studies) indicates clearly that computer instruction is effective for a wide variety of skill and concept areas.

This, however, is not an important educational question. There are many other "proven" methods of instruction. All of the methods "work," in the sense that students learn from them.

Is Computer-Based Instruction More Effective Than Other Methods?

Again, yes. There is no doubt at all that computer-based instruction is more effective than other methods. However, there are many qualifications to this answer. Before this research question becomes meaningful, one must ask three important questions:

1. What kind of computer-based instruction is meant?
2. What kind of other methods is meant?
3. What is meant by "effective"?

There are a host of computer-based instructional techniques, varying from rigid, behavioral, computer-assisted instruction (CAI) programs to free-flowing, holistic, "computer-as-a-tool" approaches. There are innumerable "other methods" with which one can compare computer-based instruction. Finally, "effectiveness" can be defined in a host of ways. For example, is effectiveness demonstrated by measurement on a standardized reading test, or by development of a lifelong love of reading on the part of students, or both?

Limitations of Computer-Based Instructional Research

When examining the research on effectiveness of computer-based instruction (CBI) that compares CBI with other methods, one must bear in mind a number of limiting factors.

First, much CBI research is based on the programmed instruction model that, though it may be effective in some ways, is presently out of favor among reading researchers and teachers. Programming of instruction involves analyzing a skill into its subskills, or a content topic into its subtopics. Each subskill or subtopic is then sequenced appropriately and divided into many small steps for presentation to students. At each step, students are tested to determine whether they understand, to reinforce correct responses, and to minimize learning errors.

Even during the heyday of conventional programmed instruction in the 1950s and 1960s, advocates were cautious about whether the techniques would lend themselves to reading instruction. Levine (1963), for example, warned that "The crucial question is whether reading can be programmed in tiny bits without teaching bad reading habits" (p. 338), such as inability to deal effectively with longer passages. These concerns have been carried over into applications of computer-assisted instruction to reading. Becker (1982) noted that CAI may have greater impact on mathematics instruction because it more closely simulates practice of math than of reading or language use.

Second, a variety of observers have indicated that the computer is not being used well in the field of education (Burns & Bozeman 1981; Holzman & Glaser 1977). Research on inappropriate applications will not yield interesting findings. Thelen (1977) has warned that "Computer-based education is a technological potential, not an educational guarantee" (p. 458). For example, the majority of studies on teaching children to program computers has yielded no improvements in problem-solving ability. In a critical reanalysis of these studies, however, Linn (1985) found that "exemplary" (as opposed to "typical") teaching yielded impressive improvements in these problem-solving abilities. Sadly, most contemporary research on reading and language arts computer-based instruction is carried out without the best software, by poorly organized and poorly funded researchers who have a minimum of experience with computers or with educational curriculum evaluation of any kind.

Third, much research has been carried out with older readers rather than younger. There is some evidence that computers may be more effective with younger students.

Four, the so-called Hawthorne effect, or novelty effect, makes it difficult to project today's results, when computers are new and therefore exciting, into a future when CBI is commonplace. The novelty of computers may result in increased student effort and persistence, but this effect may wear off with time. Kulik, Bangert, and Williams's (1983) review of secondary computer instructional studies found that longer studies resulted in significantly lower learning improvement rates, than did shorter studies. This may be due to students' becoming accustomed to CBI. On the other hand, it may be due to the greater research control possible in shorter studies.

Fifth, much older published research has been carried out without a well-established theoretical framework for instruction, by experts in computers rather than content- or skill-area experts. Research reports from computer-based reading projects often completely ignore the reading process and the software used to teach it. Instead they concentrate on the hardware used, as if the machine were the key component in instruction. A good example of this is the large body of material written about the effectiveness of PLATO, as if this system (see below for a description) were uniform in quality. Only the hardware is uniform; anyone familiar with the PLATO software will quickly realize that it varies tremendously in effectiveness.

In addition, most research has been carried out by the designers of the computer software themselves, or by those who have personal or professional involvements in the CBI projects. Reports, for example, that PLATO can raise achievement by 5 years with only 6 months of work, or that 12 hours of PLATO instruction raised reading achievement by 1.6 grade levels (Schneck 1984), are of dubious validity to anyone familiar with the teaching of reading. The great danger in such research is that false hopes may be raised. Such unrealistic expectations may do instructional computing more harm than good (Roblyer 1985a) as people come to expect microcomputers to be "a veritable deus ex machina to put all things right" (Sloan 1984, p. 541).

Sixth, Scandura (1981) and Becker (1982) have suggested that lack of quality software that accurately reflects the cognitive processes it is attempting to teach is the major impediment to CBI implementation. This problem is severe in two common cases: research projects in which software contructed specifically for the project does not have the finished appearance of top-notch commercial software, and commercial software for which publishers rarely support necessary field-testing in real classrooms prior to production. In a reaction to research reviews of CBI effectiveness, Bracey (1982, p. 53) noted:

> As I read through the literature of CAI research, I see a lot of "home-grown" [software], some of which seems to have been produced so quickly that it is likely to be of dubious quality. The fact that we still find consistently positive effects with CAI may be the most substantive endorsement of educational computing yet.

How Can Computer-Based Instructional Technology Best Be Used?

This is the formulation that must be addressed by researchers (Salomon & Gardner 1986). It raises far more complex and meaningful issues than the preceding two questions, but it cannot be simply answered with a *yes* or *no*. Effectiveness of instructional methodology is dependent on a wide variety of factors, such as the characteristics of the learners, the learning activities, the nature of materials used, and the criterial tasks by which effectiveness is measured (Brown, Campione, & Day 1981).

Clark (1983) raised the valuable point that the medium itself (the teacher, computer, tape recorder, or book) does not directly influence learning. It is what the medium *does*—the teaching—that influences learning. Is a computer more effective than a workbook for drill and practice in spelling? Yes, it is more effective, because a computer gives immediate feedback and monitors performance. But a teacher *can* give immediate feedback on workbook activities and continuously monitor performance if the class is small enough. If the teaching quality is the same—no matter what medium is being used to present that teaching—Clark's review of instructional media research suggested that the achievement results will be similar.

As a result, the primary research question to be asked about computers and reading is "What is effective teaching of reading?" The secondary research question follows logically: "How can computers help provide this effective teaching?"

Is the Computer "Just Another Teacher Tool"?

There are some who would say that computer-based instruction is not better than other techniques—it is different. It provides one more tool for the teacher to teach more effectively and the learner to learn more effectively. For example, Clark (1983), in an article surveying educational media research, argued:

> Most current summaries and meta-analyses of media comparison studies clearly suggest that media do not influence learning under any conditions. . . . The best current evidence is that media are mere vehicles that deliver instruction but

do not influence student achievement any more than the truck that delivers our groceries causes changes in our nutrition. (p. 445)

Clark's conclusions as to the effectiveness of media in enhancing achievement have been disputed on a variety of grounds (Petkovich & Tennyson 1984). His proposition that media do not affect achievement ought not to be misinterpreted, however. His meaning is that the format of instruction is the important factor: Drill and practice is equally effective, whether administered by a teacher or by a computer.

The advantage of the computer, according to Clark and Leonard (1985), lies in the possibility of its power and flexibility for increased efficiency and cost-effectiveness: Human teachers *can* provide immediate and individualized feedback for drill and practice workbook activities—just as the computer can—but this is an extremely inefficient and expensive practice.

The computer, then, is not "just another tool" that can be allowed to go the way of instructional television, dismissed as ineffective and allowed to sit on the closet shelf. The key to effective use of instructional computing lies in a recognition of appropriate applications that use computers in the most effective ways.

● How much of our students' time is spent on reinforcement and drill activities using ditto sheets or workbooks? There can be no doubt whatsoever that computer reinforcement and drill can be far more effective than traditional materials that do not provide immediate feedback or ongoing monitoring and diagnosis.

● Teachers have long faced the impossibility of requiring their students to revise written assignments. The mechanics of rewriting or retyping entire compositions have been too formidable. There can be no doubt whatsoever that word-processing software will lead to dramatic changes in teaching revision skills.

● Students learn by doing, but realistic learning activities such as chemistry lab experiments or social science simulations are difficult and time-consuming to carry out in the classroom. There can be no doubt whatsoever that computerized simulations can provide realistic experiences with a host of science and social studies concepts.

● Television can be a powerful learning device, but it lacks the monitoring and interactive capabilities to focus student attention. New video technology is already providing a uniquely effective combination of computer-based instruction and television, easy to use and relatively inexpensive.

The list could go on and on. Clark may be correct in his argument that each of these functions of the computer can be carried out in other ways. Each child could have a tutor to provide an "on-line" interactive session with workbooks or television. Each could be given a personal secretary to retype compositions as often as necessary. Each could be allowed to perform as many scientific or social experiments as desired. None of these alternatives is at all realistic, however. The computer can give reality to highly effective—but hitherto difficult to achieve—learning environments.

The important point to this discussion is not simply that the computer is effective. The point is that research on the effectiveness of the computer must address itself to each issue in turn, asking, "In what ways can the computer improve on conventional classroom effectiveness and efficiency?"

RESEARCH REVIEWS

As noted above, research on effectiveness of computer-based instruction must be reviewed carefully, bearing in mind its many limitations. A variety of authors have attempted to synthesize the present state of knowledge about CBI. Such syntheses are carried out in three ways:

1. Narrative reviews involve each author's survey of relevant research and the resulting conclusions drawn from that survey. These reviews describe selected studies and draw conclusions based on those studies.
2. Tally sheet (or box-score) reviews typically include many more studies than narrative reviews. Conclusions are based on a tally of the number of studies with results supporting either side of an issue.
3. Meta-analysis is an increasingly popular statistical technique used to draw conclusions from the results of many studies on the same topic. While other types of reviews may suffer from the subjectivity of the authors, meta-analyses have been criticized for pulling "a veil of numbers over the critical information" (Slavin 1984, p. 26), for giving a false appearance of statistical precision.

Meta-analysis has become widely accepted in recent years, but there are still many who remain critical of it (Eysenck 1978; Jackson 1980). Clark and Leonard (1985), for example, examined individual research studies used in meta-analytic surveys of CBI. They concluded that 75 percent suffered from crippling design flaws. In over 50 percent of the studies that compared CBI experimental groups with conventional instruction control groups, the CBI groups received more time-on-task than did the controls—an indication that their superior achievement could not be attributed to the computer.

Readers of the summaries described below should recognize these criticisms when they encounter supposedly exact statistics in the meta-analytic reviews. They should also bear in mind that none of the major compilations pertains specifically to reading and language arts CBI, but rather include a wide range of skill and content areas.

Research Compilations on General CBI

Vinsonhaler & Bass 1972. The reviewers concluded from a survey of ten studies that elementary age children using computer drill and practice showed achievement gains of from one to eight months over control groups. Gains in mathematics were double those in language arts.

Jamison, Suppes, & Wells 1974. This review of 20 studies led to the conclusion that CAI is as effective as traditional instruction. Younger students and students of lower ability appeared to benefit the most.

Edwards, Norton, Taylor, Weiss, & Dusseldorp 1975. The reviewers concluded that computer-based instruction is effective in raising achievement and reduces time necessary to learn. Twenty-two of 36 studies reviewed showed positive results for CBI; 12 indicated no difference; and only 2 showed negative CBI results. The authors concluded that supplemental CBI was more effective than replacement CBI. A reanalysis of the same studies by Roblyer (1985b) suggested this finding to be valid for the lower grades, but the opposite was true for the secondary grades.

Hartley 1977. This is the first study to use meta-analysis techniques with computer-based instruction. The reviewer concluded that the average effect of CBI for arithmetic teaching was to raise achievement by .41 standard deviations (from the fiftieth to the sixty-sixth percentile).

Burns & Bozeman 1981. The reviewers concluded from a meta-analysis of supplemental mathematics CAI in elementary and secondary schools that CAI was "significantly more effective in fostering student achievement than a program utilizing only traditional instructional methods" (p. 37). They found that CAI tutorials raised achievement an average of .45 standard deviations and CAI drill and practice an average of .34 standard deviations.

Kulik, Kulik, & Cohen 1980. The most impressive summative evaluations to date of CBI research have been carried out at the University of Michigan by James Kulik and his colleagues. The compilations involve a series of meta-analyses that continue to be updated on a regular basis.

In this article, the reviewers conducted a meta-analysis of 59 CBI studies at the college level. They found that achievement rose by an average of .25 standard deviations (from the fiftieth to the sixtieth percentile, considered statistically a small gain). There was no difference in course completion—whether students finished the course or dropped out—between computer and traditional instruction. CBI resulted in small gains in student attitude toward subject matter. Learning occurred in a shorter time with CBI, however. Traditional instruction required an average of 3.5 hours per week and CBI only 2.25.

The reviewers concluded that advantages of CBI were small, especially when compared with more impressive findings in elementary schools. They also noted that their meta-analytic technique involved giving equal weight to each study, no matter what the size. Had larger studies been given more weight, findings from the negative TICCIT and PLATO evaluations would have overwhelmed results from the other, smaller studies. The reviewers also noted that subject-matter content—whether "hard" or "soft" sciences, for example—did not seem to play an important role in the effectiveness of CBI.

An update of this meta-analysis (Kulik & Kulik 1986; Kulik, Kulik, & Schwalb 1986) included 101 studies and supported earlier conclusions. Achievement rose by an average of .26 standard deviations. Surprisingly, slightly higher effects were noted in "soft" content areas, such as life studies and language, than in "hard" areas, such as mathematics and science.

Kulik, Bangert, & Williams 1983.

The reviewers found in this meta-analytic review of 51 studies in grades 6 to 12 that achievement increased in 39 of 48 studies. The strongest effects were from training periods of short duration.

An update meta-analysis (Bangert-Drowns, Kulik, & Kulik 1985) was based on 42 studies of secondary computer-based instruction. Four of the studies involved the teaching of reading or language arts. Results were positive, raising posttest scores by .26 standard deviations (roughly the equivalent of raising the students' average score from the fiftieth to the sixtieth percentile). Of special interest in this study was the comparison of different types of computer-based instruction. Direct instructional applications, such as tutorials and drill-and-practice exercises, raised scores by .4 standard deviations. "Enrichment" applications, such as the teaching of programming and use of computer simulations, were largely ineffective.

Clark & Leonard 1985.

This review of CBI research supported Clark's (1983) argument that computers are not more effective vehicles for instruction, and that media research should concentrate on efficiency of delivery instead. The reviewers randomly chose 30 percent of the CBI research studies used by Kulik in his meta-analyses. Each of the studies was subjected to a detailed critique using a checklist of experimental design factors.

Results of the critique suggested that the vast majority of CBI research is so flawed as to make interpretation difficult. For example, 18 of the 40 studies analyzed by Clark and Leonard did not provide any equivalent instruction to the non-CBI control groups. In three of the studies that did provide work for the control group, CBI subjects were forced to continue work until they demonstrated achievement, while non-CBI controls were allowed to stop working whenever they wished. Other studies indicated serious problems involving dropout rates for CBI subjects, or experimental groups that were composed of higher-ability subjects than the controls. In 30 of the 40 studies, subjects were not assigned randomly to treatments, a crucial design flaw.

In all, only 15 of the studies employed methods and contents considered by Clark and Leonard to be adequate. Of these 15, only 2 resulted in significant effects in facor of CBI, and in both these cases there was an interaction effect: High-ability subjects profited from the CBI while low-ability students did better without CBI.

Clark and Leonard remained unconvinced of the effectiveness of CBI for achievement gains. CBI research, however, suffers only from the flaws that typify much educational research, flaws that are created by difficulties in carrying out laboratory-perfect studies with real human beings in real classrooms. Roblyer (1985b) has argued that conclusions as to CBI effectiveness are sound despite research imperfections: The large number of studies by different investigators in which CBI has been shown to be more effective than traditional methods "yield trends in findings and provide more reliable indications of where we should be heading with design and implementation strategies" (p. 6).

Clark and Leonard concluded that research should not concentrate on effectiveness of CBI:

> Instead, researchers are encouraged to investigate the relative efficiency and cost of CBI versus traditional instruction. . . . The contribution of the computer (and other new delivery technologies) may be to make instruction more efficient (free the teacher, reach more students with less per-student cost). (p. 15)

Winkler and Shavelson (1982) have also decried the common simplistic evaluation of CBI as obtaining predictable results: "Technology will 'win' half the time, and regular instruction will be more successful for the remainder" (p. 1). Instead of comparing the two forms of instruction, Winkler and Shavelson agreed with Clark and Leonard that effective research must examine the complex interface of three factors: the teacher, the technology, and the student.

Summary of Research Overviews

Some general conclusions can be drawn from research on CBI, bearing in mind the tentative quality of existing findings and the many qualifications that demand further research in the future:

1. The lower the grade level or ability of the students, the more effective CBI is.
2. CBI is consistently more effective than traditional instruction, but the amount of improvement is low to moderate and cost-effectiveness is uncertain.
3. Structured CBI, with emphasis on direct instruction, is more effective in producing achievement gains that unstructured CBI.
4. CBI results in considerable savings of learning time.
5. CBI results in favorable attitudes toward computers.

HISTORY OF COMPUTER-BASED READING INSTRUCTION RESEARCH

As noted above, a wide variety of research projects have been carried out in an effort to investigate the effectiveness of computer-based instruction in reading. Most of these, however, have been "research" only in the sense that they involved untested products or were grant-funded. Few have made any serious attempts to gather empirical evidence about CBI or to make important additions to existing knowledge (Thompson 1980). Mason, Blanchard, and Daniel (1983) have offered the most comprehensive collection of summaries of computer-based instructional projects for reading. Their book includes brief descriptions and detailed bibliographic references for some 14 college and university projects and some 33 school-based projects. Of these, the Stanford University and PLATO projects were two of the most important.

The Stanford Project

One of the first large-scale research projects for computer-assisted instruction in reading began in 1964 at Stanford University under the direction of Richard Atkinson. Funded by the U.S. Office of Education, the project targeted beginning readers and also contained a mathematics component under the direction of Patrick Suppes. Instruction was "traditional" CAI, consisting of tutorials and drill-and-practice exercises, though at the time these were ground-breaking methods.

A refined version of the Suppes-Atkinson material is currently marketed by Computer Curriculum Corporation on a variety of systems (see Ch. 3 of this volume). These systems have been the most commercially successful computer-based learning systems (Bork 1985). Microcomputer-based instruction has not achieved any comparable sophistication in terms of its management capabilities, because of the limited memory storage capabilities of microcomputers.

The hardware component of the project was based on an IBM mainframe computer, to which a number of student work stations were connected. Each station contained a monitor, keyboard, lightpen, filmstrip projection device, microphone, and cassette tape player with headphones. Later versions replaced the tape player with a faster digitized disk system. Both the filmstrip device and the tape player were computer-controlled. Desired pictures and messages could be accessed quickly. Students' voice inputs could be recorded for later analysis by the teacher.

Atkinson (1968a) gave the following as an example of one of the many lesson formats. The student would see on the monitor a screen similar to Figure 5-1. The cassette recorder would command, "Touch and say the word that belongs in the empty cell." If the student correctly touched the *ran* with the lightpen, the monitor display would print *ran* in the cell box and the student would be commended: "Good, you have put *ran* in the cell. Touch and

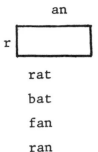

rat

bat

fan

ran

FIGURE 5-1.   Screen diagram from Stanford CAI reading
(Atkinson 1968). Used by permission of Richard C. Atkinson.

say *ran*." The lesson would then go on to the next problem. If an incorrect choice was made, the lesson would branch to one of the short remedial modules, depending on the type of error.

Simple comprehension lessons dealt with "wh-" questions. A sentence such as "John hit the ball" would be displayed on the monitor. The recorder would ask, "Who hit the ball?" If the child touched *John* with the lightpen, the recorder would respond, "Yes, the word *John* tells us who hit the ball." If the child's answer was incorrect, the recorder would say, "No, *John* tells us who hit the ball. Touch and say *John*," and an arrow would appear above *John* on the monitor screen.

The curriculum was initially sequenced in six strands:

Reading readiness
Letter recognition
Sight words
Phonics
Spelling patterns
Word meaning and sentence completion.

Initial testing of the curriculum was carried out with culturally disadvantaged first graders. Students spent varying amounts of time during the year, from short periods in the beginning up to 35 minutes per day toward the end of the project. Final posttesting indicated that the experimental CAI group was consistently superior to a teacher-taught group on a variety of vocabulary and word-recognition subtests. The two groups achieved equal scores on the comprehension subtest administered.

Criticism of the Stanford project (Spache 1967) was directed at its limited view of beginning reading as a rote memorization process of letter and word identification. Learning to read was conceived as consisting of simple repetitions of low-level decoding tasks. Virtually no attention was paid to other important components of the learning process, such as the role of the teacher and the social climate of the classroom. The students would be plugged into the self-contained curriculum, and at the end of the assembly line-like process, out would come proficient readers.

Important principles of computer-based instruction were learned from the Stanford project, however. Many of these principles continue to play a key role in computer curriculum development today.

Role of the teacher. Initial research was carried out under the assumption that teachers could be replaced by computers. The researchers concluded that such replacement could be effective in improving achievement (Atkinson 1969), but that "some aspects of initial reading seemed better left to the classroom teacher" (Atkinson & Fletcher 1972, p. 319).

It would be satisfying to most reading teachers to suggest that this conclusion was the result of the researchers' recognition of the importance of meaningful human interaction and purposeful language experiences. Atkinson's argument, however, appeared to be economic in origin: Teachers could provide certain types of appropriate instruction less expensively than computers. In its later years, the project used CAI as a supplement, not a replacement, for teacher-directed instruction.

Contemporary comprehensive projects for the teaching of beginning reading, such as IBM's *Write to Read* project (see Ch. 3 of this volume), have recognized the important role of the human teacher in providing a language-rich environment for young readers. Indeed, the goal of replacing teachers with computers has been almost entirely abandoned by the educational establishment. The realization of the need for integrated language experiences, left largely unrecognized by the Stanford project until its later years (Atkinson & Fletcher 1972), has come primarily as a result of changing philosophies of instruction and the increased interest in integrating the language arts.

Role of the computer. The recognition of the inescapable importance of the human teacher in learning to read did not obviate the findings as to the effectiveness of CAI, however. The computer instruction was consistently effective in a variety of studies (Fletcher & Atkinson 1972), but the project found that the CAI fit best into low-level decoding skill instruction rather than higher-level comprehension development.

Sex differences. Boys, traditionally slower in reading achievement than girls in their elementary years, benefited more than girls from the CAI. While both sexes achieved better with CAI than without, the boys did particularly well (Atkinson 1968b: Atkinson & Fletcher 1972).

The PLATO Elementary Reading Project

The PLATO (Programmed Logic for Automatic Teaching Operation) computer-based education project was begun at the University of Illinois in 1960 and continues today under the commercial sponsorship of Control Data Corporation's PLATO division (see Ch. 3 of this volume). PLATO has been used for a variety of reading instructional applications, including college

English (Michael & Sliger 1976) and adult preparation for the Graduate Equivalency Degree (GED) test (Elliot & Videbeck 1973). The PLATO Elementary Reading Project was started in 1971. Its purpose was to build a complete computer-based reading curriculum (Obertino 1974).

One of the great strengths of the mainframe computer-based PLATO system was its sophisticated hardware. Even in the project's beginnings, the hardware available at student work stations was more sophisticated than that available in microcomputer-using classrooms in the 1980s. The monitor, for example, was a plasma panel with clarity superior to the typical microcomputer high-resolution screen of the 1980s. The monitor screen was touch-sensitive as well. A computer-controlled slide projector provided graphics. An audio system was based on interchangeable computer disks that could each store 23 minutes of randomly accessible audio messages.

Another important issue confronted by the PLATO project was that of the relationship between computer education and the human teacher. The researchers realized early on that computers could not replace humans. Obertino (1974), for example, noted that one of the four primary goals of the project was to design a curriculum that was flexible, "so that teachers could take advantage of the lesson materials without being forced to alter their personal classroom styles" (p. 8). The flexibility was enhanced by the TUTOR authoring system that allowed fairly simple construction of computer lessons by classroom teachers. In addition, teachers could build "menus" of activities for individual students to meet diagnosed needs, and they could restructure the sequence of teaching lessons to meet the classroom's curricular needs.

Initial evaluations of the PLATO reading curricula were disappointing (Swinton, Amarel, & Morgan 1978). The poor student progress in kindergarten and first grade was blamed in part on the "slow-moving" pace of instruction and on the system's inability to recognize instances in which instruction was failing. In both the kindergarten and the first grade study, computer use apparently interfered with learning. The evaluators concluded that too much attention had been paid to the hardware and not enough to the software: "In general, *much* more attention should be devoted to courseware than has been the norm in technological innovation" (Swinton, Amarel, & Morgan 1978, p. 27).

The researchers concluded that the human teacher was essential to success of a computer-based reading program. While certain children found certain activities highly motivating (a "Concentration" game, for instance), in general the computer activities sustained interest less successfully than conventional teacher-led activities. "Since the terminal lacks the imposing physical presence of another human being three or four times the size of the little person, he will sooner desert PLATO than he will a human teacher" (Obertino 1974, pp. 10–11). The evaluators noted that teachers must be encouraged to integrate the computer learning into the regular curriculum. They also noted that there was little use by teachers of the information on student progress gathered by the computers.

SOURCES OF INFORMATION

MASON, GEORGE E., JAY S. BLANCHARD, AND DANNY B. DANIEL. 1983. *Computer Applications in Reading*, 2nd ed. Newark, DE: International Reading Association.
This book is the authoritative compilation of summaries of research and development projects carried out on computer-based instruction in reading. An invaluable and comprehensive list of bibliographic references is included.

ATKINSON, RICHARD C., AND DUNCAN N. HANSEN. 1966. "Computer-Assisted Instruction in Initial Reading: The Stanford Project." *Reading Research Quarterly* 2, no. 1 (Fall): 5-25.

ATKINSON, RICHARD C. 1968b. "Computerized Instruction and the Learning Process." *American Psychologist* 23, no. 4 (April): 225-239.
These articles describe the important Stanford University CAI reading research project carried out by Atkinson and his colleagues with beginning readers. The curriculum is described, and results of the first year of operation are reported. The articles provide interesting insight into the perspectives of early pioneers in computer-based instruction.

6

SPECIAL TOPICS OF CONTEMPORARY
RESEARCH INTEREST FOR COMPUTERS
IN READING

As mentioned in Chapter 5, the question "Is computer-based instruction effective?" is not an important issue. Instead, educators and researchers must ask, "How is computer-based instruction effective?" Researchers have looked at a variety of topics pertaining to how computers can be used effectively in the schools. This chapter surveys some of these topics.

The first major area of concern involves research on how computers are actually being used in schools. The chapter will then deal with the influences of students' socioeconomic status on computer use. Affective influences on computer-based instruction will then be discussed, followed by an extended review of research on such courseware-related issues as rate of responding, types of feedback, and learner control over program operation. The chapter concludes with discussions of social interaction and the role of the human teacher in computer-using classrooms.

SCHOOL USE OF COMPUTERS

A variety of educators have expressed concern that computer applications will be limited to low-level drill-and-practice exercises (Zaharias 1983; Balajthy 1984b). In fact, observers of classrooms report that this seems to be true (Sheingold, Kane, & Endreweit 1983; Littlejohn, Ross, & Gump 1984), though instruction in computer programming also accounts for much school use of computers.

In terms of computer-based tutorials and drill-and-practice exercises, it may be that lower-level computer applications are more effective than attempts to deal with higher-level learning. Some writers have suggested that computer instruction diminishes in effectiveness at higher levels (Kulik, Bangert, & Williams 1983; Dreyfus & Dreyfus 1984). Jamison, Suppes, and Welles (1974), for example, reviewed research to find that computer-based instruction seems most effective with remedial students. The research on this issue, however, is scanty, and confident conclusions are impossible.

Despite many heated denunciations of computer subskill drills and advocacy of moving "beyond drill and practice" to more innovative computer applications, there is no shortage of defenders of practice exercises. Lesgold (1983) has suggested that such practice can improve efficiency of decoding. LaBerge and Samuels' (1974) model of the reading process can be seen as a justification for computer drill and practice (Balajthy 1984b). Practice exercises increase automaticity of performance of lower-level cognitive processing in reading, allowing the reader's attention to be focused on higher-level analyses.

Few large-scale efforts have been made to determine how computers are actually being put to use today. Surveys that have been made are based on self-reports by teachers and administrators, a survey methodology that can lead to misleading conclusions. In addition, in a field as rapidly changing as computers in education, results of such research are out-of-date almost as soon as they are reported.

One such effort, carried out in 1983 by Johns Hopkins University's Center for Social Organization of Schools (Becker 1985a), surveyed over 2,000 elementary and secondary schools. The survey indicated that the major uses of computers in secondary schools are introductions to computing and computer programming. Of the remainder, much was low-level drill and practice. The typical student receiving such instruction used the computer only 15–20 minutes each week, hardly enough to gain proficiency in any skill being learned. In addition, schools using computers for over one year reported a decreasing amount of computer time devoted to instructional applications in subject areas other than programming.

A second survey was carried out in 1985 by Becker and his colleagues at Johns Hopkins (Becker 1986). The survey included 2,100 elementary and secondary schools. Findings indicated a 50 percent rise in number of hours per week the typical school computer was in use. Also, the typical student using the computer had more time per week at the keyboard, about 50 minutes.

In 1985, more than half of the use of computers in elementary schools was devoted to drill-and-practice and tutorial software, though programming applications still dominated in secondary schools. Elementary school teachers using computers reported that drill-and-practice activities accounted for 73 percent of computer time, and tutorial instruction an additional 24 percent. Little time was devoted to programming or word processing.

Other attempts at measuring computer applications are indirect, basing conclusions on software availability and sales. Reinking, Kling, and Harper (1985) found that about 70 percent of reading software programs on the market involved drill and practice. Rubin and Bruce (1984) found that most of over 300 language arts programs surveyed were targeted to the letter or word level of language. Rickelman (1986), among others, has expressed concern that the availability and ease of use of drill-and-practice programs will lead to overuse: "The answer to what is beyond drill and practice could be MORE drill and practice!" (p. 49).

Tally-sheet analysis of commercial language arts and reading software may be misleading, however. Advocates of holistic learning emphasize student involvement in meaningful language activities, "learning to read by reading" and "learning to write by writing." A wide variety of software, often not explicitly labeled as reading or writing educational programs, lends itself to holistic approaches (Miller & Burnett 1986b; Balajthy 1986a): word-processing software, with all the accompanying prewriting organizational programs and postwriting text analysis programs (Balajthy in press); simulations (Brady 1986); computer-mediated text presentations (see Ch. 7 of this volume); data-base research reporting; story construction software (see Ch. 1 of this volume); adventure games and interactive fiction; book selection software; and so forth.

SOCIOECONOMIC STATUS AND USE OF COMPUTERS

Some researchers have found that lower-class children and minorities are especially likely to be administered drill-and-practice exercises via the computer. Some have suggested that this subskill drill approach is a subtle form of discrimination against minorities and low-socioeconomic-status children that is likely to ensure long-term academic failure on the part of students.

Becker's (1985a) large national survey, carried out in 1983, showed indications that schools with students in the lower SES category tended to use one of two alternative strategies. Low SES schools with predominantly minority populations used their computers to administer subskill practice exercises in an effort to raise achievement of their lower-ability students. Low SES schools with predominantly white populations preferred to use computers with their higher-achieving students, teaching programming and computer skills and providing students with a challenge while teachers worked more closely with the slower students. More recent evidence from the 1985 Second National Survey of Instructional Uses of School Computers suggests that school racial composition is unrelated to computer use patterns (Becker 1986).

COMPUTERS AND THE AFFECT

Jenkins and Dankert (1981) found that student acceptance of computers in education is positive. Computers cannot, however, be considered a magical motivational cure. Obertino (1974), among others, has noted that poorly designed software will be rejected by students as quickly as, if not more quickly than, poorly designed conventional instruction.

Reinking (1984) has argued that the motivational value of many computer learning activities may actually work for students' harm rather than their good. If the motivational value is abused by subjecting students to irrelevant tasks (he offers as an example an arcade game vocabulary drill that is inappropriate because of level of words involved and of design of the activity), the computer work may actually be harmful because students may be allowed to use the program extensively in the place of more useful activities.

Simultaneously with the great growth in number of microcomputers in the schools during the early 1980s, there was a several-year fad in which video games became extremely popular. A wide variety of microcomputer video drills were created to take advantage of the high motivation associated with these games. Many, however, were poorly designed, requiring students to move too rapidly for appropriate learning to take place, or too slowly, with too much time spent on the game and graphics aspects and too little time on actual instruction. The dangers in such misuse of computers are apparent. Durkin (1978-1979) has noted that too little reading period time is actually spent in reading-related tasks. A wide variety of studies have noted the importance of time-on-task to achievement (Rosenshine 1979).

Learning Styles

"Learning styles are the cognitive, affective and physiological behaviors that serve as indicators of how learners perceive, interact with, and respond to the environment" (Keefe 1979, p. 156). Dunn and Dunn (1978) have demonstrated some success in testing the learning styles of students and matching them with appropriate teaching strategies. Some limited research has been carried out on the relationship of computer-based instruction and learning styles. It may be important for researchers to vary computer-based instructional design and development according to the various cognitive learning styles of students' information processing.

Zelman (1986) based her research on motivation for learning about computers on Dweck's (Dweck & Bempechat 1983) theories on the effects of learners' beliefs about intelligence on learning. Dweck suggested that learners are of two types, incremental and entity. Incremental learners believe intelligence consists of a repertoire of skills that can be expanded through their own efforts. Such learners would be more likely to accept the challenge of problem solving necessary for learning to use sophisticated computer software. Entity learners, on the other hand, believe intelligence is a stable trait observable by other people. Perseverance in intellectual activities is seen as risky and revealing low intelligence. Those learners exhibit "learned helplessness" behaviors and abandon challenging situations.

Sex Factors

Research literature on sex differences in learning-task accomplishment suggests that boys and girls may achieve success through different types of tasks. For example, Peterson and Fennema (1985), in a study of conventional mathematics instruction, found that girls respond better to cooperative tasks, while boys achieve slightly better in competitive tasks. Such results may indicate the importance of differential computer-based instructional approaches for each sex, or for compensatory counseling and direct instruction in optimal strategies for cooperative and competitive environments.

A variety of researchers have indicated that boys and girls respond differently to classroom use of computers. Hawkins (1984), for example, noted that "Boys want to control it" (p. 12), that is, to command the computer to perform a variety of functions. Girls tend to "stay within the dictates of the established program rather than to explore the machine's capabilities" (Schrock, Matthias, Vensel, & Anastoff 1985, p. 6). They are more likely to use software for drill and practice than to engage in programming activities of their own. PEER, the Project on Equal Education Rights, has reminded schools that "Simply having computers in the school building does not guarantee equal access for girls (Becker 1986, p. 1). Becker found in his national survey of school use of computers that many schools reported male dominance of computer time. Schrock, Matthias, Vensel, and Anastoff (1985) found that boys tended to work longer at the computer than girls, with a mean of 20 minutes for boys and 13.6 for girls.

Motivation

Research results show consistent positive student attitude toward computer-based instruction. In a survey of secondary school reading teachers using computers, Hague and Childers (1986) found 97.3 percent indicating agreement or strong agreement that students are eager to use computers. Clement's (1981) survey of computer instructional effects on motivation found an overall acceptance level of somewhere around 90 percent.

Sometimes, however, the attitude change is directed toward computers, not toward subject matter (Cavin, Cavin, & Lagowski 1981). Also, students will not be as highly motivated by poorly designed software (Gleason 1981).

Little research has been carried out to isolate the factors that contribute to motivation in computer-assisted instruction. Malone (1981) has carried out some research on computer instructional games, but his research is in need of replication and elaboration (see Balajthy 1986a). Two studies by Loyd and Gressard (1984; Loyd, Loyd, & Gressard 1986) examined attitudes of secondary and college students and found that students with more computer experience had better attitudes toward computers than those with less experience. Obertino (1974) has suggested that the physical presence of a human teacher is a more significant motivating factor for student adherence to assignments than the computer lessons.

The relationship between achievement and motivation in education is itself unclear, further complicating computer-based instructional research. Clark's (1982) meta-analysis of motivational impact on instruction has suggested the surprising finding that students sometimes learn the least from methods they enjoy the most. Schofield's findings in conventional elementary school mathematics instruction also suggested that "There is a degree of incompatibility in maximizing both cognitive and affective outcomes in children" (1981, p. 470). He explained that a concern for high cognitive achievement requires "adherence to a well-organized curriculum and exertion of pressure on children to apply themselves continually during class periods to tasks leading to content mastery" (p. 462).

COURSEWARE-RELATED ISSUES

Rate of Responding

Much of the research on rate of responding during drill-and-practice exercises has been carried out on arithmetic learning rather than on reading skills. Despite this limitation, the results are of special importance to evaluators of reading software, as many commercial reading programs employ irrelevant graphics to create a gamelike atmosphere, and thereby both slow the rate at which students complete problems and limit the time-on-task.

Evaluators must carefully observe students using programs that employ graphics before reaching judgments on the usefulness of the graphics. Vargas (1986), for example, observed students using *Alien Addition*, which requires entering a sum and shooting down a spaceship that explodes if the sum is correct. While a superficial evaluation of the graphics might lead to the conclusion that they slow student responding, in actual practice elementary students using the program worked as quickly as with an unillustrated program that required only entering the sum.

Feedback

Despite the fact that feedback is an essential part of most computer drill and practice, the function of feedback in producing learning is poorly understood. Most writers on computer-based learning point to the computer's capability of providing immediate feedback as one of its great advantages, basing their conclusions on early research by Pressey (1950). More recent research, however, is not uniformly supportive of immediate feedback. Considering the frequent use of computers to provide drill and practice, this is a crucial area for future investigations.

Some research indicates that providing students with a simple indication of whether a response is correct or incorrect is just as effective as, or superior to, providing more elaborate reinforcements (such as time-consuming graphics or "Very Good!" or "Fine Work!" statements) when the response is correct (Bardwell 1981; Robin 1978; Gilman 1969; Roper 1977; Lasoff 1981). In fact, Schimmel's meta-analysis (1983) of programmed and computer-based feedback studies found no differences in benefits between studies that provided correct answers when student responses were incorrect and studies that simply identified the response as correct or incorrect.

When learning tasks are low-level, immediate feedback may be superior (Kulhavy & Anderson 1972). For example, immediate (zero-second delay) feedback would be most effective for discrimination learning (such as word discrimination) or rote memorization tasks.

Educators have often applied the term *immediate feedback* to such practices as giving students answers after they have completed a series of problems, or even to returning corrected exercises the day after completion. The positive research results on immediate feedback, however, apply to answers that are provided *immediately* after each problem is completed.

When learning tasks are higher-level, as in dealing with verbal learning like that encountered in much reading instruction, some studies indicate that delayed feedback is best (Sturges 1972; Rankin & Trepper 1978). Other studies have offered mixed results (Robin 1978; Kulhavy & Anderson 1972). Kulhavy and Anderson varied the length of delay between response and feedback and found no consistent differences.

While research is not consistently supportive, most computer-based-instruction experts agree that students appear to learn best when they receive detailed feedback as to which answers are correct and why they are correct (Gilman 1969; Roper 1977). This is most crucial when the responses made by the student have been incorrect. Beaulieu (1985) noted that students spend twice as much time studying feedback if responses are incorrect. Lack of detailed explanations in much contemporary software is a serious shortcoming.

Learner Control

Another often-touted advantage of computer-based instruction lies in the learner's control over instruction. Learners can, for instance, proceed at their own rates. There is some controversy, however, over whether learners benefit from all aspects of this control. Reinking and Schreiner (1985) found evidence that students' metacognitive controls—their ability to recognize when they have successfully learned from their reading—may not be sufficiently sophisticated for them to benefit from learner control over computer-presented textual readings. Rubincam and Olivier (1985) reported a similar lack of ability in computer-assisted mathematics lessons for high schoolers. Steinberg (1977) reviewed research on learner control in CBI and found that motivation is increased by learner control, but improved achievement is not. Benefits of learner control may be contingent on individual student differences involving such factors as locus of control (see Ch. 7 of this volume for an extended discussion).

Haynes, Kapinus, Malouf, and MacArthur (1984) studied vocabulary learning in computer-based and traditional formats. Students were asked to estimate how well they would remember words and definitions after one week. Their estimates were far less accurate on words learned through computer presentation than on those learned through conventional formats. The researchers conjectured that students may attribute the active part of learning to the computer rather than becoming involved in the learning experience.

Research on metacognitive skill development suggests that appropriate teaching methods can improve students' monitoring of learning (Baker & Brown 1984), an apparent prerequisite to effective use of learner-controlled software. Use of self-questioning strategies can help with both narrative (Singer & Donlan 1982) and expository (Balajthy 1986c) text. Teaching exactly specified summarization rules is also effective (Brown & Day 1983).

SOCIAL INTERACTION AND ORAL LANGUAGE WITHIN THE CLASSROOM

Oral speaking skills and interaction among students in the classroom have been the focus of many computer-based learning studies. Most of these studies have, however, been carried out in the context of children's learning to program computers, often using the programming language LOGO. One of the major justifications for spending school time teaching youngsters programming languages has been that the group problem solving that occurs as students learn by discovery enhances oral language and social skills (Papert 1980). While critics have suggested that these skills can be developed through activities that are more meaningful than programming, there appears to be no doubt that properly managed classroom experiences in programming can encourage interaction among students (Hawkins, Sheingold, Gearhart, & Berger 1982).

Fears that placing students at computer work stations would make them social loners with debilitated interpersonal skills (Seltzer 1971; Lichtman 1979; Davies & Shane 1986) have consistently been shown to be unfounded. Instead, a wide variety of researchers have reported increased social interaction revolving around the computer as students ask one another for help and advice (Sheingold, Hawkins, & Chan 1984; Schrock, Matthias, Vensel, & Anastasoff 1985). Among others, Genishi, McCollum, and Strand (1985), in their observations of kindergarten and first grade LOGO activities, have suggested that the children's interactions with each other are of more importance than their interactions with the computer in the programming activities.

Increased Interaction

Seventy-five percent of computer-using secondary reading teachers indicated disagreement with the statement "Computers isolate students from one another" in a survey carried out by Hague and Childers (1986). Hawkins (1983) and Sheingold, Hawkins, and Chan (1984) have suggested that the increased interaction noted in classroom computer applications has been due to the fact that microcomputers remain a new phenomenon in classrooms. The traditional taboos about doing one's own work have not yet begun to control teacher and student behaviors.

In addition, functional computer applications such as programming, word processing, and data-base research lend themselves to the establishment of a cooperative working environment (Hawkins & Sheingold 1986). There is a job to be done, a task to be learned, and students and teachers quickly recognize the value of cooperation. It is not the computer, per se, that increases amount and quality of interaction. Instead, interaction is increased by the purposeful working environment that accompanies these classroom computer uses.

One weakness of techniques such as peer tutoring and cooperative learning is that the learners involved often lack content expertise and effective teaching-learning strategies. In computer-assisted cooperative learning, the computer provided direct instruction, monitoring of learning, and reinforcement. The peer learners were responsible for modeling and analysis as they performed the reading-study procedure in pairs. Evaluative testing indicated superior performance in the trained group over a control group untrained in the study strategy. There was no superiority to another group trained in the study procedure but without either computers or cooperative learning.

Problems with Interaction

Early writings on computer applications in the classroom suggested that computers would have an almost magical effect in improving student interaction. Recent research in the quality of interactions among students using computers has raised new concerns. Schrock et al. (1985), for instance, in an observational study of microcomputer use among second and third graders, noted that much of the verbal behavior was not task-oriented. When the discussions were on task, they were frequently less than satisfactory from a pedagogical viewpoint. For example, when two or more students were working at a computer, hoarding of the keyboard, reprimands, and pushing away of hands were common. In a composition situation, one student might question the writing competence of another (Dickinson 1985). Much of the work was not truly collaborative, in the sense that students had different purposes in mind for the task at hand, and much of the interaction involved struggle for possession of the computer controls (Schrock et al. 1985).

Dickinson noted that off-task behavior was also a problem in collaborative writing tasks, taking up to 25 percent of the time in some sessions. He did, however, also note several instances in which one student would admonish another to stay on task.

In early observational studies, researchers noted a tendency for one or two students in a class to take on the role of class expert. Teachers were advised to take advantage of this natural tendency for some students to become more involved than others. Class experts could be trained as aides, for example, to relieve the teacher of responsibility for low-level mechanical details and questions (Balajthy 1986a).

Recent research has suggested that the teacher must take a more active role in dealing with the issue of class experts than was originally realized. Schrock et al. (1985), for example, observed one classroom and concluded:

> The "child expert" sought to dominate the machine. . . . He was insensitive to [other students'] needs for approval and frequently denied it. . . . He was ingenious in creating bogus reasons to usurp control of the machine. . . . On the balance, in the judgment of these investigators, this "child expert" interfered significantly with the computer skills acquisition of other children in the class. (p. 8)

Schrock et al. also noted that the child expert did not have a repertoire of mature teaching styles and tended to solve problems of his classmates himself rather than showing the children how to solve them. In fact, other children in the classroom who did not have as much computer knowledge were more likely to exhibit skillful teaching behaviors.

In her observational study of sixth grade classroom word processing, Michaels (1986) noted that in the classroom where a single child, Richie, was dominant in computer knowledge, other children referred their problems to him rather than learning text-editing commands themselves. In the classroom where the teacher remained dominant, many more students became independent in their computer operations. In Richie's classroom, girls were especially handicapped, as Richie would spend more time advising other boys.

Wepner, Feeley, and Strickland (1987) have suggested that teachers use a variety of thought-provoking awareness activities to help children understand the problems involved with access to computers. Teachers need to observe computer use in their own classrooms and employ problem-solving discussion techniques to ensure fair access for all.

The Teacher Factor

One crucial determining factor in quality of social interaction is the teacher. Computers can be used effectively, but they can be misused as well. Genishi, McCollum, and Strand (1985), for example, noted that an effective teacher was able to transmit enthusiasm and confidence to the children. While a part of the interaction among students occurred automatically because programming problems encountered were constant and teacher availability was limited, the crucial factor was teacher encouragement of cooperation among the students.

In their analysis of teacher interaction with students using the computer, Schrock et al. (1985) noted that little of the interaction was substantive. Much had to do with monitoring behavior in the computer area and with indicating whose turn it was to use the keyboard.

Dickinson (1985), on the other hand, in an observation of a first and second grade classroom in which writing experiences using the computer were being carried out, considered the computer experiences successful. He found that collaboration at the computer resulted in about as much on-task behavior as solitary paper-and-pencil writing. Solitary computer writing resulted in the greatest amount of on-task behavior. The successful implementation of collaborative computer writing was attributed to a variety of factors, most of which were teacher-centered. The teacher was in the second year of establishing a process-oriented writing program in her classroom. Prior to the microcomputer being brought into the room, the students had been writing about 45 minutes per day, with effective teacher monitoring and insistence that they remain on task. In addition, assignments were interesting (shared experiences or topics studied during the school year) and purposeful (for class publication or for sharing with parents).

Observational studies of classrooms employing microcomputers in process-oriented writing programs almost unanimously report surprisingly positive results. Serious problems and failed attempts appear to be rare. These successes seem to result from tendencies on the part of naturalistic researchers to look at exceptionally talented or dedicated teachers. A skeptic might also suggest that published observational research reported by those who are attempting to carry out naturalistic research in the field or writing—computer-based or not—tends to give a uniform glow to writing in process-oriented classrooms that is somewhat unrealistic and rarely found in real-life situations.

ROLE OF THE TEACHER

Teachers and Curriculum Change

Past technological innovations have failed to significantly influence education, largely through lack of appropriate teacher training. While information on teacher training in instructional applications of computers has only recently become available, the field of education offers a rich body of knowledge on staff development during educational change. Guskey (1986), in a survey of research, suggests that teacher trainers be aware of two major guiding principles:

1. Recognize that change is a difficult and slow process for teachers.
2. Provide continued support for the teachers both during and after initial training.

As in any field change presents great difficulties to educators. Lortie, in his well-known *Schoolteacher* (1975), noted that teachers are reluctant to risk failure. They recognize that the stakes are high in education: Failure of a new experimental methodology will lead to failure of student learning, and teachers have a strong, personal commitment to student success in learning. Fullan (1985) has noted that major changes, such as implementation of computer instruction, are best introduced gradually with a minimum of disruption or extra work.

Michaels (1986) noted in her observations of word-processing implementation in two elementary classrooms that the technology itself did not alter writing instruction in any meaningful way. Organization and pacing of instruction remained unchanged. The teachers were trained in use of the word-processing curriculum Quill, which included emphasis on two goals: establishing collaborative writing and writing across the curriculum. Yet there had been little of either prior to introduction of computers into the classrooms. Without this prior commitment, teachers simply used the computers in ways that were least disruptive to existing classroom management patterns, for instance, as replacements for the typewriter in preparing a final published draft.

Luehrmann (1986) argued that the popularity of word processing in elementary classrooms is due in large measure to this very phenomenon: that it only marginally affects the existing system of instruction in terms of its effects on the teacher-student relationship and the teacher role.

Staff Development

Staff developers should adhere to several basic principles when implementing computer instruction in the schools.

First, focus on application, not operation. Teachers must learn how computers can be used effectively in their classrooms. The key to effective integration of word processing in an elementary classroom lies in demonstration of how word processing fits into the classroom curriculum. How can students be scheduled to use the computers available? What lesson plan organization is required? What problems typically occur in organizing the classroom for word processing? Teacher training should center on the answers to such questions. Simply teaching teachers to use word-processing software misses the point.

Second, follow-up support is crucial. The vital role of ongoing support for teachers once the initial implementation of computers is past has been underscored by Guskey's (1986) contention that changes in teacher beliefs and attitudes occur *after* the implementation of new methods. It is only after the innovation has proved itself workable and has demonstrated improvement in student learning that teachers commit themselves to the new methods. In addition, teachers need time to experiment and develop their expertise in the new methods. No matter how good the prior training, it is when teachers actually try to use the new ideas that they encounter the most serious problems and doubts (Fullan 1982).

Third, training should be targeted to specific goals in the curriculum. If the decision has been made to use computers to develop reading skills, training should deal specifically with the concerns of computer-based reading skill instruction and with the software to be used in those efforts.

While there is a good deal of material available for general evaluation of software, there is little other teacher training information for classroom computer applications in reading and language arts. An increasing number of graduate courses designed specifically for reading and language arts teachers have become available (Modla 1986; Reinking 1986b; Rickelman 1986; Balajthy 1986b; Prince 1986).

As teachers become more familiar with computers, their anxieties about using this new technology decrease, and they develop more positive attitudes about computer-based instruction (Gressard & Loyd 1985). Stasz and Shavelson (1985) conducted a survey of computer-using teachers in 49 California schools to identify perceived needs pertaining to training in computers. They found that teachers recommended the following topics, in order from the highest priority to lowest. The number in parentheses indicates the number of teachers recommending that topic.

> Operation of microcomputers (47)
> Programming (30)
> Selection/evaluation of courseware (30)
> Instructional uses (29)
> Computer literacy (28)
> Integration with instruction (22)
> Administrative uses (10)

In addition, 12 teachers specifically recommended that no programming be taught.

This 1983 survey probably is not completely representative of contemporary computer-using teachers, as the population of such teachers has expanded tremendously since that time. In particular, the desire for programming knowledge has probably declined in recent years, as the benefits of teaching programming to children have been called into question and as more teachers have recognized the difficulties involved in programming their own courseware.

Teacher as Monitor

Observational studies have noted the serious problems confronting computer-using teachers. Teachers are frequently interrupted when working with other children by questions about computer operation (Schrock et al. 1985). The burden of monitoring computer use is imposing. Schrock et al. (1985) noted that the teacher being observed frequently had to instruct students to leave the computer station. Smith and Davis (1986), in their comparison of reading instruction as delivered by microcomputer software versus the minicomputer-based WICAT integrated learning system, indicated that the increased burdens on teachers of dealing with a fragmented microcomputer-based curriculum were substantial.

It is a common expectancy that computer-based instruction will allow a higher teacher-to-student ratio. Roblyer and King's (1983) findings that low teacher-to-student ratio makes the single largest contribution to achievement in computer-based reading instruction indicates a need for some caution in this area. It does not seem appropriate to justify the costs of CBI on the basis of eliminating teacher positions. Instead, justification should be based on using computers to improve the ability of teachers to deliver effective instruction (Roblyer 1985a).

Bork (1985) described the change in his role as university instructor of phsyics as a change from lecturer to tutor, an illustration of future teacher roles. Bork used computer-assisted instruction to deliver basic course content. Should a student fail to pass a computer-administered test after four tries, the computer referred the student to Bork for tutorial instruction. In this way, students who did not respond well to the computer's curriculum were provided an alternative form of instruction.

Student Independence in Learning

While some studies suggest the benefits of teacher supervision of computer-based instruction, other studies have demonstrated successful applications that can be carried out independently of teacher supervision, especially for older students. Feeley and Wepner (1986) demonstrated the effectiveness of the *Speed Reader II* program in increasing student reading speed as measured by the Fast Reading subtest of the Stanford Diagnostic

Reading Test. A major advantage cited by the researchers was the savings of teacher time. In traditional reading-rate instruction, teachers must allocate great amounts of time to administering timed reading drills. In Feeley and Wepner's study, all timed drills were carried out independently of instructor supervision. Balajthy, Bacon, and Hasby (1985) also reported successful independent use of reading-rate software with college students. In addition, Balajthy (1986b) reported successful use of an independent computer-based module of instruction designed to prepare preservice teachers in the fundamentals of using computers in the classroom.

Future Roles of Computer-Using Teachers

If increased independent learning through computer aids is the norm in education, what kind of functions may the teacher play? In most classrooms today, equipped at most with one or two microcomputers, the teacher's function is not changed. In a future with greater availability of hardware, teachers' roles may be altered considerably. The hardware-intensive PLATO systems allowed consideration of such alterations in computer-using teachers' roles.

Teacher construction of CBI courseware.   One of the major aims of the PLATO system (see Ch. 5 of this volume) was to encourage teachers to author computer instructional lessons. The authoring-language TUTOR was developed to be used by teachers for this purpose. An experienced teacher could construct an hour of student work in an estimated 26.4 hours, while it would take an inexperienced teacher some 237 hours for the same task (Hoyle 1983). TUTOR was only one of several CBI construction languages that facilitate lesson development. The best-known authoring language is PILOT.

Though PLATO-using teachers constructed a wide array of educational programs, a variety of problems were encountered in the project. One problem has to do with teachers' sense of professional purpose. Most teachers have not entered the profession with the goal of constructing educational materials; their goals are more person-oriented. They want to work with children and young people. As Hoyle (1983) pointed out, "They do not wish to individualize instruction as much as to personalize it" (p. 60). As much as possible, they would like to return to the days of tutors, in which instruction was offered on a one-to-one basis (Schneck 1984).

Increased personal instruction.   Experience shows that in most contemporary classrooms, the hardware shortages and software insufficiencies place an increased burden on microcomputer-using teachers. An ultimate goal of computer instruction, however, is to provide computer assistance with the management and clerical chores confronting teachers. This will free them to work with students for whom other learning resources have proved insufficient (Bork 1985). Once again, in the PLATO environments where hardware and software needs are met more effectively, instructors perceived that they have more contact with students than before use of computers. Alderman, Appel, and Murphy (1978), for example, reported that 39 percent of PLATO-using instructors reported that they had more contact with students because of PLATO, while only 15 percent indicated their student contact was decreased.

This human teacher component in education will remain a vital factor, in part because the Western learning tradition is human-centered. If it were not, human instruction would have been phased out with the invention of the printing press. In addition, as Davy (1984, p. 16) points out, schooling involves far more than cognitive training: "At the heart of real life is working with people, being with people, understanding people. . . . As long as classrooms include real teachers, cognitive development cannot in the nature of the situation, be divorced from emotional, social, and moral experience."

In her survey of research on instructor/student interaction, McCombs (1985) found that adequate opportunities for contacts between computer-using instructors and their students are consistently related to successful achievement outcomes. On the other hand, time spent by instructors in instructional management, administration, and clerical tasks was ineffective. McCombs suggested that human instructors function to augment the computer-based instruction. They also help students develop positive attitudes and act as guides to learning and as models for self-management skills.

In conjunction with the increased ability to deal personally with students, however, must come training for teachers. Most teachers have little understanding of the differing purposes of small-group versus large-group instruction. In addition, most are not familiar with tutorial and conferencing methods.

Teacher as researcher.   The capability of the computer to collect and report data on student achievement can be valuable in increasing understanding of how students learn. In addition, this capability allows teachers to evaluate the effectiveness of particular programs. Since much instructional programming can easily be changed by the simple addition of some lines of code, this ongoing evaluation by teachers is an important function. With appropriately conceived computer instruction, teachers need not throw up their hands in frustration when an explanation is insufficient or out-of-date. They can make changes themselves or order consultants to make the changes.

THE FUTURE OF COMPUTER-BASED INSTRUCTIONAL RESEARCH

An imperative for research is the need to identify computer-based instructional advantages. Without a clear indication of effectiveness, schools will be unable to obtain further financial support for educational technology. As Becker (1985b) pointed out, however, the "catch-22" in this situation is that proof of effectiveness is being required without sufficient computers to permit integration into classroom teaching patterns.

SOURCES OF INFORMATION

REINKING, DAVID (ed.). In press. *Computers and Reading: Issues for Theory and Practice.* New York: Teachers College Press.
This valuable text contains chapters on a variety of reading-related issues. Some of the chapters offer review of research related to their topics. Others provide descriptions of specific computer-based educational projects. Topics range from artificial intelligence research, the technology of print, and computer analysis of written materials to eye movement technology and computer speech. The special strength of this book is that its chapter authors are knowledgeable about research in reading and in computer-based education.

CULBERTSON, JACK A., AND LUVERN L. CUNNINGHAM (eds.). 1986. *Microcomputers and Education: Eighty-fifth Yearbook of the National Society for the Study of Education*, Part 1. Chicago: University of Chicago Press.
This text is a compilation of articles on a wide variety of computer-related topics, including future implications of widespread use of computers, computer literacy, cost-effectiveness of computer-based instruction, and local area networks. The writers occasionally display three tendencies characteristic of proponents of computer-based education: lack of knowledge about computer-based educational research other than that carried out in conjunction with their own work, unwarranted faith in computers to solve all educational problems, and placement of blame for the contemporary problems with CBI on educators who are "unwilling to face the future." Janice H. Patterson and Marshall S. Smith offer a particularly valuable chapter, "The Role of Computers in Higher-Order Thinking."

VDT NEWS: THE VDT HEALTH AND SAFETY REPORT. P.O. Box 3000, Dept. JJ, Denville, NJ 07834
This newsletter reports on research, legislation, and allegations pertaining to the effect on health of VDTs. Articles in a typical issue have included "NIOSH Epidemiological Study Controversy Continues," "Michigan Pregnancy Study Downplays VDT-Miscarriage Link," and "Comprehensive Canadian Utility Study Finds No VDT Risk." For up-to-date information, this is a reliable reference on a topic about which the mass media are uninformed.

HUMAN FACTORS: THE JOURNAL OF THE HUMAN FACTORS SOCIETY. Human Factors Society, Box 1369, Santa Monica, CA 90406
This journal publishes research on the factors involved in human interaction with computers, including effects of monitors and lengthy use of computers on health and the psyche.

7

COMPUTERS AND LEARNING
FROM TEXT

Viewers of the "Star Trek" television series will be familiar with pictures of *Enterprise* crew members relaxing with good books. Whether it was Scotty studying an engineering manual, Uhuru enjoying a novel, or Spock contemplating scientific research, reading was a fairly common pastime of those space-exploring heroes. The books read, however, were not printed on paper and bound in cloth. Instead, their pages appeared on the ubiquitous computer monitors scattered throughout the starship. With a few simple commands, any text stored in the huge memory banks of the *Enterprise*'s computer system could be called up for viewing.

What promise does computer presentation of text hold for the future? A variety of topics in this area are described in this chapter. The problem of screen clarity and legibility is considered briefly. While this is a problem for the moment—many people do not respond well to prolonged periods of computer monitor reading—improved technologies are already available and within a few years this will no longer be an issue. The problem of computer memory storage is considered in Chapter 10. For large amounts of print, computer storage is not efficient, but again, new technologies such as CD-ROM will soon provide remedies for this problem.

The flexibility of text presentation on a computer monitor holds tremendous potential for improvement of education. Words can be highlighted in text, questions interspersed, definitions of unknown vocabulary requested, more or less complex explanations provided, and so forth, all at the command of the reader or under the control of the software authors. The ease of revising and updating text presentation could lead to substantial developments in the science of text engineering, with computer-presented textbooks being revised as frequently as necessary, perhaps even at the local level by teachers who are using them.

The bulk of this chapter will deal with the engineering of instructional and informational computer text presentation. The purpose and design of interactive text systems and of large-scale hypertext systems are considered. Then a variety of issues having to do with improving the effectiveness of text are discussed, including use of highlighting devices, graphics, and glossary-like aids. The debate concerning the advantages and disadvantages of user control over text presentation is considered in conjunction with important findings from metacognitive "learning-to-learn" research. Before dealing with those topics, however, the important technological issues of computer monitors and text legibility are considered.

CONTEMPORARY TECHNOLOGICAL LIMITATIONS

Is Prolonged Reading at Computer Monitors Hazardous?

The increased use of computers for presentation of text means longer times spent in front of video display terminals (VDTs). A variety of concerns have been raised about possible health hazards supposedly caused by prolonged use of VDTs, including headaches, backaches, eye strain, stress, fatigue, and more serious problems such as radiation poisoning, problem pregnancies, and development of cataracts. In a survey of research on VDTs, EPIE (Educational Products Information Exchange 1986) contested commonly held fallacies about such claims and concluded that there are no known health hazards:

1. No reputable scientific evidence shows that VDTs expose users to harmful radiation.
2. VDT use does not affect eyes any differently than other reading activities.
3. VDTs themselves do not cause muscle discomfort any more than other activities that require a fixed position for long periods of time.

VDT users can follow several recommendations to minimize discomfort:

1. VDTs should be 18-24 inches from the user's eyes.
2. The top of the VDT screen should be level with the user's eyes.
3. Users should adjust contrast controls as needed for greatest personal comfort.
4. VDT users usually function best with slightly lower lighting than in the typical office.
5. Users should take a rest period every two hours.
6. Keyboards should be set so that user's wrists are slightly (10-20 degrees) elevated.
7. Adjustable chairs and desks provide greatest flexibility for comfort.

Text Legibility

In his comprehensive survey of text legibility on computer monitors, Daniel (in press) bemoans the lack of research on this topic. He notes that the large body of findings pertaining to hard-copy printed text (Tinker 1963; Watts & Nisbet 1974) are only marginally applicable to text legibility on a computer monitor. A number of recent studies, however, have been directed to this issue.

Care must be taken in interpreting the educational significance of these studies, as it is too early to draw final conclusions on many issues. In comparisons of printed text and text on a VDT, a variety of factors must be considered. For example, VDTs vary in clarity. A study carried out with one model VDT is not necessarily transferable to another model. Font types will also affect findings, as will varied settings of the contrast controls. Unfortunately, most studies to date are small in scale and do not deal with a sufficient number of variables to yield convincing results.

VDT text presentation versus printed pages.   Kruk and Muter (1984) found that readers were up to 24.1 percent slower in reading text on a VDT than on a printed page. Heppner, Anderson, Farstrup, and Weiderman (1985) found test scores to be lower on a standardized test displayed on a VDT than on the same test in paper copy.

McNinch, Creamer, and Shaffer (1985), on the other hand, found no differences in fifth graders' comprehension scores when reading an identical story on a VDT, a typed page, and a filmstrip projection. Gambrell, Bradley, and McLaughlin (1985) found that children as young as eight years old could read computer-presented text with the same comprehension as printed text. The students involved in their study had extensive prior experience with computer-based learning. In general, scores of reading tests administered on computer monitors are equivalent to scores of paper-and-pencil tests (see Ch. 4 of this volume).

Reinking and Schreiner (1985) tested fifth and sixth grade students, and found that both better and poorer readers achieved higher comprehension scores on printed material than on identical text presented on a VDT. Their findings suggested that an interactive effect may exist due to passage difficulty. Comprehension of the groups on high-difficulty passages was about the same. The group reading the printed text had superior scores on low-difficulty passages.

Upper- and lower-case presentation.   Early microcomputers were unable to easily present lower-case letters. One of the most substantial findings of older print legibility research clearly indicated problems created by all-upper-case text. Watts and Nisbet (1974), for example, surveyed a convincing body of literature to conclude that children functioned better with mixed-case text (that is, both upper- and lower-case) than with upper-case alone. This limitation of the early microcomputers has been largely overcome for most educational text presentation needs. Read-only memory modifications and greater random-access memory capacities allow microcomputers to present both cases, and often several different font styles and sizes, as well.

Image polarity. Cushman (1986) has studied visual fatigue resulting from reading. He found fatigue to be greater with the positive-image presentation of text in microfiche, in which the letters are dark and the background light. Visual fatigue was no greater for negative-image VDT presentation of text than for ordinary printed materials. Reading speed was slower for the negative-image VDT than for printed pages, but comprehension was equal across all conditions.

Chunking of text. A variety of studies suggest that text "chunked" by inserting extra spaces between phrase and clause units may increase rate and comprehension. Hartley (1982) suggested that line endings in computer-presented text be determined by such syntactic groupings. On the basis of such recommendations, Jandreau, Muncer, and Bever (1986) carried out reading-rate studies with community college students. They found that increasing the space size at major phrase boundaries improved rate, and inserting spaces at minor phrase boundaries helped even more.

Screen page width. A page width (sometimes called line length) of approximately 65 characters is standard for business letters. Two-column page formats in magazines typically have a line length of 25 to 30 characters per column. Frase (in press) chunked computer-presented text into phrase and clause boundaries and analyzed varied page widths to find which widths yielded the greatest number of occurrences in which one complete chunk was presented per line. He found that optimal automatic chunking of fourth-grade-level material occurred at 44 characters per line, tenth grade material at 50 characters per line, and eighteenth grade material at 56 characters per line. No actual testing of reading performance was carried out, however.

Right justification. Use of word processors has increased the propensity to right-justify—that is, to line up the right margin just as is standard procedure with the left. Right justification is sometimes called full justification. This practice has been roundly criticized by Daniel (in press), who cited research on chunking text by inserting extra spaces between phrase and clause units. Such chunking frequently led to improved rate and comprehension. Researchers who randomly chunked text, however, by inserting extra spaces at random points within text, as occurs when computers right-justify text, invariably found that comprehension was reduced.

Trollop and Sales (1986) have compared college students' performances on computer-presented text readings that are right-justified with readings with a standard ragged right margin. Groups did not differ in comprehension, but right justification slowed reading rate. Muncer, Gorman, Gorman, and Bibel (1986) also found that right justification disrupted reading for college students. Findings indicated greater disruption for good than for poor readers.

Single versus double spacing.   Kruk and Muter (1984) found that reading of single-spaced text on a VDT was 10.9 percent slower than reading of double-spaced text.

INSTRUCTIONAL TEXT ENGINEERING

We read for different purposes. We learn from text in different ways and at different rates. Publishers of textbooks recognize these differences and make available a variety of textual aids for improved learning from text. Researchers in reading, for instance, have found evidence that learning from text can be enhanced in many ways (Anderson & Biddle 1975; Fleming & Levie 1978; Mayer 1980):

• Structured overview diagrams present a picture of the basic chapter organization.
• Adjunct questions can be used for a variety of purposes. Postquestions, for example, appear to increase general retention of text. Prequestions focus attention and learning on targeted information.
• Headings provide a sense of organization and can serve as the basis for reader self-questioning.
• Introductions and summaries focus attention on key ideas and provide repeated exposure to that information.

Each of the text learning aids mentioned above can be incorporated into computer text presentation as desired by publishers. Computer presentation of these aids offers many advantages over traditional text applications, largely through the flexibility and control possible with computers. In traditional texts, once a book is printed, it is impossible to change. Later editions may be revised by the publisher, but only at significant cost. In computer text, if it is designed for flexibility, changes can be made simply and quickly—as simply as inserting or deleting, using a word processor. Updates can be distributed in disk formats by the publisher. Under appropriate conditions, classroom teachers can update and change the text to better reflect course content and focus. Crucial passages could be highlighted, for example, and material that merely repeats in-class presentations deleted or stored in a secondary file accessible by students who were absent or who want review. As Obertino noted, in comparison with printed hard copy, software "has no inherent propensity to fossilize" (1974, p. 10).

Research on traditional text adjunct study aids, such as use of headings and questions, has often had mixed results. While some studies indicated that the aids could be used effectively, a major stumbling block was that many students did not use the aids. They read a chapter, for instance, skipped over the questions, and failed to look for an overall chapter organization as indicated by the headings.

Reinking (1984) has suggested that, to some degree, the ineffectiveness of these study aids is due to their inability to actively confront the reader. They are static components of the textbook. A major theme underlying much of Reinking's research on computer text presentation has been that the increased engagement possible on computer monitors will greatly improve learning from text. Computer presentation of text must not be considered a simple case of transferring a printed page to a monitor screen, involving qualitatively the same cognitive operations as evidenced in reading the printed page. Instead, "Computer technology makes available a number of previously unavailable manipulations of text that in turn may lead to the use of a different set of mental skills to derive meaning from text" (Reinking in press). To emphasize the differences possible between traditional printed text and text presented on a computer monitor, Reinking uses the terms *computer-mediated text* and *dynamic text* (Reinking 1987) to describe displays of connected text under the immediate control of a computer program.

Interactive Text

Weyer (1982) put a social studies textbook on computer at the Xerox Palo Alto Research Center. Readers were led to browse through the contents of the text to find information on topics about which they were questioned. The on-line book had an index. If the reader selected a topic in the index, the monitor displayed the appropriate information immediately. Words selected from the index were highlighted. This latter approach, putting a text in electronic form so as to allow search operations, is often called an interactive text.

The Comprehension Connection is a commerical software series for grades 4–9, based on Reinking and Schreiner's research (1985; see discussion below) on use of interactive text for comprehension and metacomprehension development. Students read content area passages on the monitor, answer questions, then receive feedback as to success or failure of comprehension. At any point during reading, students can reread the text, or they can access a variety of comprehension aids: an on-line dictionary, an easier version of the passage, a summary of the main idea, a graphic.

Videotex and Teletext

The origin of videotex and teletext is sometimes traced to the 1964 World's Fair and its display of AT&T picture telephones. British scientists who studied the development could see no major implications for viewing other speakers in a telephone conversation, but they did realize the implications for delivery of a new medium of information into homes: electronic displays of textual information.

Ten years later, the world's first videotex system, Viewdata, was developed in Britain and shortly afterward a teletext version of the same system, Ceefax, appeared (Pfaehler & Carey 1985). Videotex refers to any system of displaying textual information on a television screen or monitor at the viewer's command. Communication is two-way, with users capable of both sending and receiving information. Information is usually delivered over phone lines. A teletext system involves one-way display of textual information originating from a broadcast.

Many people believe that in 20 years, cities will be wired with communication grids to link homes, schools, and businesses to libraries, information data bases, and large computer facilities. Among the more popular videotex services in the United States are CompuServe and The Source. Both provide access over phone lines to a variety of information sources.

Some limited research and development has been carried out using videotex in the United States. The University of Wisconsin, for example, used electronic text to support a 26-part Public Broadcasting System series called "Congress: We the People." The series was designed as part of an undergraduate course in political science. Students accessed the electronic text curriculum in one of two ways: using disk-based lessons on an Apple microcomputer or using home videotex equipment accessing the curriculum through CompuServe. Pfaehler (1985) reported generally positive results, especially in terms of student attitudes about the convenience of such instruction.

Hypertext and Hypermedia

In scholarly work, learning involves making connections between knowledge sources. The academic library, with its massive storage capabilities, allows scholars access to the information necessary for formation of complex webs of knowledge about specific topics. These connections are made explicit in traditional text through the use of footnotes and references to outside sources. Searching out those references, however, is laborious and time-consuming. Scholars may be forced to consult several different libraries to get access to the information they want, and much time will be spent walking the aisles of each library.

Electronic text, as envisioned by theorists and experimental developers, will put massive webs of immediately accessible information at the fingertips of learners and scholars. Rather than involving searches for printed books and articles, relevant texts will be immediately available through electronic data storage and retrieval. A student studying one of Auden's poems, for example, might be able to call up relevant articles by a wide variety of literary critics, or perform a key-word search through the corpus of Auden's poetic works. Should one of the critics mention some relationship between Auden's theme and a contemporary poem by Eliot, the student could immediately access

Eliot's poem and a web of critical commentary about it. These interlocking webs of information could, in theory, go on practically forever, providing an unparalleled capability of "augmenting human intellect" (Englebert & English 1968).

Carmody et al. (1969) used the term *hypertext system* to describe a text editing system capable of dealing with construction and reading of such an interlocking web of text. Hypertext is

> . . . nonsequential writing and reading. Both an author's tool and a reader's medium, a hypertext document system allows authors or groups of authors to *link* information together, create *paths* through a corpus of related material, *annotate* existing texts, and create notes that point readers to either bibliographic data or the body of the referenced text. Hypertext can allow the creation of an automated encyclopedia of sorts. Readers can browse through linked, cross-referenced, annotated texts in an orderly but nonsequential manner. (Yankelovich, Meyrowitz, & van Dam 1985, p. 18)

At the heart of such systems would lie a large data base of information. Readers would use computer data-searching techniques to find and organize information on topics or on relations between topics in the data base. Yankelovich, Meyrowitz, and van Dam (1985) warned that the problem of spatial organization would be a serious one for users of hypertext systems. It is easy to become disoriented, not to know where one is located, within a three-dimensional web of related information. They suggested that such systems be provided with schematic diagrams of the overall structure of information nodes. Such maps might indicate all path options, as well as show paths that the reader has already taken. These maps would have to be constructed at a variety of hierarchical levels, from an overall global view of the system to detailed depictions of specific topics within the system.

McClintock (1986) has studied the benefits to education and scholarship of such hypertext systems and concluded metaphorically that computer-based education to date has not even left the starting gate. Because of memory and design limitations that continue to hinder development of hypertext systems, computers are still "objects of study, not its tools, because nothing yet available is quite ready to serve the educational functions anticipated for it" (p. 2).

As an example, he estimated the size of the web of information (he referred to this web as a "knowledge tree," with varying levels of depth) necessary for an undergraduate course in a liberal arts college. Such a course might include reading a book a week and completing a serious term paper based on two or three more books. At one to two megabytes (million bytes; a typical classroom microcomputer of the mid-1980s has a maximum memory of only 65 kilobytes, that is, 64,000 bytes, a small fraction of a megabyte) of information per book for electronic storage, this would require that the class would have access to 20 megabytes of required readings and an additional 5 megabytes of source materials for each student that would be read in detail and 25 megabytes per student for cursory readings, in preparation for the term paper. This adds up to 620 megabytes of information for a class of 20 students. McClintock estimated that a typical high school course would require a knowledge tree of about 138 megabytes.

Needless to say, present computer text storage capabilities come nowhere near being adequate. This, McClintock claims, is the reason that computers have not yet left the starting gate in the race toward fulfilling educational expectations:

> We have here the stark and simple reason for the chronic mediocrity of educational software: educational software has been deficient in the quantity of its information content by a factor of about one thousand, doing in kilobytes tasks that in other media have been done in megabytes. (p. 6)

McClintock notes that a number of factors beyond mere hardware technological issues continue to hinder development of satisfactory data bases, including legal and economic restrictions on the entry of copyrighted text into electronic form.

Kamil (1982) has calculated software sufficiency by comparing printed text contents with computer memory equivalents. To provide a 10-chapter textbook for each of grades 1 to 12, 120 chapters are required. If 5 8-kilobyte (8K) programs equal a chapter, 600 8K programs are needed to provide an equivalent amount of information.

Provenzo (1986), among others, has suggested that most specialized and technical information will soon be placed in electronic form rather than in books or printed journals. Scholarly works in every field will be readily available on-line, and authors will be required to submit manuscripts in electronic form in order to eliminate the expense of keyboarding the articles from printed text. In fact, in many cases technical information is already being stored electronically, and many publishers will accept manuscripts in electronic form for direct typesetting.

Several publishers of microcomputer software have constructed limited text data bases to provide students with simplified experiences in working with such information sources. *Poetry and Mythology Databases* includes biographical data and poems of selected poets, as well as summaries of major Greek myths with data on their themes and characters. *Literature and Composition Databases* includes information on 75 fables, with summaries and morals. Both data base disks are designed for use with an ordinary data base program, *Scholastic pfs: File*. While the data bases can be used to provide students with a basic understanding of how electronic information systems may work, they do not contain anywhere near the amount of information envisioned for actual hypertext systems.

Feiner, Nagy, and van Dam (1982) reported the development of an experimental system that goes beyond hypertext to hypermedia. Called *The Electronic Document System*, this has text construction systems and an overall hypertext control system. It also has sophisticated graphics capabilities, including ability to incorporate animation with text presentation.

The system has been used to create a maintenance manual for sonar equipment. Readers may study the manual by selecting topics from a menu, or they can follow a prescribed path through the document. The authors have prearranged several paths for the needs of differing readers: a novice, an intermediate, and an expert path. In addition, readers may use a key-word system to specify presentation of specific topics.

Two map diagrams of the system are provided for readers. One illustrates the path that the reader has followed. The other illustrates the position within the system at which the reader is now, with all possible paths to that point and from that point.

RESEARCH ON COMPUTER-MEDIATED TEXTUAL MANIPULATIONS

The computer offers unprecedented flexibility of design for textual displays, and research has only begun to scratch the surface of its potential.

Author or User Control?

One of the key issues in design of computer text presentation will be that of author versus user control over the text manipulations. Readers read for different purposes and from different points of view. Pichert and Anderson (1977), for example, found that readers who read a story from one point of view remembered different information than those who read the same story from another point of view. Van Dijk (1985) has pointed out that key information in a text can be considered "important" only insofar as the reader and author are separately concerned. Information can be important in two ways: Textually important information is important in terms of the author's structure and emphasis; contextually important information is important to the reader.

Author control of text manipulations would have the purpose of presenting textually important information more forcefully. For those readers who wish to control the reading process for their own purposes, however, user control—the ability to select or refuse specific manipulations—would be a valuable asset. Research on traditional printed text indicates that for some readers, under some conditions, use of text aids and special study strategies can actually impede comprehension and retention (Balajthy 1986c). Many readers can perform most effectively by managing their own reading and study strategies.

Learner control over pace of learning has long been cited as an advantage of computer-based instruction (Grubb 1977). The major advantage was that the learner could make decisions about the learning process more appropriately than a computer or the designers who created the computer program. Merrill (1980) argued that program control over learning would make students more dependent on the computer system. Independence of decision making would improve students' ability in learning how to learn.

A number of studies have indicated that poor metacognitive functioning—that is, inability to accurately monitor success or failure of learning—hinders learning in situations where students are given control, as opposed to situations in which control is exerted by the computer (Steinberg 1977; Tennyson, Tennyson, & Rothen 1980). Balland et al. (1985), for example, found that in an instructional program about the human heart, students performed worse with self-pacing than with moderate computer control. Rubincam and Olivier (1985) surveyed 11 studies that included comparisons of achievement in learner-control versus nonlearner-control situations. Five of the studies indicated superior performance under nonlearner control and only two under learner control. Four studies showed no difference.

One basic problem appears to be that students do not develop clear-cut learning goals. Brown (1986) described a common student behavior when using computer-based instruction as "wandering about the courseware":

> They will start one program and then soon tire of it. They then try another and another, until they have operated every program on the disk for five or ten minutes. They will then ask for another disk, asserting that they have "completed" the one they have. (p. 28)

Balajthy, Bacon, and Hasby (1985, in press), in an examination of content-area vocabulary learning via microcomputer instruction, found that another basic problem is that students terminate instruction prematurely, with little sense of whether the learning task has been completed successfully. Computer-based studies indicating such metacognitive inabilities support studies using more traditional forms of instruction (Brown, Campione, & Barclay 1979; Robinson & Robinson 1984).

Garhart and Hannafin (1986) tested the relationship between college readers' self-assessments of comprehension and their actual comprehension based on factual and inferential posttest questions. Little or no correlation was found between self-assessments and posttest scores.

Gay (1986) investigated the possibility that prior knowledge of a topic may influence learners' effectiveness in monitoring their own learning when using a computer. Using a biology topic for instruction, she found that learners with little prior knowledge of the topic performed better under program control than when they controlled instruction. They tended to practice too little and to avoid unfamiliar or difficult subtopics. Learners with a high degree of prior knowledge, on the other hand, performed as well under their own control as under the computer's. Gay suggested that direct teaching of how to use control options may be effective for improving learning.

Reinking and Schreiner (1985) compared performance of fifth and sixth grade readers in three on-line conditions. In one condition, readers were simply presented textual material, then posttested. In another, readers had the option of referring to a variety of text learning aids, including graphics, summaries, vocabulary definitions, and a revised version of the passage written at a lower readability level. In the third condition, readers were presented the text learning aids under computer control. For both high- and low-difficulty passages, the group that received computer-controlled presentation of all learning aids scored higher than the other two groups. The group that was given optional access to the learning aids did no better than the group that was given the text alone.

Rubincam and Olivier (1985) interviewed students who were involved in making decisions about instruction in computer-based learning. Students decided whether to take a pretest on instructional objectives to determine needs or to begin immediately on an instructional module designed to teach that objective. They found a high degree of consistency of choice. Individual students either typically chose to take the pretest or not to take it. Postinstructional interviews led the researchers to conclude that decisions were based on a personality variable that ranged from cautious to confident. The educational problems created by this type of decision making may be the result of an interaction between metacognitive inability and personality variables such as locus of control. External locus of control may result in lack of reader attention to computer-provided text learning aids.

Improvement of Comprehension Monitoring

Comprehension monitoring involves an awareness on the part of a reader of success or failure of understanding. Anderson (1980) has described the "click" of comprehension success—a sudden feeling that one has understood the concepts contained in text—and the "clunk" of comprehension failure. A variety of studies have found that younger and poorer readers have poor self-monitoring ability (Markman 1979; Owings et al. 1980), often proceeding in reading without realizing that comprehension failure has occurred and, as a result, not using any "fix-up" strategies such as rereading, looking ahead, or referring to a dictionary or another text.

Comprehension monitoring is one component of the more general processes known as metacognition (Flavell 1979) or, when referring specifically to reading, metacomprehension. *Metacognition* refers to an individual's control over cognitive functioning.

No research to date has yielded evidence that the computer's capabilities can be used to improve metacognitive functioning (Reinking 1986b). There is evidence, however, that computers can be used to improve comprehension of text by regulating readers' processes through use of external controls as a supplement to independent internal comprehension monitoring.

Anderson et al. (1974) demonstrated one technique in which computers might be able to help students with poor self-monitoring abilities. College students read a short assignment and were immediately administered a computer multiple-choice test. Those who failed the test were sent back to reread the assignment. While the test was administered and scored on a computer, the actual reading assignments were off-line. Students in the experimental groups scored significantly higher on their course final exam than students who read and studied without the computer monitoring.

L'Allier (1980) also used the computer to monitor comprehension. Comprehension was automatically monitored by the computer in two ways, reading rate and answers to questions. Any student whose speed and/or answers indicated a need was provided an on-screen revision of the reading passage that had been rewritten to a lower readability level. High schoolers in the experimental condition scored higher in a comprehension posttest than control groups reading the original versions without computer monitoring. In fact, the lower-ability students in the experimental group scored as high as the high-ability students in the control. An average 7 percent increase in time-on-task for the computer monitoring group resulted in a 22 percent gain in comprehension.

Conversational Text

Encouragement of active reading has long been a goal of reading teachers. A variety of cognitive learning strategies have been proposed in an effort to teach this active reading. Most are based on generative learning models similar to that proposed by Wittrock (1974).

Singer (1978), for example, defined active reading as asking questions of oneself during reading (called self-generated questioning). Pauk (1974) suggested that interaction between the college reader and text be increased by advising students to spend 50 percent of reading time with the book closed, thinking about facts and ideas presented. SQ3R (Robinson 1961), the best-known of many study techniques, encourages interaction in a variety of ways, including surveying text material before reading, developing questions about important material, and reading to find the answer to those questions.

These active, generative behaviors have been found to be effective in increasing comprehension, especially if students receive training and practice in their use. Research by Singer and Donlan (1982) indicated that self-generated questioning can improve comprehension of stories. Balajthy (1986c) found that self-generated questioning can also be effective when used with the more varied organizational structures of expository prose.

Interactive computer presentation of text has even greater potential to change the nature of reading into an act more like conversation. A serious limitation on effectivness of cognitive strategy research and instruction has been student involvement. For many strategies, such as the ITT self-generated questioning technique (Balajthy 1982), in which students are trained to construct questions to predict paragraph content and organization based on their reading of topic sentences, activity is internal and cannot be monitored. In other words, students generate questions in their minds, and researchers and teachers have little control over the quality of questioning—or, indeed, over whether questioning is being carried out at all.

Interactive software offers much more control over processing than is possible for authors and teachers using traditional textbooks. Interaction can be exactly specified and enforced. In addition, extended training programs in which appropriate interactive strategies are modeled may lead to increased transfer of these strategies to noncomputer reading. Researchers in the area of study skills have long believed that extended training—beyond the scope of most study skills sessions—is necessary if students are to be convinced of the value of using the study skills they are taught.

Blohm and Whiteside (1986) studied the effects of computer-presented interspersed decision statements on college students' comprehension. They interspersed two types of decision statements between paragraphs in continuous text. One, a rote memory/knowledge-level statement, asked readers to identify whether a particular sentence had appeared in the paragraph just read. The second type of decision statement was a semantic memory/analysis-level statement. It required that readers make higher-level decisions about ideas in the text. Results confirmed findings from printed text research (for example, Rickards 1976) that higher-level decision-making tasks improve comprehension of text.

Typographic Cues

The usefulness of typographic cues to topic importance is generally accepted in printed texts. Authors frequently make use of headings, italicized type, bold print, underlinings, and so forth. The flexibility of computer presentation of text makes serious consideration of typographic cues of key importance. Presentation of such cues could be under author control, or readers could be offered varied options for cuing. Text might, for example, include inverse highlighting of main idea sentences. Color coding could differentiate levels of importance or interrelationships between ideas in the text.

Blohm and Whiteside (1986) investigated the effects of color-coding text on a computer screen. College students were presented paragraphs in which main idea statements were printed in white, explanation and definition statements in orange, and examples and details in green. No significant effects were found for this color coding.

Graphics

Visuals play a variety of roles in improving learning based on verbal material (Wisely & Streeter 1985). They can function to attract and sustain attention, to simplify or explain, and even to present inaccessible processes such as a movie of open heart surgery. In optimal circumstances, one picture may indeed be worth a thousand words for improvement of learning from reading (Rankin & Culhane 1970).

In many circumstances, however, graphics offer no help or actually harm performance. There is no evidence to support the use of graphics for the simple purpose of improving attractiveness of screen layout. There is some evidence that presentation of extraneous graphics may interfere with children's concentration on print (Samuels 1967).

Glossary-like Aids

McConkie and Zola (in press) used a computer program that gives a voice-synthesized pronunciation of any word touched by the user when it is displayed on the monitor screen. Preliminary results of evaluation indicate that the adults for whom the system was designed are able to read text well above their instructional reading level when oral pronunciations are available. In addition, the unfamiliar vocabulary is apparently learned by the readers, as words selected for pronunciation by specific readers are chosen less frequently later on in the reading.

Chomsky (1986) used a computer-driven videodisk to simulate reading aloud to children. A story is displayed one page at a time on the screen. The child controls forward and backward movement through the story. As the page is displayed, a voice reads the words aloud. The words being spoken are highlighted to help children follow along.

Reinking and Schreiner's (1985) study of interactive text, described above, involved presentation of expository materials. One of the options available to readers was to request vocabulary definitions for unfamiliar words and technical terms.

As Brown (1983) has suggested, use of electronic pronunciation and dictionary systems may lead to development of bad habits, a persistent negative reliance on technology. He compared such help to use of the graduated-length method of learning how to ski, in which students find early success on short skis that improve control, balance, and turning. Such task simplification may lead to bad habits, but a good coach can circumvent these problems by knowing how to prevent and remediate them.

Provision of Supplemental Information

Reinking and Schreiner's (1985) innovative programs allowed readers to request two types of supplemental text information in addition to graphics and vocabulary discussed earlier. If the reader required additional background information on the concepts presented, or if a summary of passage content was desired, either could be requested. The summary was presented in the form of an outline of the passage structure.

Blohm (1982a) carried out a study in which college student readers of text on a computer screen could request paraphrases of technical passages.

```
1
    One of the most  universal  findings to   emerge  from  recent
<
psycholinguistic research is the marked degree to which a  learner
                                                         >
applies prior knowledge of a topic to facilitate future cognition.

IN OTHER WORDS, THOSE WHO STUDY THE  PSYCHOLOGY AND LINGUISTICS OF
READING HAVE FOUND THAT WE   USE KNOWLEDGE WE  ALREADY HAVE TO GAIN
UNDERSTANDING  OF  NEW  INFORMATION WE  IDENTIFY IN  OUR  READING.
2                            <
In fact, most contemporary delineations of comprehension allude to

the role of prior knowledge as a  "yellow brick road"  to  compre-
                        *
hending  written  discourse  [THE IDEAS  CONTAINED  IN  THE TEXT].
3
Recent experiments conducted by  cognitive  psychologists  provide
-
explicit demonstration of the prominent role prior knowledge plays
                                4
in text comprehension.   For example,....
```

FIGURE 7-1. Example of glossed version of screen text. The lines in all capitals have been added to the screen text at the request of the reader (Blohm 1982).

The text was coded with the commands necessary to ask for help (see Figure 7-1). Those students with the option recalled more information from the passages than did students who read from the computer screen but did not have access to the paraphrases. The use of the glossing required no more study time than was required by readers without the glossing aid. Blohm also found that low achievers tended to make more frequent use of the help options than high achievers, indicating that they found the option particularly useful.

SOURCES OF INFORMATION

YANKELOVICH, NICOLE, NORMAN MEYROWITZ, AND ANDRIES VAN DAM. 1985. "Reading and Writing the Electronic Book." *Computer* 18, no. 10 (October): 15-30.
This article summarizes contemporary research and development in formation of electronic hypertext networks of information for learning. Several existing systems are described, and principles of development are discussed.

SOFTWARE REFERENCES

The Comprehension Connection
Milliken Publishing Co.
1100 Research Blvd.
PO Box 21579
St. Louis, MO 63132

Poetry and Myth Databases
Literature and Composition Databases
Scholastic pfs: File
Scholastic, Inc.
P.O. Box 7502
2931 E. McCarty St.
Jefferson City, MO 65102
Apple II series

8

VOICE SYNTHESIS

Computer-based speech-processing devices have become a normal part of everyday life. Talking watches and household appliances, and cars that tell drivers "The door is ajar" are common. More specialized devices, including inexpensive reading machines for the blind and speaking aids for the deaf, are under development.

One of the rapidly expanding facets of computer-based instruction in the mid-1980s has been the incorporation of speech into instructional programming. Computer speech, or voice synthesis, appears to be particularly useful for software targeted to younger readers who are making the transition from oral language to print. Children beginning their schooling already have a rich knowledge of oral language. Voice synthesis can help smooth the transition from listening and speaking to reading and writing.

Voice synthesis has also been a valuable tool in other instructional circumstances where oral language is crucial to learning. English as a second language and English as a foreign language learners can read print and hear it spoken aloud simultaneously. Remedial readers can listen to stories as they read along on the computer monitor. Blind students can be provided an oral version of printed material necessary for their studies. Many computer-based learning experiences can be improved by provision of speech capabilities, as speech is a preeminently "natural" form of communication. Listening is practically automatic and requires little conscious attention, so that other learning tasks can be carried on at the same time.

This chapter considers the two major types of voice synthesis devices, digital and phonemic, listing the advantages and disadvantages of each.

Research on perception of computer-produced speech is discussed at the end of the chapter.

TYPES OF SYNTHESIZERS

Two major types of hardware devices and software programs are presently available to produce computer speech. Each has advantages and disadvantages. Voice synthesis using the sophisticated memory and processing capabilities of larger computers has significantly higher quality than voice production on microcomputers.

Digitized Voice Synthesis

In digitized voice synthesis (also called stored speech or speech coding), a human speaker is recorded on audio tape using a microphone and a tape recorder. A device known as an analog-to-digital converter then analyzes this speech and converts it to the binary code readable by computers, a process known as digitizing. This binary code is then stored in computer memory. When called upon to reproduce the speech sounds, the computer reads the code and converts it back to speech, using a digital-to-analog converter.

The actual process of digitizing speech is more complex than outlined above. During the initial analysis of the tape-recorded speech, the converter takes many rapid samples of the sound waves composing the speech. These are stored in digital form.

Literally thousands of digitized samples can be made and stored for each second of speech. A ten-second sentence might require tens of thousands of samples, each stored in computer memory. The more samples taken per second, the higher the quality of speech production. When fewer samples are taken, the quality is decreased.

Needless to say, the computer memory storage requirements for digitized speech are enormous. In computer-based instruction, as vocabulary requirements for the learning task become larger and larger, this approach to voice synthesis becomes more and more impractical. Digitized speech tends to be most effective in tasks where vocabulary is limited, as in multiple-choice activities, or yes-no or true-false problems, or when limited sets of instructions must be given.

Another disadvantage of digitized speech involves the difficulties of constructing new sentences from existing words stored in computer memory. When sentences are formed by combining words that have been individually recorded, the results do not have normal pitch and intonation. The sentences are unnatural and mechanical. Intelligibility of such sentences can be poor (Greene, Logan, & Pisoni 1986), even though the quality of the individual words composing those sentences is quite good.

In addition, microcomputer systems employing digitized speech do not allow users the capability of creating their own words and sentences. In the microcomputer-based *Ufonic* system, for example, users can create their own sentences only by choosing from a list of prerecorded words already digitized and stored on disk.

The key advantage of digitized voice synthesis is the fine quality of speech possible, since the process of digitizing begins with the recording of a live human voice. The original speech that was recorded can be reproduced with a quality that exceeds the quality of telephone speech. In the *Ufonic* system mentioned above, for example, voice production can be as good as could be obtained from a typical tape recording.

Phonemic Voice Synthesis

In phonemic voice synthesis (also called unrestricted text-to-speech synthesis or rule-based synthesis), words typed into the computer are converted into speech by a series of linguistic rules. Most of the rules deal with phonics, the correspondence rules of printed language and oral language. In the word *knife*, for example, the initial *kn* might be analyzed using a rule that specifies the *k* is silent. When the word is synthesized and produced aloud by the computer, only the *n* would be pronounced.

The actual process involved in phonemic voice synthesis is more complex. In fact, depending on the sophistication of the system, the process can be incredibly complex, involving hundreds of word recognition and production rules dealing with phonemics, syllables, and morphemes. Syntax, or grammar, rules can also be incorporated into the system to aid in word identification and sentence pronunciation. Input is first converted to computer code (ASCII code), and can be analyzed to identify words whose pronunciations do not fit standard rules, as well as numerals, abbreviations, and special symbols. Other rules can specify the pitch, stress, and timing of pronunciation.

The more rules incorporated into the system, the closer to natural speech the results can be. As Greene, Logan, and Pisoni (1986) note, "You get what you pay for" (p. 105). Limited memory capabilities of microcomputers dictate limited sophistication of the systems used. Results sound mechanical and robotic. This poor speech quality is the crucial disadvantage in applications of phonemic synthesis technology to instructional software.

Research and development of phonemic systems continues at universities and commercial research centers. *MITalk-79* was developed at Massachusetts Institute of Technology (Allen 1976, 1981) as a research tool for use on a DECSYSTEM-20 computer. The system was divided into several modules. Textual input was segmented into morphemes (meaningful word parts). Each morpheme was then looked up in a 12,000-item dictionary.

If the morphemes composing a specific word were not found, another module was used to develop the pronunciation. This second module contained some 400 letter-to-sound rules. Still another module then performed a syntactic analysis on each sentence to determine prosodic information such as timing and stress. A final module synthesized the results for output. The complexity of *MITalk-79*'s operation slowed response time considerably, but high quality was achieved. Greene, Logan, and Pisoni (1986) found only a 7 percent overall error rate in word identification when using *MITalk-79*.

Digitized synthesizers have traditionally had the advantage in speech quality over phoneme synthesizers. Over the last few years, voice synthesis researchers have investigated letter-to-sound rules and blending of sounds within words. As a result, phoneme synthesizers have improved greatly, especially when using the memory capabilities of larger computers.

A second limitation is also due to the limited memory capabilities of microcomputers and the resulting limitation on the number of linguistic rules included in the system. If the rules involving actual pronunciation of a word are not included in the system, and if that particular word is not included in the system's list of exceptions to rules, the word will be mispronounced.

One popular voice synthesizer for microcomputers, for example, mispronounces the *y* in *psychologist* as the long *e* sound. Instructional programs typically solve this problem by allowing users to edit input so that the word can be respelled to accommodate the rule system: *Psykologist* yields the correct long *i* sound for *y*, as the vcv rule (a vowel followed by a single consonant and another vowel is usually long). The subprogram that allows customization of pronunciation is sometimes called phonetic mode of input. Some microcomputer-based systems, such as The Alien Group's *Voice Box*, store the pronunciation of such exceptions in an on-disk dictionary for future reference, and the words will be pronounced correctly when they recur.

The major advantage of phonemic voice synthesizers is that any text can be spoken by the computer. This allows for easy construction and adaptation of software. Microcomputer phonemic voice synthesizers typically will run a BASIC program and speak all PRINT statements aloud. Teachers can easily construct a program to have the computer read a story aloud to students by typing the story in programmed PRINT statements (with allowance made for special spelling adaptations to fit the synthesizer's rule system). In instructional programs that include teacher utilities, such as spelling games that allow teachers to use their own lists of words, any word typed by the teacher can be read aloud to the students.

DEVELOPMENT AND RESEARCH ON RULE-BASED SPEECH SYSTEMS

How well can computer users understand computer-synthesized speech? Pisoni, Nusbaum, and Greene (1985) have suggested that a variety of factors complicate the answer to this apparently simple question. Each factor must be considered when evaluating the effectiveness of synthetic speech. While their work on evaluation of synthetic speech at the Speech Research Laboratory at

Indiana University has not specifically targeted student populations or pedagogical applications, many of their findings have implications for instruction.

The complexity of tasks confronting a student while listening to speech
affects performance in speech perception. Some tasks, such as listening for a
spelling word chosen by the computer from the week's list of ten words, are
simple. Others, which may involve listening while engaging in some other task
that requires attention, are more complex. A whole variety of task-related
factors can affect performance, including instructions given to the students,
their subjective expectancies, the amount of context available for decision
making, cognitive load, and task uncertainty.

The human information-processing system is inherently limited in its
ability to perceive, encode, store, and retrieve information. Short-term memory limitations, for example, place an important cap on possibilities of processing sensory input (Shiffrin 1976). As speech quality deteriorates, the strain on
short-term memory increases.

These processing limitations are affected by the ages and abilities of
student listeners. Short-term memory limitations are overcome in part by
application of a variety of information-processing strategies. Human listeners
can draw upon a variety of knowledge domains to analyze what they hear.
Speech perception and understanding depend upon a combination of both
"bottom-up" sensory input, the sound, and "top-down" information, the lis-
tener's background knowledge of phonology, vocabulary, syntax, and semantics. The more sophisticated those domains and strategies, the better the
perception and recognition of the message.

Humans can quickly learn strategies to improve performance on speech
recognition tasks. Any research on speech perception must account for this
variable. As students experience more and more synthetic speech, their perceptual abilities with it will increase (Waterworth & Lo 1984; Pisoni, Nusbaum,
& Greene 1985). Many people experience a similar phenomenon when listening to a speaker with a foreign accent. After a few minutes of listening,
comprehension improves dramatically.

A message might consist of isolated words, individual sentences, or complete passages. A synthesized word identification program, for example, might
pronounce words differing by only one phoneme, as in *met, mat, mitt,* and *mutt.*
A comprehension exercise, on the other hand, might require more complete
activation of the listeners' phonological, syntactic, lexical, and semantic knowledge systems.

The structure and quality of the speech signal refer to how closely the
synthesized speech signal matches the phonetics and prosody of naturally
produced speech. Pisoni, Nusbaum, and Greene (1985) reported a series of
studies carried out to compare phonemic synthesized speech with naturally
produced speech. In one test, the Modified Rhyme Test (House, Williams,
Hecker, & Kryter 1965), listeners identified a single word by choosing one of
six possibilities. Each of the word choices differed by only a single phoneme, in

either the initial or the final position within the word. All the choices were single-syllable words with a cvc (consonant-vowel-consonant) pattern. For example, listeners might have heard the word *ban* pronounced aloud. They would then have to choose the correct item from a list of six: (a) bad, (b) back, (c) ban, (d) bass, (e) bat, (f) bath.

Findings indicated that adult subjects scored an average of 99.4 percent correct when listening to natural speech. Performance with the computer-synthesized systems varied from 94.4 percent to 66.2 percent correct. Of the eight rule-based systems tested, five obtained scores of over 90 percent. The lowest score was obtained by the one microcomputer-based system tested, a system typical of those used in classrooms during the mid-1980s.

In another study reported in the same article, subjects dealt with actual reading passages read aloud. The synthetic-speech groups showed dramatic gains in comprehension over time. Apparently, as they became accustomed to the synthesizers' outputs, they improved in their understanding. In the last half of the test, the synthetic-speech groups slightly outperformed a group listening to natural speech. No microcomputer-based synthesis system was used in this study, however.

In still another study reported in the article, Pisoni, Nusbaum, and Greene (1985) tested for gains in recognition of synthetic speech using a low-cost, microcomputer-based device, the Votrax Type-'N-Talk. Initial performance on a word identification test was poor, about 25 percent correct. After ten days of practice, adult performance increased to almost 70 percent. These gains were retained by subjects over a period of six months with no intervening contact with synthetic speech.

Luce, Feustel, and Pisoni (1983) have suggested that listeners' problems in comprehending synthetic speech stem from a limited short-term memory capacity. Synthetic speech lacks many of the linguistic cues typically found in natural speech, such as clear segmentation cues. As a result, listeners must devote more of their cognitive capacity to the listening task. To demonstrate this, Luce, Feustel, and Pisoni arranged to have subjects listen to speech while attempting to remember series of digits visually displayed on a computer monitor. They found dramatically decreased digit retention during synthetic speech as opposed to natural speech. They suggested that word identification efforts when listening to synthetic speech so taxed short-term memory as to leave decreased capacity for secondary tasks such as the digit memory task.

Some limited research has been carried out with younger children, a target population who might benefit greatly from synthetic speech used for instructional purposes. In a test based on the Peabody Picture Vocabulary Test, Greene and Pisoni (in press) tested kindergartners and second graders using natural- and synthetic-speech vocabulary items. The synthesized speech was produced by the *Prose 2000* system. When each word was pronounced, the children had to point to the corresponding picture among four pictures on a card. Kindergarten children correctly identified 94 percent of the natural-

1. Does the program have an easy-to-use play-back feature that allows children to immediately replay a word or sentence that has not been understood?

2. Does preliminary field-testing of the program indicate a satisfactory recognition rate among the students?

3. Is the voice synthesis device to be used often enough to allow students to improve in their recognition abilities?

4. Does the program allow children to devote full attention to the computer-produced speech, or must they perform other activities while simultaneously listening to the speech?

5. Does the voice output play an important role in the program?

FIGURE 8-1. Evaluating a voice synthesis program

FIGURE 8-2. Choosing a voice synthesis hardware/software system

1. What educational software will you be using on the system? Choose the software first, then choose the system that fits the software.

2. Is the system compatible with your computer?

3. Will you be constructing your own programs? If so, how easy is construction?

4. If vocabulary is resident (prepared), how many words are available? Must additional vocabularies be purchased separately?

5. What is the quality of voice production?

speech words and 82 percent of the synthetic words. Second graders identified 98 percent of natural-speech words and 94 percent of synthetic words.

Many teachers have expressed concern that children will find computer-produced speech impossibly confusing. Recent research suggests otherwise, however. In fact, ability to access synthesized vocabulary words during reading improves comprehension of readers (Oslen, Foltz, & Wise 1986). While synthesized speech is not as accurately recognized as natural speech, it nonetheless is recognized at a satisfactorily high rate. In addition, classroom teachers find that children expect robotic speech from a computer and are not bothered by its unnatural sounds. Some principles for teachers to follow when evaluating voice-synthesis instructional lessons are listed in Figure 8-1. Choosing a voice-synthesis system can be an expensive proposition. Guidelines are provided in Figure 8-2.

SOURCES OF INFORMATION

ROSEGRANT, TERESA J. 1986. "It Doesn't Sound Right: The Role of Speech Output as a Primary Form of Feedback for Beginning Text Revision." Paper presented at the American Educational Research Association, San Francisco, April.

Rosegrant, the developer of Scholastic's *Talking TextWriter,* has carried out some of the only applied research in actual classroom implications of voice synthesis. *Talking TextWriter* is a word processor for beginning readers and writers that incorporates speech output. Children are able to hear their text as they type.

COMMERCIAL SOFTWARE/HARDWARE

Echo Speech Synthesizer
  Street Electronics Corp.
  1140 Mark Ave.
  Carpinteria, CA 93013
  The *Echo* is used by a wide variety of educational software publishers, including Scholastic (*Talking TextWriter*)

Talking TextWriter
  Scholastic
  PO Box 7502
  2931 E. McCarty St.
  Jefferson City, MO 65102
  Apple II series

Super Talker
  Mountain Computer, Inc.
  300 El Pueblo Rd.
  Scotts Valley, CA 95066

Voice Box Synthesizer
  The Alien Group
  27 W. 23rd St.
  New York, NY 10010

Votrax Personal Speech System
  Votrax
  500 Stephenson Highway
  Troy, MI 48084

Ufonic
  Borg-Warner
  600 W. University Dr.
  Arlington Heights, IL 60004
  Ufonic is a digitized voice synthesizer that has a wide variety of educational programs available for it.

9

INTERACTIVE VIDEO

Interactive video technology combines the interactive instructional capabilities of computers with the full-color picture and sound of television. An undergraduate teaching major can, for instance, watch a short video lecture on the philosophy underlying the language experience approach. The interactive video lesson might then include a computer-assisted instructional lesson designed to review and reinforce the concepts presented by the lecturer. Another video then might show a sample LEA lesson presented by a master teacher to a class of second graders. At each step in the lesson, the video would stop and a series of questions would be presented to the viewer to promote thoughtful analysis of the procedure.

Interactive video lessons of this sort offer great promise for expanding instructional design and dialogue possibilities for computer-using educators. Promoters of this technology, however, tend toward the "Gee whiz!" school of education. "You thought your old microcomputers were good stuff, eh? Wait till you see what we've got now!" Like all innovations, interactive video has its drawbacks, and no one can be certain that these new developments will affect classrooms in a positive way. After all, instructional television, a closely related technology, did not achieve the hopes raised for it in the 1960s. Chambers (1987), among others, has argued that future applications of interactive video will be limited by high production and hardware costs, a limited demand, and competition from other technologies—including traditional print and ordinary, noninteractive video. To this point, at any rate, existing interactive video lessons are less than enthralling, and few are on the market.

Despite a great deal of excitement about the possibilities of interactive video, there has been little empirical research on its effectiveness (Hannafin 1985). Bosco (1986) surveyed a wide range of studies on the topic, most of which are open to procedural criticism. The studies included curricula from elementary schools to college and the military, on topics from Spanish to tumbling to lift truck safety. None involved reading or language arts instruction. In 24 of 39 statistical tests comparing an interactive video training group with a control group, the research findings indicated that interactive video training was more effective than other methods. Only about 50 percent of those studies reporting positive results actually found an increase in achievement. Benefits most often reported involved improved user attitude and decreased training time.

The purpose of this chapter is to describe in detail the two major technologies of interactive video: video cassette and videodisk. Both are based on a combination of computer-assisted instructional lessons with video players much like those commonly available in homes. Procedures involved in integrating the two technologies will be described in some detail, as well as examples of relevant research and development projects in educational applications. Finally, the chapter will discuss the problems facing those who advocate implementation of this technology in classrooms.

Video-based programs are often categorized according to their degree of interactivity. A Level 0 system, for example, includes no interaction at all. The video is simply meant to be played from beginning to end.

Level 1 systems also involve no computer components. The video hardware allows a viewer to move forward or backward, to slow down or to speed up motion. Most products designed for home entertainment are of this sort.

Level 2 video players contain a built-in microprocessor of limited memory size (1K or less). It is capable of decoding instructions encoded on a videodisk, for example. Students can interact with the instruction in a limited fashion, answering questions, for example. Such systems are not widely available.

Level 3 systems involve a computer-controlled video player. Most ongoing research and development are carried out with this kind of system. Schaffer and Hannafin (1986) compared a Level 3 lesson on the topic of preparation of video graphics with Level 0 and Level 1 lessons. Each lesson used the same video materials but had a different degree of interactivity. High school subjects learned more under the fully interactive version, but they also took the longest time. The simple linear videotape presentation (Level 0) took the shortest time and as a result obtained the highest rate of learning. This chapter is concerned with Level 3 systems.

INTERACTIVE VIDEOTAPE

Interactive video cassette technology involves the linkage of a computer with a video cassette recorder (VCR). The recorder must be equipped with a remote plug that allows an outside device, in this case the computer, to control its on-off functioning. An interface device provides the linkage between the computer and the recorder. Often this device is a circuit board plugged into a slot within a microcomputer. The circuit board is connected to the VCR's remote plug by a cable.

An interactive video instructional lesson consists of two major components, the program code and the video sequences. The program code contains the computer-based instructional frames, which may be of any type of computer-based instruction. For example, the program may present a traditional tutorial computer-assisted instructional lesson in woodworking. It may involve students in a simulation of a trip to the moon. It may drill students on identification of paintings or types of rocks. The computer code is recorded on the computer's standard data storage medium, such as a floppy disk.

The video sequences are designed to provide enhanced visual and sound accompaniment to the computer-based instruction. Each step of a tutorial on woodworking tools may include a demonstration of a master craftsman using the particular tool under discussion. The simulated trip to the moon may have pictures of spacecraft launchings and moon craters. Each question on the drill-and-practice exercise may be accompanied by a picture of the appropriate painting or rock. These video sequences are stored on a standard videotape.

The computer program that presents the tutorial, simulation, or drill-and-practice exercise also contains special codes that order the VCR turned on and off. The interface device recognizes these codes and controls the on-off switch on the recorder.

One major advantage of the interactive video cassettes is that schools already have most of the necessary equipment. All they need buy is the interface device, which usually comes with utility software that helps a teacher create the computer-based lessons.

Designing a Lesson

The design of an interactive video cassette lesson requires all the planning of a standard computer-based learning lesson. Goals and objectives must be decided. Frames must be charted out, with appropriate instructions and questions. Finally, the lesson must be programmed in a standard programming language or by using an authoring system. As with standard computer-based authoring systems, video authoring systems allow for text presentation, computer graphics, branching, and record keeping of learners' performance.

In addition, the interactive video lesson designer decides the points in the lesson at which the VCR will play. The video segments are then videotaped and edited, and the computer is programmed, including the simple commands that order the recorder on and off.

Details in the construction of the lesson vary slightly from one manufacturer of interactive video systems to another. Often the next step involves adding a signal track on the videotape's second audio channel (the first audio channel contains the sound track of the video). This signal track is added quite simply, using the interface and accompanying software. It basically involves numbering frames on the videotape to use as a kind of pagination device, so the interface can find appropriate spots to turn the recorder on and off.

Once the signal track is established, the lesson designer views the videotape to choose the start and stop points for the various video segments. Marking each start and stop point is carried out by pressing a few keys on the computer keyboard.

Advantages and Disadvantages

As noted above, a major advantage of interactive video cassette technology is its easy availability to many classroom teachers. For the purchase price of the interface, a school can own its own system. Teachers familiar with programming computer-assisted instructional lessons, whether in a programming language such as BASIC or an authoring language, will find it fairly easy to adapt to constructing interactive video lessons for their students. Videos can be inexpensively obtained by taping television broadcasts, though there are legal ramifications involving copyrights.

Constructing video lessons might make a fascinating class project involving significant amounts of reading and writing. While the quality of the final result might not be on the commercial level, the project can be a valuable learning experience for youngsters. Howe (1984) has described a project in which his students constructed a lesson based on their home city of Philadelphia.

Another approach to class projects in interactive video involves using commercially prepared videotapes and teacher- or class-prepared computer-based instructional lessons. Teachers can turn a video movie, drama, current events show, or science show into an interactive lesson, though there may be legal difficulties involved in using copyrighted video material. A wide variety of educational magazine articles describe such classroom projects.

Teacher preparation of interactive video lessons suffers from many of the same problems (and offers many of the same advantages) of teacher preparation of traditional computer-based learning software. The time involved in actual construction can be tremendous, far beyond the capabilities of most classroom teachers. Unfortunately, many teachers who want to construct an interactive video lesson are tempted to save time by skimping on the planning phase of software construction. Writing objectives, general lesson plans, and frame-by-frame screen diagrams are often seen as a waste of time. The final results are thus less than satisfactory.

A commercially successful interactive video curriculum project, one that is worth exporting to other schools, requires integration of a team of planners and workers. Virtually no one is an expert in all the components necessary for interactive video production. A project requires someone who understands instructional television. Videotaping involves a good deal more than simply pointing a portable videotape camera and pressing the button. An effective videotape is planned frame-by-frame to fulfill specific objectives. Angle of each shot, background materials, music accompaniment, and verbal material must all be planned beforehand and integrated in a natural way. Videotaping is an art form that is rarely accomplished effectively by amateurs.

The project also requires someone who understands the nuances of computer-assisted instruction. Interactive learning is a complex field of study with a rich research base. Unfamiliarity with construction of computer-based learning experiences will inevitably lead to an outcome that may confuse students more than it helps them.

At the project's heart must be someone who understands the task or concepts to be taught to the children via the interactive video lessons. The skills or content-area specialist provides the heart of the lesson, without which the best of video experts and computer-assisted instructional designers cannot function. Many inferior computer-assisted instructional projects have the root of their inferiority in lack of attention to the material to be taught.

Finally, a project requires a good deal of adjunct help. Actors or speakers must be gathered and rehearsed. Plans must be reviewed by outside consultants to ensure quality. Preliminary results must be field-tested on classes of children.

Construction of a commercially viable product, then, is a major undertaking. Relatively few interactive video cassettes are available for educational purposes. Most of those available are results of federally funded research projects and are experimental in nature.

Another complicating factor that seriously limits availability of educational interactive video cassettes is the lack of standardization within the industry. Each manufacturer's interface device will operate only with software specifically designed for that device. Just as Apple software cannot be used on an IBM microcomputer, so interactive video cassette software will operate only on the device for which it was designed. Since no manufacturer is yet dominant in this field, commercial distribution of interactive video cassettes is limited.

Alvermann (1985) used an interactive video cassette lesson to teach education majors to administer informal reading inventories. Students were able to see a professionally administered IRI and responded to questions about it. Alvermann compared performance of these video-trained subjects with subjects trained using printed text. Video-trained subjects performed better on a test, but not on a free-recall task in which they were asked to write down what they remembered. Alvermann qualified her positive conclusions, noting that video-trained subjects spent a greater amount of time on the learning task.

INTERACTIVE VIDEODISKS

As with video cassettes, videodisk technology is now familiar in many homes. A videodisk is about the size of an LP record and can store audio, visual, and digital information.

There are two major formats used for home video entertainment, though others are being developed. RCA's system uses capacitance electronic disks (CEDs). A diamond stylus in the videodisk player actually touches the disk as the disk spins. These disks are capable of holding a great deal of video information, which makes them optimal for storing movies for home entertainment. They are unsuitable for interactive video applications for a variety of reasons. Frames cannot be "frozen," since the stylus is constantly moving on. The playback is linear: As with video cassettes, there is no random access to specific frames. There is only one audio channel, and the disks are subject to wear and tear, just as phonograph records are.

Optical-encoded disks (also called reflective disks or laser disks) are used in interactive videodisk applications. Disks are made of thin aluminum sheets encased in a protective plastic shell. There are two types of optical-encoded disks. CLV (continuous linear velocity) disks have 60 minutes of motion video per side. They are often used for movies because of their longer playing time, but frames cannot be frozen for still pictures. They are of limited usefulness for most educational applications.

CAV (continuous angular velocity) is used more often for educational purposes. A CAV disk has the capacity to store 54,000 tracks on each side. Every track contains microscopic pits. A low-power laser shines through the protective surface layer of the disk. A light-sensitive device in the videodisk player determines whether the laser light is reflected or a pit has stopped the reflection. This information is translated into electrical current as binary 0's and 1's.

Each track corresponds to one video frame that can be frozen and played over and over with no wear and tear on the disk, though sound is not available for a frozen frame. Maximum playing time is about half an hour for motion pictures. Any frame on the disk can be accessed by the computer in between 3 and 12 seconds. There are generally two audio channels.

Advantages and Disadvantages

Videodisks must be manufactured commercially, using highly specialized equipment. New information cannot be stored on the disks by home or school users. This technology therefore does not lend itself to classroom production projects that involve filming of new material.

The videodisk's random-access feature is invaluable for classroom instruction. On a videotape, information is stored linearly. One segment must follow the other in unvarying order. On a videodisk, any segment can be called up onto the screen at any time. A student studying dinosaurs might, for example, be given a choice of four motion picture lessons, each on a different species. Almost immediately after making the choice, the student will be able to view the appropriate lesson. This feature allows for branching on the basis of student need.

As with video cassettes, interactive videodisks require an interface between the computer and the player. No industry standards for these interfaces have yet gained dominance, so that disks made for one manufacturer will not run on another manufacturer's system.

While a videodisk does not have a long playing time for motion pictures, it can store large amounts of visual material for archival purposes. An archival disk (or visual data base) contains a collection of still frames, motion sequences, or some combination of both. The entire collection of the Metropolitan Museum of Art, for example, could be stored on a single disk. Jet Propulsion Laboratories has produced a disk with thousands of photographs from NASA space exploratory missions.

A crucial problem, however, is image size and clarity. The limits of the television monitor are imposed on the image resolution. No work of art pictured on a television screen will be as clearly portrayed as is possible in a book or on a slide. Detailed diagrams, often of crucial importance for educational purposes, will also be limited in resolution. Monitors in the higher price range give surprisingly clear pictures, however, and video projection technology is available for large-group presentations.

Laser disks are durable, an important feature in classroom applications. Since the laser does not actually touch the disk as it is read, the quality of the disk's video image will last indefinitely.

Examples of Applications

Because videodisk hardware is in short supply in schools, publishers have made few efforts to develop software for interactive purposes. Researchers have also been hampered in software development by limited federal funding for educational research and development. Most projects have been directed toward topics where federal funding is greatest, such as science and math education (Withrow 1985–1986) and special education. Davidove (1986), for instance, decribed a 14-step development process for construction of interactive videodisk programs at Gallaudet College. The major applications of videodisk learning technology have been in business and government/armed forces training, where development has been extensive (Blanchard 1984).

Business, the government, and the armed forces find videodisk technology particularly effective because most of their training involves "how-to-do-it" presentations. A picture is worth a thousand words, especially in training a salesperson how to close a sale or teaching a welder how to fashion a type of weld. For example, Warner Lambert, a medical technology company, uses the QUEST videodisk tutorial system to train its sales personnel in the basics of anatomy and physiology. Ford Motor Company uses a videodisk tutorial to train its mechanics in the use of engine diagnostic devices. A great deal of research and development has been carried out for use of videodisks in business and technological applications.

Much of the limited research and development in educational applications has been done with already existing videodisk materials. Project VIDALL (Videodisk-Assisted Language Learning), a project funded by the New Jersey Department of Higher Education and sponsored by Jersey City State College, constructed lessons for limited-English-proficient students using the QUEST authoring software and an existing video series titled "Master Cooking with Craig Claiborne" (*Quest Promptlines* 1986). The interactive videodisk curriculum used cooking lessons as the basis for learning vocabulary, sentence structure, and numerical adverbs. The policy of using existing videos to meet new learning goals is called repurposing or reformatting.

The Educational Technology Center at Harvard has also repurposed videos in its research with interactive videodisks. They have pilot-tested *Seeing the Unseen*, a series of four science lessons based on Public Broadcasting System shows. For example, the lesson "How Does Light Affect Plants?" uses time-lapse photography to have learners formulate and test hypotheses about phototropism.

Minnesota Educational Computing Corporation has developed several interactive laser disks of its own for commercial release. *Introduction to Economics* and *Trigland* are both designed for high school students. *Improving Teacher Effectiveness* is designed for in-service professional education.

Chomsky (1986) gave a preliminary report of a reading/ language arts application of interactive videodisk, though her findings were sketchy. Text was displayed on the video screen one page at a time. A voice read it aloud as the child followed along in the text. The spoken portions were highlighted as the voice read, helping the child keep his or her place. The child controlled turning the pages forward or backward. Vocabulary, spelling, and comprehension exercises followed the story presentation.

Because of the expense of videodisk hardware and software, publishers recognize the reluctance of schools to use interactive videodisk technology for individual or small group instruction. After all, if schools cannot afford to individualize instruction using sufficient numbers of microcomputers for each student, they certainly cannot afford work stations that require a videodisk device in addition to a microcomputer. Therefore, commercial interactive videodisks are presently marketed to schools largely as lecture tools. An instructor can, with a few commands to the computer, locate and display still photographs or moving pictures to illustrate a lecture.

Ease and flexibility of use make this lecture technology far more convenient than slides and films. This capability can be especially important in development of content-area vocabulary. In Optical Data Corporation's *Earth Science* disk, for example, an instructor discussing *alluvial plane* or *alpine glacier* can quickly display illustrations to a class by simply typing the terms into a microcomputer hooked to the videodisk device. The same technology will lend itself to individualized computer-based instructional applications as interactive laser disks and the necessary hardware become more readily available.

FUTURE DEVELOPMENTS

As explained in Chapter 10 of this volume, CD-ROM technology is already available for some classroom applications. Research and development of further CD-ROM applications are presently under way. The result will be a new category of media based on optical data storage. It will be capable of generating motion pictures, still-frame photographs, text, and high-fidelity stereo sound. This future medium is presently referred to as CD/I, compact disk-interactive media systems. The Sony Corporation and North American Phillips Corporations are cooperating on development of this new technology.

SOURCES OF INFORMATION

The interactive video markets are highly volatile at this point, with new companies being formed and old companies going out of business or merging. Comprehensive, up-to-date lists of manufacturers and publishers can be located in educational technology magazines. Most manufacturers and publishers cater to business and government.

The listing below provides information on selected leading sources of interactive materials that are of special interest to the public school market.

SCHWARTZ, ED. 1985. *The Educators' Handbook to Interactive Videodisc.* Washington, DC: Association for Educational Communications and Technology.
This 93-page book offers a tremendous array of information about educational applications of interactive videodisk. The introductory material presents a brief overview of videodisk hardware and its use. The bulk of the book consists of directories of information sources, including hardware, software, authoring languages, and manufacturers.

1986. "DIRECTORY OF VIDEO PRODUCTS FOR EDUCATION." *T.H.E. Journal* 14, no. 1 (August): 84-86.
This includes a listing of manufacturers of interactive videodisk and videotape technology.

1986. *THE VIDEO SOURCE BOOK.* Syosset, NY: National Video Clearinghouse.
This vast listing of video—especially videotape—resources includes sections for movies, sports, fine arts, education, health, science, business, and industry. The book contains tens of thousands of titles and hundreds of distributors.

Interactive Video Hardware/Software

Manufacturers of interactive videodisk systems maintain catalogs of software publishers who market materials for their particular systems. Many manufacturers of video hardware also support their systems by supplying software. Little software is presently available for reading/language arts applications.

ALLEN COMMUNICATION, 140 Lakeside Plaza II, 5225 Wiley Post Way, Salt Lake City, UT 84116
Allen offers a sophisticated authoring system, QUEST, to accompany the Pioneer LD-V1000 disk player. Allen also offers an optional touch-screen package to accompany its video hardware.

Grolier Electronic Publishing Co., Sherman Turnpike, Danbury, CT 06816
> The Grolier *Knowledge Disc* contains only text: The nine million words of Grolier's *Academic American Encyclopedia*. A table of contents and an index are on the disk itself.

Optical Data Corp., PO Box 97, Florham Park, NJ 07932
> Optical Data's Living Textbook series of educational products enhances ease of access to videodisk contents. Each disk is divided into "events" that are indexed in accompanying manuals. If a teacher or student wants to play the "Physiology: Contractile Viruses: Narrated Movie" event, a simple command to the microcomputer immediately puts it on the screen. Optical Data also offers an authoring system, *Laser Writer*.
> A partial listing of laser disks available: *Principles of Biology, Earth Science, Astronomy, The Sun/ Universe, Voyager and Viking, Grolier's Knowledge Disc, National Gallery of Art.*

Educational Interactive Video Projects

Readers interested in an up-to-date source of information on interactive video projects should consult recent ERIC indexes.

Educational Technology Center, 337 Gutman Library, Cambridge, MA 02138
> The Center sponsors research on videodisk in its New Technologies Group, and it publishes a newsletter, *ETC Targets*.

Minnesota Educational Computing Corp., 3490 Lexington Ave. N., St. Paul, MN 55126
> MECC has developed three interactive videodisks: *Introduction to Economics, Trigland,* and *Improving Teacher Effectiveness*. MECC's newsletter, *MECC Network*, keeps readers up-to-date on its interactive videodisk development.

10

SPECIAL HARDWARE-RELATED TOPICS

Research in computer technology has resulted in production of so much new hardware that it is hard to keep up with it all. New products appear on the market every week, and existing products are constantly being improved. Prices usually are high initially, but after the new products have been on the market for a couple of years, the prices often decline markedly.

The purpose of this chapter is, first of all, to review the present situation in terms of educational hardware. The bulk of the chapter will deal with hardware developments that have not yet reached common use in the classroom. Three important technologies will be discussed: CD-ROM, telecommunications, and local area networks (LANs). Each hardware technology will be described, along with its advantages and limitations in terms of reading and language arts instruction. A list of references and information sources is also provided.

COMPUTER HARDWARE IN THE SCHOOLS TODAY

During the early 1980s, Apple Computer Corporation gained control of the educational microcomputer hardware market with its Apple II series. Since that time, Apple's dominance has been challenged many times by competing corporations, yet in no case have those challengers made any serious impact. Apple's closest competitor in the educational market, IBM, discontinued production of its PC-jr, the version of the IBM-PC that was to have been the Apple II's competitor. While there is an increasing amount of educational software available for the IBM-PC, much of this is sold to the home market, where families may own PC's for business purposes. Few schools have felt the need to switch to the IBM for instructional purposes other than, perhaps, business courses.

The Apple II series remains dominant for a variety of reasons, despite the superior sophistication of many newer models of microcomputers, including Apple Computer's own Macintosh.

1. Apple II hardware is inexpensive, especially if the purchaser is satisfied with the older editions of the Apple II series. While competing new models such as the IBM-PC and the Macintosh are sophisticated, this sophistication is insufficient to balance their higher prices.
2. The Apple II series is versatile. Slots and plugs within the microcomputer housing allow users to plug in a wide variety of devices, including adapted keyboards for special learners, speech synthesis and recognition devices, light-pens, and graphics tablets. These devices have been readily available for some years (Balajthy 1986a).
3. Apple Computer has shown a consistent loyalty to this series since its inception in 1978. Other models come and go, but the Apple II endures. Software developed in 1978 is still usable on the newer models, such as the Apple II +, the Apple IIe, the Apple IIc, and the Apple IIGS.
4. Apple's marketing strategy has included a constant series of upgrades for the series, each of which is compatible with the older models. A newer model, the IIc, for example, is better equipped for use of a mouse and is more portable than earlier models. The IIGS, introduced in 1986, has dramatically enhanced graphics and voice synthesis features and a larger memory. Rumors of future developments are constant, another factor that keeps Apple II users loyal.
5. Apple's encouragement of software development by third-party companies has proved to be an important strategy. No other model has anywhere near the amount of educational software availability as the Apple II series. Many educational publishers produce software that runs only on that series.

While many computer enthusiasts worry about the possibility that educational computing is stagnating with the "Model T" technology of the Apple II, educators are by and large unconvinced of any need to switch to newer models.

CD-ROM

The advent of CD-ROM (compact disk read-only memory, sometimes called by the more generic name OD-ROM, optical disk read-only memory), has been made possible by the recent mass production of low-cost laser technology for sound and video entertainment purposes. A CD-ROM disk looks like the disks sold in record stores for compact disk stereo players. It is 4.75 inches in diameter. Disks are etched in a factory and covered with a plastic coating for greater durability.

The drive is able to read digital information from the disk by using a low-power laser beam to reflect light off the disk's shiny surface. In a standard microcomputer floppy-disk drive, the drive reads magnetized particles to gather the 1's and 0's that make up digitized information. A CD-ROM drive, however, distinguishes between light reflected from the shiny disk surface and the decreased reflection from the countless pits etched into the disk. The pattern of reflected light is then translated into 1's and 0's for the computer to process.

Since a laser can be focused into a narrow beam of light, information can be packed tightly onto the disk. A single CD-ROM disk can store up to 600 megabytes of data, the equivalent of many floppy disks. Any information that can be stored digitally can be stored on the disk, including computer programs, text, high-quality graphics, and stereo-quality sound. A disk can store up to 15 hours of audio information and 15,000 color images.

The etching of digital information onto the CD-ROM disk must take place at a factory. Hence the *ROM* term, *read-only memory*, indicates that a microcomputer user cannot change any of the data on the disk or add anything to what is already stored.

In 1985, Grolier helped pioneer CD-ROM production with the publication of its *Electronic Encyclopedia*, a version of the *Academic American Encyclopedia*. The entire 20 volumes fit on a CD-ROM disk, 9 million words in all. Users can perform a word processor-like "search and find" operation for specific terms in the encyclopedia. Use of any word or word combination can be located in less than one minute. Search results can be printed out, saved on disk, or transferred to a word-processing file (a real boon to the typical sixth grade research paper writer).

Grolier's publication is an example of an application ideally suited to contemporary limitations on CD-ROM technology. The encyclopedia is text only, as the industry has not yet established an agreed-upon standard for audio and video integration. No complicated arrangements were required between a variety of authors and publishers. The publication of the disk probably will not create any serious competition to Grolier's premier quality encyclopedia line. The contents of an encyclopedia do not quickly grow out-of-date, and the material that does become dated is probably best researched in periodicals anyway.

Primary use of CD-ROM disks appears to be limited to reference material for the foreseeable future. Microsoft's *Bookshelf* CD-ROM disk, for instance, contains the contents of ten reference tools, including the *American Heritage Dictionary*, *Roget's Thesaurus*, *The Chicago Manual of Style*, and a U.S. zip code directory. While it would be quite possible to develop a single disk with, for example, the contents of many best-selling novels, the price of that disk would necessarily be enormous. Actual production cost of the disk would be negligible. The necessary author and publisher fees would account for the bulk of the cost. Most book publishers will be slow to agree to any alternative form of publication that will compete with their book publication profits. The same will hold true for software publishers.

Another factor that limits CD-ROM applications is the inability to update material on a disk. This will not be a problem in, for example, publication of classical works whose copyright date is past, or out-of-print books. The Educational Resource Information Clearinghouse (ERIC) has a CD-ROM subscription system for its indexing system. It deals with the update problem by sending subscribers a new disk each quarter that will contain both old and new information. Old disks are discarded.

A variety of other professional and technical data bases are already available in CD-ROM formats (Chen 1986), including *Books in Print*. The Institute of Electrical and Electronics Engineers, a professional organization, for example, has begun preliminary development of a sophisticated system that could eventually bring a research library of technical information to the fingertips of an engineer. An engineer interested in a particular topic could access a listing of relevant articles. Another command could access the abstract of any of the articles, and still another command could bring up the entire paper on the screen—text and illustrations (Kaplan 1986). There is no doubt that such an information retrieval system for educational periodicals would have made writing this book a lot easier.

As mentioned above, a number of problems stand in the way of CD-ROM implementation: copyright problems, inability to integrate sound and video, lack of an industrywide standard for software developers to follow, and inability to update disks. In addition, there is no standard interface between CD-ROM drives and microcomputers, leading to incompatibility of systems. To date, reference libraries using CD-ROM for reference purposes typically use "dedicated" computers—the computer is dedicated to only one information data base.

Another problem involves the relatively slow rate of data access, sometimes called a long "seek time." CD-ROM drives function more slowly than magnetic disk drives, such as inexpensive floppy-disk drives. Data pickup is much too slow for high-quality audio or broadcast-quality motion video. Manufacturers must carefully analyze the best way to arrange information on a disk before putting the data on it. Also, while prices have dropped, CD-ROM hardware and software are expensive.

Finally, it seems a safe bet that few will invest in CD-ROM for their classroom microcomputers until some software becomes available. A look at the CD-ROM literature, which includes books and magazines about a technology that, for most practical purposes, doesn't exist yet, would give the reader an impression that a tremendous amount of software is on the market. Hoffman has wryly noted that CD-ROM has had a tremendous introduction: "Very few technologies come with their own fanfare before they are generally available to the public" (1986, p. 65).

In fact, most of the software mentioned by bandwagon CD-ROM enthusiasts, who are perfectly willing to cite specifics about titles and manufacturers, is still "vaporware"—supposedly under development. Most products under development are oriented to technological fields with higher-paying dividends than the educational materials market (O'Connor & Moore 1986).

Hiscox and Hiscox (1986) surveyed a broad range of possible public school applications for CD-ROM, from textbook replacement to individualized instruction to maintenance of school operating records. They concluded that while CD-ROM is a powerful and versatile technology, there are nonetheless few instructional applications that require its unique combination of characteristics.

TELECOMMUNICATIONS

The ability of computers to communicate with other computers over telephone lines, or computer telecommunications, could impact education in a wide variety of ways. Any type of digital information can be sent over telephone lines, whether it be text files, audio, or graphics. For the moment, most telecommunications applications of computers are limited to activities of more interest to computer hobbyists than to classroom teachers. A decision to use telecommunications as an educational tool should be made only after a close examination of the problems involved and of the alternatives.

Telecommunications applications involve a set of specialized equipment and software that gives rise to a set of technical terms. The device that allows a computer to send and receive messages over telephone lines is called a modem (for modulator-demodulator). The modem may be an integral part of the computer unit, a removable board within the computer unit, or an external peripheral device. It converts electronic signals from its computer in order to transmit them over telephone lines to another computer. Once the signals arrive at the second computer, another modem is required to reconvert the signals so as to be interpretable by that computer.

Most modems for microcomputers are direct connect modems. These do not require an actual telephone. Instead, a cable from the modem is plugged directly into a telephone jack. Another type of modem is the acoustic coupler, into which a telephone handset is inserted directly.

Different modems send information at different rates of speed. The faster the speed, or baud rate, the less a user need pay for telephone bills, an important consideration, especially when communicating over long distances. Modems rated at 1,200 baud or more are becoming increasingly popular for microcomputers.

When one computer is actively connected to another using modems, they are considered to be on-line. Software known as telecommunications programs facilitates the transfer of information. Some such software is capable of receiving and sending information automatically, without a computer operator's presence. The act of sending a file to another computer is called uploading. The act of receiving a file is downloading.

Computer operators frequently use a central computer through which they telecommunicate, rather than making direct contact between their own computers. This central computer, which may be operated by a commercial network, by a user group of computer hobbyists, or by the operators' central organization (for example, a corporation or university), is generally operating at all hours. Users simply turn on their own computers whenever they want to access the central computer for information. These central computers often offer a bulletin board service, on which users may leave general announcements or messages for specific colleagues. Telephone calls between computers are often sent over special telephone networks designed to decrease their cost, such as TYMNET and TELENET.

The primary advantages of telecommunications capabilities are speed of information transfer and access to remote (that is, not local, not immediately available on site) information sources. In situations in which teams of people are working together under time constraints on projects that involve large amounts of information, the instantaneous communications available via computer telecommunications can be crucial. Businesses that are decentralized can share information on production and inventory. Researchers from different universities involved in a team project can keep in touch. In situations where necessary information is stored on a computer in a different location, such as the Educational Resources Information Index (ERIC) files, telecommunication allows a computer user quick access to the information.

In many other situations, however, telecommunication offers little or no advantage over other information transfer media. In most research projects, data and text can be transferred less expensively and with less bother by mailing printouts, disks, or tapes. Urgent messages can be communicated with a simple telephone conversation. Rather than researching information in an on-line encyclopedia, a trip to the school library may save time and money, and yield more information. Dissemination of information for professional organizations is usually carried out more efficiently and with better quality through carefully edited newsletters and journals than through bulletin board services that have no quality controls.

A variety of telecommunications applications are of interest to reading and language arts educators. Each has its drawbacks, however, and must be evaluated on its own merits.

Telecommunications Information Networks

These networks offer a variety of services, but at a cost that can quickly mount up for schools. Special interest groups operate bulletin board services through these networks, including Educational Products Information Exchange (EPIE), Educator's Forum, and Educational Research Forum. The networks also offer services including on-line newspapers, ERIC, free public-domain software downloads, *Grolier's Encyclopedia*, and many others. It is even possible to take a college course on-line. Users must pay membership fees and on-line rates that vary depending on the time of day. The typical school day is during top rate hours. In addition, many of the services charge extra fees above the basic membership cost.

Before becoming a member of one of the networks, users should shop around for the one that best meets their needs. Rates vary significantly, as do the services available.

Local Bulletin Board Services

A less expensive alternative for those interested primarily in communicating with other users is a local bulletin board service. These are often operated by user groups, which can be located by contacting computer stores. Schools that might want to trade student compositions or newsletters on-line could use one of these services. The services often allow users to download public-domain programs as well.

On-line "Publication" of Student Writing

One means of allowing students to publish their writings is electronic publishing: making the texts available via an electronic bulletin board or sending texts over telephone lines to other schols, to be printed out in hard copy (see Figure 10-1 for a listing of ideas). Such projects have been piloted in a variety of circumstances, with mixed results (Garrett 1984; Riel 1985). Difficulties usually center on the user unfriendliness of much telecommunications software.

Lake (1986), for example, estimated that six to eight hours of training in telecommunications is required even for teachers who are familiar with computers and word processing. His project involved use of a telecommunications package specially designed for classroom use, *The Newsroom*'s "Wire Service" component. Students from a variety of schools wrote articles, which were collected on-line in a central computer and printed out to form a newspaper.

With all the complications involved, critics might question whether it would be more efficient simply to have each student mail a printout or disk to the central location, or have each school print its own newspaper and send copies to other schools by mail. Lake, however, reported that students were highly motivated to write for electronic publication.

High student motivation was also reported by Eastman (1984), who had eighth grade students use a commercial telecommunications network to access an on-line encyclopedia. The students indicated a preference for using the computer to access information over using a print encyclopedia. Eastman noted that the students claimed that the electronic encyclopedia was easier to use, despite clear evidence to the contrary.

Ideas for Educational Telecommunications Projects

1. A collection of articles about local industries and vocational training and opportunities for each.

2. A collection of book, movie, television, or music reviews.

3. Analyses of characters from various literary works.

4. Summaries of classroom project results from science or social studies.

5. Student poetry or short short story anthologies.

6. Community issues.

7. Trade information with classrooms located in different parts of the country or world. Professional educational associations and educational computer user groups (such as the International Reading Association's Special Interest Group on Microcomputers in Reading. Dept. of Elementary & Secondary Education & Reading, State University of New York at Geneseo, Geneseo, NY 14454) can serve to enlist teachers interested in such projects.

8. Foreign language newspapers.

9. Collections of college reviews for college-bound secondary students.

FIGURE 10-1. Ideas for Educational Telecommunications Projects

LOCAL AREA NETWORKS

A local area network (LAN) is a system designed to interconnect microcomputers within a small business office or a school. Perhaps the best-known of these is the Ethernet, developed by Xerox Corporation for businesses. Office workers can store word-processing or numerical files that can be accessed by anyone within the network. By the mid-1980s, one-third of U.S. corporations used LANs for information handling (Brilliantine 1985).

An educational LAN typically consists of fewer than 40 student work station microcomputers, a central disk storage system, and printers. All components are linked together by cables. The usual purpose of a LAN in education is to improve efficiency of a microcomputer laboratory. Integrated learning systems (ILSs) with student work stations connected to a central minicomputer are also classified as LANs and are discussed in Chapter 3.

Efficiency of the laboratory operation is improved largely due to the central storage device, usually a hard disk capable of containing many educational programs. In order to load a program, students or teachers need only issue the appropriate command and the program is loaded into the microcomputer's memory. There is no need for floppy disks, as all programs are contained on the central hard disk. Different students can work on different programs—or the same program—at the same time.

In addition, each student work station can directly access the laboratory printers and send files to be printed out in hard copy. This represents a marked improvement over laboratories in which students must hand-carry their disks from their own work stations to another microcomputer that is hooked up to a printer.

Since programs are loaded into the microcomputer work stations from the central storage device, there is no absolute need for disk drives for each microcomputer. Most LANs, however, include drives for at least some of the work stations, in order to use software that cannot be stored on the central device. As a result, there is usually no significant financial savings in purchasing a LAN, as opposed to purchasing completely independent microcomputers.

The decision to purchase a LAN must be made carefully, after a full assessment of a comprehensive list of advantages and disadvantages like that suggested by Vogt (1984). One major concern should be the availability of software for the LAN. While any kind of public-domain software can be loaded directly into the central disk's storage system, anything that is copy-protected—and that includes almost all commercial software—cannot be. The LAN manufacturer must negotiate an agreement with the software publishers for each program to be stored on the system. If an agreement is reached, the publishers will provide unprotected copies of the program to be loaded into the system for a licensing fee. If the LAN purchaser wants a large number of such programs, the licensing fees can be substantial. *Bank Street Writer*, for example, may cost $500 to implement on a hard disk system. Some LAN systems provide hundreds of educational programs, and others provide few.

Another major concern has to do with the maximum number of work stations allowable on the system. The greater the number of users, the slower the system will operate in such processes as loading and storing programs. While in theory a LAN can have an almost unlimited number of users, in practice the greater the number of work stations, the less convenient the system is for use of the peripheral devices—the printers and the central storage system. Systems differ in the speed at which they operate. Also, some system designs are more efficient than others.

Since the LAN is a good deal more complex than a lab of independently operating microcomputers, purchasers should be particularly aware of the need for professional installation and servicing. If the LAN breaks down, the laboratory is out of operation until a service person arrives, unless the micro-computers have their own disk drives for independent functioning and the laboratory is equipped with floppy disks of software.

SOURCES OF INFORMATION

While each of the following technologies is serviced by a variety of manufac-turers and publishers, most are oriented to business and industry. The follow-ing select list includes those who have directed some efforts toward the educational community.

Networking Devices

"DIRECTORY OF NETWORKING DEVICES FOR EDUCATION." 1986. *T.H.E. Journal* 13, no. 9 (May): 89-93.
This includes a comprehensive listing of LAN manufacturers, with brief descriptions of some 57 products. LANs for both microcomputers and mainframes are included.

CORVUS OMNINET, Corvus, 2100 Corvus Dr., San Jose, CA 95124.
The Corvus central storage device is a hard disk. Corvus is the best-selling LAN (Birkhead 1986) and has done substantial work in securing software for its system. Many MECC (Min-nesota Educational Computing Corporation) programs are available for Corvus, for example.

TANDY CORP./RADIO SHACK, Network 1, Network 2, Network 3, Network 4, Tandy Corp./Radio Shack, Education Division, 1400, One Tandy Center, Fort Worth, TX 76102.
Tandy offers three different LANs, of varying complexity, designed for its microcomputers. Another system, Network 4, is based on a hard disk/microcomputer combination.

CD-ROM

LAMBERT, STEVE, AND SUZANNE ROPIEQUET (eds). 1986. *CD-ROM: The New Papyrus*. Redmond, WA: Microsoft Press.
This compilation of articles on the technology and implications of CD-ROM discusses both sides of the major issue: the side represented by those who think CD-ROM will bring about a Gutenberg-like revolution and those who think CD-ROM will fizzle.

ROTH, JUDITH PARIS. 1986. *Essential Guide to CD-ROM*. Westport, CT: Meckler Publishing.
This introduction to CD-ROM technology includes a detailed glossary and directory of pub-lishers and manufacturers. A CD-ROM disk is included that contains over 8,000 public-domain software programs for the IBM-PC.

Hardware

A wide variety of CD-ROM drives are available or under development. Some of the first on the market were the following:

Hitachi, 59 Route 17 S., Allendale, NJ 07401
MicroTrends, 650 Woodfield Dr., Suite 730, Schaumburg, IL 60195
Phillips, 100 E. 42nd St., New York, NY 10017
Sony, 23430 Hawthorne Blvd. #330, Torrance, CA 90505

Software

ELECTRONIC ENCYCLOPEDIA, Grolier Electronic Publishing, 95 Madison Ave., New York, NY 10016. 212-696-9750

BOOKSHELF, Microsoft Corporation, PO Box 97017, Redmond, WA 98073. 206-882-8080

TELECOMMUNICATIONS RESOURCES

Telecommunications Information Networks

COMPUSERVE, 5000 Arlington Centre Blvd., PO Box 20212, Columbus, OH 43220.

THE SOURCE, 1616 Anderson Rd., McLean, VA 22102.

Information Sources

GLOSSBRENNER, ALFRED. 1985. *The Complete Handbook of Personal Computer Communication: Everything You Need to Go Online with the World.* New York: St. Martin's Press.
This is a definitive book for beginners interested in learning more about telecommunications.

MILLER, ELWOOD E., AND MARY LOUISE MOSLFY (eds.). 1985. *Educational Media and Technology Yearbook, 1985,* Vol. 11. Littleton, CO: Libraries Unlimited.
This annually published yearbook contains a compilation of data bases of interest to educators. This volume lists 17. Each listing includes a brief description, with addresses and phone numbers. This yearbook is published by the Association for Educational Communications and Technology and by the American Society for Training and Development.

Telecommunications for Educational Purposes

NEWSROOM
This program allows children to write articles, then arranges the articles in a newspaper to be printed in hard copy. Students can integrate graphics by using the "Photo Lab" application. Articles can be sent to other schools via modems by using the "Wire Service" application. The Scholastic edition includes many useful ideas for classroom uses of *Newsroom,* such as the creation of "historic" newspapers. *Newsroom* is published by Springboard and by Scholastic.

Springboard Software, 7808 Creekridge Circle, Minneapolis, MN 55435

Scholastic Software, PO Box 7502, 2931 E. McCarty St.,
Jefferson City, MO 65102
IBM-PC, Apple II series, Commodore 64

11

NATURAL LANGUAGE FOR READING
INSTRUCTIONAL SOFTWARE

In order for computers to communicate most effectively with students, software must be developed that can understand and produce natural language—that is, human language such as English or French rather than the artificial programming languages such as BASIC or Pascal. In essence, computers must be taught to read and to write. Chapter 12 will deal with "cutting-edge" research on natural-language artificial intelligence systems. The present chapter deals with materials that are on the market. It will discuss the limitations of such software and the reasons for those limitations. This chapter begins with a discussion of how computers can carry out "coversations" with students for teaching purposes. The later sections demonstrate how these interactions are becoming more complex and how the computer's role is becoming more "human like" in terms of giving intelligent responses to students.

Most critics of computer-based software take aim at the workbook-like qualities of materials on the market. Programs consist of "pages" of drill-and-practice exercises, sometimes accompanied by marginally helpful text instructions. These computer drills do offer some advantages over workbooks. They include graphics, sound, limited interaction as the computer responds to student answers, enhanced motivation, and management subprograms that keep track of student progress. As such, they enhance subskill instruction in reading (Lesgold 1983; Balajthy 1984b).

Yet the most frequent response of teachers to microcomputer software has been disappointment. Computers are not at present capable of carrying out the kinds of instruction that most teachers think should be carried out. To understand just where computers can fit into the teaching of reading and language arts, both today and tomorrow, it is necessary to understand a little bit about how computers operate when dealing with what we call "natural language"—real-life English, French, or whatever a person's speaking language may be. This leads naturally to a discussion of artificial intelligence, as efforts to enable computers to think and communicate like human beings are subsumed under that term.

YESTERDAY'S APPLICATIONS OF COMPUTERS

Designers of computer-assisted instruction realized the capacity of the computer to deliver mechanical instruction early on, as computers became available for such uses. During the 1960s and 1970s, extensive software development was carried out to teach reading and writing skills (see Ch. 5 of this volume). Several large-city school systems were active in producing such courseware. For example, Philadelphia's Computer-Assisted Reading Development (CARD) program, some of which was later published for microcomputers by Radio Shack, provided subskill tutorials and drills. In addition, a variety of research projects, often funded by the federal government for use at the college level, were carried out by using mainframes to teach reading and writing skills.

These curriculum developers recognized the power of the computer to deliver rote, mechanical forms of instruction. Their efforts were largely misdirected, however, in that the limits of their programming skills determined their instructional approaches, allowing "the tail to wag the dog." Newman (1984) has suggested that the ultimate lack of acceptance of these programs was due largely to their lack of solid grounding in language development theory.

The field of reading, for instance, was moving away from linear, subskill models of the reading process and toward psycholinguistic (Goodman 1967) and interactive (Rumelhart 1977; Lesgold & Perfetti 1981) descriptions that deemphasized exact, letter-by-letter, word-by-word aspects of reading. These newer approaches highlighted the influence of reader expectations and background knowledge on comprehension of text. Simultaneously, researchers and theorists were suggesting that language is a holistic process to be learned in an integrated way that closely relates the key processes of reading and writing (Graves 1983; Moffett & Wagner 1983).

The abundant and unimaginative subskill drills offered by software manufacturers are diametrically opposite to these educational theories (Kindman-Koffler 1984-1985). Rubin (1983), for example, surveyed some 317 reading and language arts programs. Only 21 required students to read connected text. The vast majority dealt with isolated letters, words, or phrases.

The limitations of such software have led to many teachers' disenchantment with computers as tools for instruction. Similarly, the large-scale federally funded projects that were simply the old programmed instruction formats transferred to the computer screen never met with widespread acceptance despite industrious public relations efforts. Today, even those teachers who use video game format drill-and-practice programs often do not value them as teaching tools. These colorful games, highly popular with students at least for the moment, are used more for their motivational value than for serious instruction (Becker 1983b).

TODAY'S APPLICATIONS OF COMPUTERS

Though it has not been generally realized by the public at large or even by the teaching profession as a whole, the cutting edge of educational computing underwent a dramatic change of focus as microcomputers gained popularity. No longer are computers seen primarily as instructional delivery systems—as tutors and drillers. Instead, students and teachers are beginning to realize that today's immediately relevant application of the computer is as a tool (Taylor 1980). It is a tool for many of the same functions for which businesses use computers—the handling of information.

Teachers of composition, for example, have recognized that word-processing software is revolutionizing written communication. Revising, long advocated by theorists of the writing process—but long ignored by teachers and students alike as too mechanical and painful for practical use—is now possible with the pressing of a few keys. The potential for use of word processors as a tool for teaching of composition is enormous (see Ch. 1 of this volume). In addition, their impact in business offices indicates that knowledge of word processing is an important job skill in and of itself.

Use of the computer as a tool has many additional applications in the classroom. Spelling-checker programs can be used to flag misspelled words in compositions. Data-base programs help students organize and file information for research projects and class book report files. Use of computer-based data systems is an important library research skill. Text analysis programs perform analyses of compositions for grammar and usage errors.

Creative teachers are also encouraging student growth in language and thinking by encouraging thoughtful student responses to computer-based activities. Computer simulations of social or scientific processes can be used to encourage discovery-oriented thinking in analyzing cause-and-effect relationships. The popular adventure game software, in which computer users are detectives solving a crime or heroes fighting dragons and trolls, can be the basis for a wide variety of creative writing activities. Video games and computer adaptations of board games such as *Nim* or *Towers of Hanoi* can be the basis of strategy analysis in which teachers lead students to learn more about their metacognitive thinking strategies and problem-solving abilities. For younger students, the simple computer graphics programs such as *Facemaker* (in which youngsters create and animate humorous cartoon faces using computer graphics) can be the basis for language experience stories.

In all these applications, however, whether the computer is being used as a tool or as a device to which students can respond with problem-solving or expressive activities, the human teacher is essential to provide feedback and to facilitate instruction. Indeed, the human component gives meaning to the tasks, providing the basis for interaction. It is on this point—involving the fundamental interactive nature of language—that the computer fails. Contemporary limitations on the computer's ability to process natural language—limitations caused by software, hardware, and the state of knowledge about the interrelationships of cognition and machine operation—justify teachers' reservations about using the computer for direct instructional purposes.

APPROACHES TO NATURAL LANGUAGE PROCESSING

Interaction by "Exact Match"

How does the computer interact with humans? Even novice computer users quickly become aware of the computer's limitations in comprehending language. The "language" used by most microcomputers is called BASIC. Like all programming languages, BASIC consists of a limited number of command words that must be sequenced exactly, according to specified rules. At a more fundamental level, the computer cannot even understand BASIC. Its knowledge of programming languages is based on an intricate pattern of microelectronic on and off switches translated into 0's and 1's. As a result, if a student types the words "Hello, it's a nice day" into a computer, unless the computer has been programmed to recognize that exact string of characters, it will respond with a message to the effect "I don't know what you're talking about."

In their quest to simulate human interaction, computer programmers use a variety of techniques. Each can be effective in certain circumstances.

The most frequent technique, and perhaps the simplest, involves instructing the computer to examine input for an exact match. The user is given a "prompt"—a question or command to type an input. *Hello* (Ahl 1978) is a short program designed to be typed into a computer. It is a simple attempt to simulate a "conversation" between the user and the computer "psychologist."

The program asks, "What kind of problems do you have?" and offers four possible choices. When you type your reasons, BASIC commands within the program look like this in substance:

1. Examine the input.
2. If the input is MONEY, then print out the following: "I'm broke too. Why don't you sell encyclopedias or marry someone rich or stop eating so you won't need so much money?"

3. If the input is JOB, then print out the following: "I can sympathize with you. I have to work very long hours for no pay—and some of my bosses really beat on my keyboard."

And so on through the four choices. Finally, if the input looks like none of the above, indicate that the choice is not understood and ask the user to try again.

This "exact match" paradigm of human-computer interaction is the foundation for the tutorials and drills that compose so much of reading and language arts software. The computer asks a question, receives an input from the user, and looks for a match to something stored in its memory.

The match may take a variety of forms. It may be a letter or number. Such matches are easy to program, and as a result much software offers human-computer interaction of a multiple-choice format. The match may be a word chosen by the user from a specified set of choices, as in the *Hello* program described above. Even video game drills have their basis in this exact match pattern. If the child's launching of a rocket "matches" the appearance of the correct vocabulary word in a definition exercise, for example, the rocket strikes home and the child earns a point.

The limitations of interaction to "match-no match" statements is serious for language arts instruction. Only the simplest of learning tasks lend themselves easily to such a format. Open-ended questions are disallowed. Even short-answer questions must have strict constraints. *Herringbone Stories* is a public-domain comprehension program developed by the author based on WH- questions about short passages. Students are asked to type in "WHEN?" a particular story occurred. The target passage states that events took place "in the late 1890s." Correct answers could be phrased in many different ways: 1890, 1890s, nineteenth century, 1890's, eighteen nineties—the computer has been instructed to accept over 15 possible answers as correct, and there certainly are more. Programming for such almost unlimited variant possibilities is usually prohibited by time and finances.

Open-Ended Responses

In order to escape the constraints of the exact-match pattern and to allow for the open-endedness characteristic of quality language instruction, a variety of programs have been developed that avoids the problem altogether. They do this by removing meaningful responses by the computer to the student's input.

A simple example involves the name input routine often used to personalize instructional programs. The computer asks, "What's your name?" The student types "Mark." The computer continues with "Hi, Mark! Today we are going to study adjectives!" The name input is received and used by the computer without any semblance of meaningful recognition. The student could type "MXFARTHINGOBUL" and the computer would dutifully print "Hi, MXFARTHINGOBUL!"

A variety of programs use such nonjudgmental approaches to encourage and structure student writing. Poetry generators such as *Poetry Express* ask students to generate highly structured poems in a mechanical fashion, following styles popularized by Koch (1970). Students respond to requests such as "Type a noun" and "Type two words ending in -ing that describe your noun." The computer is unable actually to understand or respond to what the student types. It simply prints it out in poetic line formats.

Composition starters (sometimes called "composition heuristic" or "rhetorical invention" programs) lead students through organized prewriting planning procedures. "Write a statement about your topic" and "Give two reasons to support the accuracy of your statement" are among the thought-provoking questions typically asked. The computer makes no judgments on responses. Answers are simply organized and printed for reference during the actual writing of the composition.

The Puzzler is one of the first programs to use this nonjudgmental technique to develop reading ability (see Ch. 1 of this volume for a detailed description). Students are presented a portion of a passage and are asked to make predictions as to the passage's topic. Each passage on the disk is sufficiently ambiguous to encourage guessing—there are no "right" answers. As the program proceeds, further portions of the passage are provided, and the student types in new predictions that are progressively refined.

As with the prewriting programs described earlier, inputs are open-ended and are not "understood" by the computer. Instead, teachers can use the activity as a focus for discussion of reading as a process of hypothesis generation/testing, the "psycholinguistic guessing game" (Goodman 1967; Burnett & Miller 1984). Large-group follow-up discussion would center on students' reasons for their guesses. "Why did you make that guess?" and "Which sentence in the passage supports your guess?" would be typical questions addressed to the students by the teacher. After the teacher models one or two such exercises in class, students quickly learn to work in small groups on the passages, independent of teacher direction. The group discussions follow the questioning and reasoning patterns established by the teacher earlier in large-group discussions. Miller (1987) has labeled software, such as *The Puzzler*, that lends itself to higher-level thinking and discussion as "hands-off software."

Skeptics about the usefulness of computers in reading and in language arts are rarely satisfied with either the exact-match or the open-ended type of programs. The latter is said to provide little or no guidance to students. Some critics, apparently under the impression that open-ended programs attempt to fool students into believing the computer understands their inputs, charge that students quickly realize that the computer can generate no intelligent response to their input. Of what use is a program, they ask, in which students can generate nonsense or outlandish responses with no appropriate reaction by the computer?

Such criticisms are based on uninformed expectations of computer performance and on lack of understanding of the function of the computer as a tool. The general principle of computer performance has always been GIGO—garbage in, garbage out. Experienced computer users recognize that computer tools such as word-processing and data-base management software do not judge inputs—they simply allow the user to manage information more readily. In similar fashion, open-ended instructional programs function as tools for presentation and management of information—no more, no less. These tools can be of great value, but they have their limitations.

Is the inability of the computer to deal with natural language—to understand and respond intelligently to user inputs—a critical failing? Certainly not. Even in their present "stupid" state of development, computers offer unique advantages if the user recognizes their limitations. But if computers were capable of intelligent responses, how much more valuable would they be as tools for the intellect?

We are therefore led to ask two questions: What are the computer's capabilities—both present and future—to understand natural language? How can these capabilities be tapped for the purpose of reading and writing instruction? Both questions lead to a discussion of artificial intelligence.

Artificial Intelligence

The classic test of whether a machine has been given comprehensive intelligence is known as the Turing test. Alan Turing, an early and important computer scientist, proposed a test called the "Imitation Game" (1950). Place an individual in a room with a keyboard and teletype that may be connected to either of two possible sources—a human or a computer. Allow the individual to carry on a conversation with the computer. If the individual is afterward unable to determine with whom he had been communicating, human or computer, the computer is "intelligent." It is to this basic end that the field of artificial intelligence is devoted: to develop a computer that can respond to natural language in human fashion.

The challenge is enormous. The ability to communicate with language is perhaps the most complex of all human processes. Meaningful communication involves stores of information about a great variety of topics. It involves the interrelationships among these various stores of information, both literal and figurative. It involves control of language systems. It involves the ability to think—to draw upon background knowledge and to construct linkages with that knowledge in order to use higher levels of cognition, such as drawing conclusions and making judgments. It involves the ability to deal with new information, to connect it in logical fashion with existing knowledge for memory purposes.

While the field of artificial intelligence (AI) is of course involved with computer programming, its relationship to the field of reading and writing is almost as intimate. After all, a truly intelligent computer must be able to "read" input and "write" output.

As a result, researchers on AI are interested in how the human mind operates in language processes. Cognitive research on comprehension is of particular interest to AI people. How is background knowledge stored in the mind? How are these stores brought to bear on material being read? How does the mind use background knowledge to determine levels of importance of ideas within text—finding the main idea, for example? How does the mind draw upon this background knowledge to integrate new information, while in the process making judgments and inferences and drawing conclusions? These questions, so central to the teaching of reading, are just as central to the objective of programming an "intelligent" computer.

AI researchers face many challenges in their task—challenges faced by reading teachers as well. Take the following sentences, for example.

> The car was driven by the bank.
> The car was driven by the woman.

Both appear to be grammatically identical on the surface. In fact, the relationships among the nouns are quite different. As human speakers and proficient readers, we recognize the differences automatically. However, how can a computer be programmed to recognize differences in such sentences? The ability to understand these relationships depends on sophisticated grammatical understanding of the types of phrases and on a thorough store of background knowledge about driving.

Take another sentence: "As Mary Ann sat back against the tree, staring at the clouds, she heard a slither in the grass near her foot and a faint rattling sound." What will happen next? Will a poisonous snake slide into view? Will it strike? Will Mary Ann jump up and scream? Will she freeze in fear? What will happen if the snake bites her? All the possibilities automatically come to mind as a mature reader reads the sentence, yet all demand inferential predictions based on our past knowledge of snakes and people. Is it possible for this background information and inferential ability to be programmed into a computer?

As a result of such questions, AI is centrally concerned with the study of the human mind. Schank, director of the artificial intelligence project at Yale University, has suggested that the most fruitful avenue of research in AI is to program computers to simulate human cognitive processes as closely as possible (1982a, 1982b) (see Ch. 12 of this volume). In order to succeed in this task, it is first necessary to understand those cognitive processes—a goal of psychologists for generations.

One of the cognitive processes of most interest to AI researchers is comprehension. Reading involves not only letter recognition; computers can recognize the input of letters, numbers, and other characters. This reading task will not succeed if limited to word recognition. Computers can recognize the input of words—they can do the equivalent of "word calling."

If the reading task is to succeed, computers must be programmed to understand—to comprehend—at the sentence level, at the paragraph level, and at the passage level. They must be programmed to make inferences, to draw conclusions, to understand figurative language, and to learn in order to process incoming information (Schank 1982b). These reading tasks are of interest to AI researchers just as much as they are to reading teachers. The computer is a "remedial reader" in the sense that component processes of reading must be analyzed and explained—programmed—in detail.

INTERACTION BY NATURAL LANGUAGE TODAY

A variety of programs on the market today illustrate the potential of the computer to interact with humans using natural language. These programs are extremely limited in their topic areas, their vocabulary knowledge, and their ability to use varied sentence structures. As a result, their applications to classroom situations are awkward. They do, however, suggest that future developments could enrich students' work with computers incredibly.

One program that has received widespread attention from teachers interested in the use of natural language with computers is *Eliza*. The original version was developed by Joseph Weizenbaum in the mid-1960s for a mainframe computer. *Eliza* simulates the role of a nondirective psychotherapist à la Carl Rogers. The computer-using "patient" types in comments, and the computer responds with startlingly intelligent answers. Weizenbaum (1976, pp. 3-4) offers the following sample conversation. User responses are in italics.

> "Patient": *Men are all alike.*
> "Doctor" *Eliza*: In what way?
> *They're always bugging us about something or other.*
> Can you think of a specific example?
> *Well, my boyfriend made me come here.*
> Your boyfriend made you come here.
> *He says I'm depressed much of the time.*
> I am sorry to hear you are depressed.
> *It's true. I am unhappy.*
> Do you think coming here will help you not to be unhappy?

Some people respond amazingly to *Eliza*, carrying on the conversation for great lengths of time. They find some limited therapeutic value to the program.

Eliza's ability to respond to user comments is only a shallow simulation of an actual therapeutic session, of course. The program does not actually understand what the patient types, nor does it have any of the sensitivity and insight of a trained therapist. As a matter of fact, many of its responses are nonsequiturs, nonsensical in context, and many "patients" quickly lose patience with *Eliza*. The following is a sequence from another version of the program, designed for microcomputers, that more clearly illustrates how *Eliza* masks the lack of understanding with nonsequiturs.

> "Doctor" *Eliza*: May I help you?
> "Patient": *I have got some problems.*
> I see.
> *Do you have any suggestions?*
> We were discussing you—not me.
> *My job bothers me.*
> Why do you think your job bothers you?
> *My boss is really mean.*
> Why do you think your boss is really mean?
> *I do not know.*
> Come, come elucidate your thoughts.
> *I do not want to go to work today.*
> What would it mean to you if you got to go to work today?

The Rogerian therapeutic style, in which the counselor responds to the patient by rephrasing comments into questions to draw out more information, uniquely lends itself to the type of programming used by Weizenbaum. *Eliza* recognizes certain key words in user input as "exact matches" to words in its memory and gives a certain type of response based on that input. If no key words in the input are recognized, the computer may give a randomly chosen response: "I notice that you have not mentioned your relationship with your mother."

Responses to *Eliza* vary. Some users are fascinated. Others are quickly bored by the basically meaningless routine. *Eliza*'s conversation gives a superficial appearance of perceptivity. At its core, however, the program is simply throwing the users' words back at them. While this technique works passably well in a simulation of Rogerian therapy, it is hard to imagine any other suitable contexts. Its appropriateness for educational uses is doubtful.

A more advanced use of natural language for communication with the computer can be seen in computer adventure games. Dozens of these games are commercially available. They range from mysteries and war games to romances or science fiction and fantasy. In an adventure game, the user assumes the role of an adventurer. In the highly successful *Zork* series, for example, the player searches through an underground maze of rooms for hidden treasures. Along the way she or he will encounter dangerous traps and enemies such as trolls and thieves.

The user's participation in these games involves giving commands to the computer. E, W, N, and S are standardized commands to move in the directions of the compass. U and D move the adventurer vertically up stairs and down holes in the floor. Early adventure games were largely limited to use of such simple commands.

Today's games are capable of understanding much more complex inputs. In *Zork*, an adventure game published in 1979, the adventurer encounters a house with a window slightly ajar. The commands "Open the window" and "Climb in the window" are understood by the computer, and the user is able to maneuver around and perform actions within the adventure scenario by using natural language. "Attack the troll" will elicit the response "With what?" If the player's answer is "bare hands," he or she will suffer the consequences of such an unwise decision. If the answer is "with sword," the player has a much improved chance of surviving the encounter.

The program is capable of understanding these constructions because of a component called a parser that recognizes certain nouns and verbs, as well as adjectives, prepositions, and other parts of speech. By the mid-1980s, Infocom, a publisher of many of the more complex adventure games, had designed sophisticated parsers equipped with vocabularies of up to 1,200 words per game.

At its heart, however, the interaction between the computer and the user remains on a simple, exact-match level. The computer is programmed to respond in certain ways to certain vocabulary words and sentence constructions. The extent of vocabulary programming need not include the entire English language. Only those words likely to to be used in the game are included. Action words (jump, run, attack, go, take) and nouns used in the program (lamp, rope, troll) must be recognized. If the user phrases a command in an unfamiliar manner ("Leap over the stream"), the computer responds with "I don't understand." The user then tries to rephrase the command in words the computer will understand: "Jump over the stream." Sentence complexity is generally limited to a command-object relationship: "Attack the troll," "Take the golden egg," "Open the door."

The amazing ingenuity of game programmers in functioning within these parameters helps the games come alive within players' minds. The more complex series of games, such as *Zork* and *Wizardry*, offer players literally months of spare time action and a fair amount of reading as well. The adventure game *Deadline*, for example, has 25,000 words of text. The challenge of communicating with the computer is part of the attraction of these games.

One of the first microcomputer adventure games, suitably called *Adventure*, was written by William Crowther, who had studied at MIT. *Adventure* had a two-word text parser that could analyze sentences such as GO EAST or TAKE HAMMER (Addams 1985). Several companies have relied on such crude parsers for their games. Sierra, for example, has emphasized graphics rather than language sophistication for its programs, though it did begin marketing a full-sentence text parser with its 1984 *King's Quest* fantasy game.

As the microcomputer industry boomed in the early 1980s and users searched for challenging adventure games, Infocom established itself as the developer of the most intricately designed adventures. At the heart of programs such as its *Zork* series were text parsing programs that allowed use of quite sophisticated sentence structure—compared wuith parsers produced by other companies—and that accessed large software dictionaries. Infocom continued to dominate the adventure game market through the mid-1980s, largely as a result of its sophisticated text parser.

The battle for supremacy in the lucrative adventure game market continues to revolve around text parser development. The 1985 release of *Star Trek: The Kobiashi Alternative* included a software dictionary that contained every word from the setting and event descriptions and from conversations with other characters within the science fiction scenario. A later model (Addams 1985) of the text parser in Spinnaker's *Telarium* adventures (which includes literary titles such as *Fahrenheit 451*) could deal with ten items of grammar, including adjectives, nouns, verbs, and direct and indirect objects.

Yet, as with *Eliza*, the language constraints under which these games function do not lend themselves to many instructional situations. For one thing, users must learn to function under the rules of such interaction—use of simple sentences and common vocabulary. Another problem involves the range of possible user inputs within a computer game. This range is limited in comparison with possible reader inputs to general reading passages. When confronted by a menacing troll in a room with only two exits, the player has only three choices: Attack, run through exit number 1, run through exit number 2. A computer can be programmed to recognize a variety of responses as corresponding to one or another of those three choices. In a reading exercise, though, if the reader is asked to draw conclusions from a passage, the range of possible responses is enormous, as any teacher of reading will verify. Thus, adventure games may be a promise of what is to come, but the programming techniques used in this software are not immediately useful in many instructional situations.

The first major application of these programming techniques to microcomputer instructional software is *Story Machine*, a program designed for preprimer readers. *Story Machine* is an animated language-experience activity with a 50-word vocabulary. Students may choose words from a dictionary including nouns (girl, boy, tree, house), verbs (run, jump, sing), pronouns, prepositions, and function words. They type sentences into the computer, and the sentences are acted out in high-resolution animation on the monitor screen.

THE BOY GOES TO THE TREE yields a picture of a boy and a tree. As the period is placed at the end of the sentence, the boy walks over to the tree. HE SINGS causes notes to be sounded from the computer's speaker. Children can string together simple sentences to form a story that will be acted out in sequence on the screen. The activity is charming to both the preprimer children for whom it was designed and to older students and adults, though the simple vocabulary and sentence structure render it educationally valueless for older users.

As with adventure games, *Story Machine* supplies the computer with a specified set of vocabulary words. In adventure games, the player must find out just what is contained on the set of words. This time-consuming activity would have no useful function in an instructional program, so children are informed from the start as to which words will be recognized by *Story Machine*. Also, as with adventure games, only certain sentence constructions and combinations of words are recognizable. THE BOY DANCES is allowed, but THE BOY SINGS AND DANCES is not.

Unfortunately, the limitations on vocabulary and sentence structure can be frustrating for children. The traditional ending of stories, ". . . and they lived happily ever after," contains unrecognizable words. Sentence constructions that are composed of legitimate vocabulary words are not always recognized by the computer, sometimes for reasons that even adults cannot understand.

Of course, a little frustration is not necessarily a bad thing. Children ought to be encouraged to use a problem-solving approach to determining which sentence *can* be acted upon by the computer, rather than allowing themselves to get bogged down by failures. As with all software designed for such young children, close adult supervision is required, especially when children are first learning to use it. *Story Machine* is a motivational activity despite its limitations. Even better, it is a promise of things to come as educational programming takes advantage of more sophisticated techniques and as computers are provided with larger memory storage to allow complex processing.

INTERACTION BY NATURAL LANGUAGE TOMORROW

When will computers have the ability to engage in free-flowing interaction in the manner of Arthur C. Clarke's HAL in the movie *2001: A Space Odyssey*? Certainly not by 2001. Computer hardware developments are taking place at incredible speeds. The development of software will not keep pace, however, until psychologists have a more complete understanding of how the mind operates.

Rose, in his *Into the Heart of the Mind* (1984), a popular history of research into artificial intelligence, describes the problems involved in the seemingly simple matter of teaching a computer the common sense to "come in out of the rain." Common sense, the ability to draw conclusions based on past experiences, is a major obstacle in AI researchers' efforts to construct computers that think like humans. Until psychologists determine just what processes underlie common sense, the goal of teaching operations will not be achieved.

More common developments can be expected in the "expert systems" approach to artificial intelligence (see Chapter 14 of this volume). Rather than attempting to model human cognitive processes on a global scale, researchers in expert systems limit their attention to one focused topic of interest: decision making. MYCIN, for example, is a medical diagnostic program that is capable of responding intelligently to diagnostic inputs in much the same fashion as a knowledgeable medical specialist would. The necessary background information is stored in memory, and the computer is directed to follow certain logical "thought processes" in its analysis of a patient's condition. As with adventure games, the possible vocabulary inputs are limited and thus can be handled by the program. The necessary background knowledge that must be brought to bear on the various diagnostic inputs is also limited. Within these constraints, the program apparently functions well in replicating the analyses of trained physicians.

Business and government are actively supporting research into these expert systems. Think of an "expert" computer-controlled fighter plane, capable of flying, monitoring radar, managing weapons systems—all simultaneously and without human involvement. Businesses could capitalize on computer control of complex manufacturing processes. Design of computer chips, for example, has become so complex as to overwhelm human engineering ability. Computers are already programmed to help in design of microelectronic components. In a sense they are being taught to create themselves.

Expert systems could well play a key role in education in the not-too-distant future. Software might be available to deal with particular content or skill topics. One program might function well in carrying on a pedagogical discussion with a student about automobile safety, for example. Another program might discuss dinosaurs. The possibilities are endless.

WHAT CAN I DO TODAY?

We come back at this point to complete a full circle in order to deal with our original issue, today's applications of the computer to reading and language arts instruction. What should teachers recognize about the use of AI and computers in the classroom?

We must recognize the central role of the human teacher in instruction. Computers will not change this. Some computer advocates are still suggesting that computers will replace teachers. Koetke (1984), for instance, pointed to the burgeoning market for educational software for home use as parents buy programs for their children. Will classroom educators be superseded by a home-based educational system in which children pound away on their micros in isolation from peers and teachers? Not many take such an idea seriously. Most software purchased by parents goes the route of all traditional Christmas toys—used one day and forgotten on a shelf afterward.

Computers will not replace the human teacher. What roles, then, must computers assume in the classroom to be viable today? First, computers must be used as tools. The computer is a tool for the teacher, providing better management of instruction (for instance, record keeping) and individualized instruction to students with specific needs. The computer is a tool for the student, providing experiences otherwise unavailable (such as science and social studies simulations) and more efficient information handling (word processing and data-base research). Unless those who control the purse strings of school systems are convinced of the value of the computer in these key areas, microcomputers in education will go the same route as the older computer-assisted instruction of the 1960s—into obscurity.

Second, teachers and administrators must provide an intelligent market for well-designed programs as they are published. Yes, much commercial instructional software is cut-and-dried workbook-like tutorials and practice materials. As more sophisticated programs appear, however, the schools must recognize them, purchase them, and use them. Publishers need convincing that the extra effort and expense needed for development of such materials are worthwhile.

Educators have not heard the last of complaints that "There is no good software out there," complaints that indicate a lack of knowledge of computer materials and lack of willingness to change in the face of developing technology. There is a lot of good software available today. Developments are occurring quickly, as a brief comparison of typical educational software of the late 1970s with today's sophisticated materials will demonstrate clearly. Educational computing has a long way to go, but it has made a strong start. Now it is necessary for teachers and schools to seize the opportunities presented.

SOURCES OF INFORMATION

SCHANK, ROGER C. 1984. *The Cognitive Computer: On Language, Learning, and Artificial Intelligence.* Reading, MA: Addison-Wesley.
This book is written at a nontechnical level as an introduction to artificial intelligence. Schank, director of the Yale Artificial Intelligence Project, is one of the foremost leaders in AI research. This text gives a history of Yale's research in the development of computer systems that understand natural language. The final section of the book gives some of Schank's predictions about the present and future impact of computer technology on education and on society in general.

ROSE, FRANK. 1984. *Into the Heart of the Mind.* New York: Harper & Row.
This book, written at a nontechnical level, details the work of Robert Wilensky, one of Schank's former students at Yale and now a leader in his own right in the study of AI. Wilensky is presently at the University of California at Berkeley. He and his students are studying commonsense reasoning and natural language. The book is written in a relaxed, informal style. Some readers may be irritated with the author's apparent inability to keep to his topic, but Rose tries to give his readers an experience of what it is like to solve AI problems, rather than simply communicating facts.

COMMERCIAL SOFTWARE

Deadline
Infocom
125 Cambridge Park Dr.
Cambridge, MA 02140
Apple II series, Macintosh, Atari, Commodore 64, IBM-PC, TRS-80, and others

Eliza: The Computer Psychotherapist
This program is available from a variety of sources, including
Artificial Intelligence Research Group
921 N. La Jolla Ave.
Los Angeles, CA 90046

Facemaker
> Spinnaker Software Co.
> Kendall Sq.
> Cambridge, MA 02139
> Apple II series, Commodore 64, IBM-PC

Fahrenheit 451
> Spinnaker Software Co.
> Apple II series, Commodore 64

Poetry Express
> Learning Well
> 200 S. Service Rd.
> Roslyn Heights, NY 11577
> Apple II series, Commodore 64

Puzzler
> Sunburst Communications
> 39 Washington Ave.
> Pleasantville, NY 10570
> Apple II series, IBM-PC, Commodore 64

Zork
> Infocom
> Apple II series, Commodore 64, Macintosh, IBM-PC, TRS-80, and others

12

HISTORY OF NATURAL LANGUAGE RESEARCH

One purpose of this chapter is to provide general background information on the progress of research in natural language processing, both past and present. A second major purpose is to discuss the varying viewpoints on the future of natural language research and, more generally, the future of cognitive science. In any such discussion, there is strong temptation toward the interminable listing and description of existing programs that simulate human use of language. This chapter attempts to avoid this temptation: Details as to the wide variety of programs developed to date are available elsewhere (see "Sources of Information" at the end of the chapter).

The first of two major parts of this chapter deals with the history of research into natural language processing, beginning with computer-based translation efforts and culminating with findings of the past decade. The second major part of the chapter deals with the implications of these research efforts for future developments. The contemporary debate about these implications is rooted in both philosophy and psychology, and some background information is given about the frequently unrecognized relationship between the two fields.

MACHINE TRANSLATION

The early 1950s saw a flurry of interest in using the new digital computer technology to translate foreign languages. The basic assumption of such attempts was that translating from one natural language to another was a rather direct process with relatively little higher thinking involved. Waltz (1982) described the assumptions underlying such attempts: "Translation is a process of dictionary look-ups, plus substitution, plus grammatical reordering" (p. 5).

Computers were programmed to identify a word from an original sentence and identify a matching word from the target language based on a software dictionary listing of words. This matching word was then substituted for the original: *man* for *hombre*, for example, in a translation from Spanish to English. Finally, any necessary reordering of sentence parts would take place. For a translation into English, for example, subject nouns would be placed before their matching verbs.

The interest in machine translation came to an early end as developers recognized the need for true understanding as a prerequisite for accurate translation. Simple word-by-word matching was clearly insufficient. The most often cited example of this insufficiency is a probably apocryphal translation from English to Russian of the sentence "The spirit is willing but the flesh is weak." The final result read "The vodka is strong but the meat is rotten."

THE SEMANTIC INFORMATION-PROCESSING ERA (1962–1973)

As interest in machine translation died out, renewed interest in the study of natural language processing was characterized by what Waltz (1982) has called "engineering approaches." That is, researchers limited their scope and objectives to specific problem areas. They sought to program computers to deal with those problem areas without necessarily modeling the ways in which humans dealt with them. That is, researchers were not primarily interested in developing computer models of internal psychological reality, as long as the output—the actual problem solution—was viable. In order to achieve this viability, the scope of their efforts was narrowed to specific subject areas.

The key development occurring at this time was based on work carried out at the Rand Corporation think tank under Allen Newell, Herbert Simon, and Clifford Shaw. Until their formative work in the late 1950s and early 1960s, computers had been used largely as number crunchers, solving mathematical problems too complicated or too time-consuming for humans. Newell, Simon, and Shaw pioneered efforts to use computer manipulation of symbols that represented real-world objects, such as words or chess pieces. Their program *General Problem Solver* was an attempt to simulate human problem solving for a wide range of topics (Newell & Simon 1963).

Exact-Match Systems

Exact-match (or key-word) systems are described in Chapter 11 of this volume. ELIZA, the well-known party game microcomputer program, is a good example and is described in detail in Chapter 11. Like its counterparts

DOCTOR (Weizenbaum 1967) and PARRY (which simulates a paranoid person: Colby, Weber, & Hilf 1971), ELIZA has no actual understanding of the dialogue. Its capabilities are based on an exact-match system (sometimes also called key-word or pattern matching rules). Inputs are analyzed for specific words, which in turn cause ELIZA to produce specific phrases.

Translating English into a Formal System

The 1960s also saw first attempts at translating natural language into more formal and precise "languages" such as mathematical equations and data-base commands. Bobrow's (1968) STUDENT program was designed to translate algebra word problems into sets of equations, then to forward the equations to another program that could solve them.

BASEBALL (Green, Wolf, Chomsky, & Laughery 1963) was one of the first "front ends" to data bases that could translate natural language questions into commands to sort the data base for specific information.

In some ways adventure games are ideal for use of text parsing efforts (see Ch. 11 of this volume). Use of natural language is important. Since most players use a variety of games, learning a different complex set of commands for each game would be impossible. Also, the effects of a text-parsing failure— misinterpretation or incomplete understanding of a command, such as "Run quickly to the weapon," is not serious—except in terms of the "life" of the fantasy hero. A failure of natural language communication in some other settings—the main computer at Strategic Air Command headquarters comes to mind—would involve a great deal more trouble.

A serious application of natural language techniques that has received a good deal of attention is in the translation of English into the formal command structure involved in questioning data bases, in use of a front-end sub-program—a link between the user and the actual data base program. Ordinarily the command structure of a data base is rather complex and can take many hours of study to master (though some simple programs, such as *Bank Street Filer* and *PFS: File*, can be learned quite quickly).

Suppose a business person were to request the popular data base management system *dBASE II* to research a data base for an answer to the question "Which companies in New Jersey have sales over $1,000,000?" He or she would have to be familiar enough with the *dBASE II* command structure to generate the following: LIST ALL COMPANIES, STATE, SALES87, FOR STATE = 'NJ'. AND. SALES87 > 1000000." Needless to say, unless such a command system were used on a daily basis, most users would quickly forget its nuances and would be forced to spend great amounts of time learning and relearning.

Two categories of natural language front-ends (sometimes called inter-face languages or user interfaces) have been developed to aid in use of data bases. Both are possible at today's primitive stage of natural language technology for the same reason that text parsers for adventure games are possible:

the limited scope of vocabulary usage and sentence structure necessary for success in the desired tasks (Petrick 1976).

The first approach has involved the development of menu-driven front ends, a somewhat unsophisticated version of multiple-choice command options. Users are presented a menu page of optional statement parts. By moving a cursor around the screen, the user can choose from a variety of words and phrases to form a coherent question. The program then "translates" those choices into the appropriate commands. Texas Instruments *Natural Link* programs have been developed as menu-driven front ends for database systems such as *Lotus 1-2-3* and *dBASE II*, as well as word processors such as *WordStar* and disk operating systems such as MS-DOS. IBM-PC users will recognize, for example, the command "DISKCOPY A: B:." Rather than being forced to remember such a command, a *Natural Link* user can select the following phrases from the menu page: "I want to—copy—both sides of the disk in—drive A—to—drive B—and check the accuracy of the copy."

Menu-driven programs are easy to use, but their operation can be slow. An experienced user can issue a complex word-processing command in a split second by the touch of two or three keys. It takes a good deal longer to move a cursor around the screen to choose statement parts and form them into a complete sentence. These programs are best suited for occasional program users.

A second approach to data-base front ends involves use of commands typed in English. As with adventure-game text parsers, these programs work by incorporating the linguistic models and rules that were developed through artificial intelligence research. The English sentences typed in by the user are translated into formal command structures.

In *Cash Management System*, for example, a simple sentence such as "Who are my customers in Philadelphia?" commands the system to list all Philadelphia customers. "Who gets paid weekly and has a pay rate under $10?" lists the names, their pay schedules, and their pay rates.

Schneiderman (1980) noted that natural language front ends will be most helpful for system users who have a knowledge of the general concepts involved in the computer application (for example, word processing or programming) but lack knowledge of the specific command system. He distinguishes these two types of knowledge as semantic and syntactic, respectively.

Contemporary natural English front ends tend to get stuck when unknown words or misspelled words are offered. They are also slower to use and less precise than the formal command structures. As with the menu-driven front ends, they are of most value to infrequent users or the "naive" user who does not have specialized training. Natural language approaches appear to be of limited usefulness in the many application areas where users have the opportunity to develop expertise in the command system (Turner et al. 1984). In the long run, a frequent user of *WordStar*, for example, would find it easier to learn and use the complex command system rather than a natural language front end.

BEGINNINGS OF COGNITIVE SCIENCE

Winograd's (1972) SHRDLU program worked within a limited "world" of blocks and shapes arranged on a table to deal with natural language. It could answer questions specific to that world. Its data base was composed of information about the blocks and about how blocks can be moved.

At about this time, Schank (1980, 1982a, 1984) began working on a series of projects that has continued to the present. Schank has dealt with a far less constrained "world," one that is primarily concerned with human actions. This work has been based on the assumption that such actions can be grouped into a small number of "primitives." Each primitive is associated with a "frame" that specifies information usually conveyed in association with that primitive. For example, the primitive MTRANS (that signifies "transfer of mental information") must be associated with an intelligent source and an intelligent receiver for that mental information.

LESSONS OF THE 1970s

From AI research carried out during the 1970s, several important lessons were learned that point to the incredible complexity of natural language processing. Many of the lessons had major impacts on the "cutting edge" of reading research during that time. To some extent, perhaps, leaders in the field of reading were so impressed with AI research—or so influenced by the research monies available from federal funding sources associated with AI— that attention shifted from reading instruction improvement toward the development of psychological models of reading that were in tune with the influential AI perspectives.

Knowledge Representation

A variety of questions about the relationship of background information to language processing have been raised. Among them are

How can memory be accessed?
How can memory be organized?
How can memory be updated?
How can inconsistencies in memory be handled?
How can decisions be made as to what information is important (or unimportant) to any given situation?

Researchers have dealt with the issue of knowledge representation in a variety of ways.

One of the key issues is that of "common sense," a vital factor in terms of inferencing. The reading field, in its analysis of comprehension, has traditionally indicated that the lowest level of comprehension is the literal level—the level at which the reader comprehends information that is explicitly stated by the author. Contemporary research suggests, on the other hand, that such low-level processing simply doesn't exist—or is far less pervasive within the reading process than previously thought.

Instead, comprehension has come to be thought of as primarily an inferential process in which the reader is continually making connections between knowledge gained from the text and his or her background knowledge. A reader knows a great deal about human behavior, for example, and supplies that knowledge to form completed versions of what he or she is reading. In this sense, some theorists have come to describe the reading process as a process of "composition"—as the reader composes a meaningful and complete picture of the topic under consideration (Petrosky 1982; Tierney & Pearson 1983).

Analysis of the reasonableness of these interpretations seems to occur automatically in good readers. Yet work with computers indicates such commonsense analysis is far from simple (McCarthy 1968). Waltz (1982) offers the example "We were afraid the milk might make the baby sick, so we boiled it" (p. 26). A misunderstanding is possible unless the computer recognizes the plausibility of differing possible interpretations: People might boil milk, but ordinarily they would not boil babies.

The school of reading researchers known as schema theorists has attempted to find parallels between the human mind engaged in reading, on the one hand, and artificial intelligence approaches to understanding communication, on the other. These researchers have drawn the bulk of their theoretical orientation from AI and related cognitive psychological research.

A variety of research studies, for example, have investigated the issue of how readers "fill in the blanks" to make inferences during reading. One study had groups of readers from India and the United States read a wedding story (Steffensen, Joag-Dev, & Anderson 1979). The story did not include explicit mention of the color of the bride's dress. Yet, when questioned, American readers indicated the dress was white and Indian readers indicated it was red. Both groups had used their background knowledge of typical bridal dress colors to inferentially "compose" a part of the story that had not been made explicit.

In similar fashion, if computers are to "understand" stories as humans understand them, they must be capable of drawing upon their store of background information to make reasonable conclusions about missing information. Many efforts continue to be made to develop such understanding.

Frames

Marvin Minsky (1975), founder of the Artificial Intelligence Laboratory at MIT, has suggested that background memory is organized into units that he has called frames (within the reading field, a frame is often called a schema). A frame is a mental outline of a topic containing slots for information typically related to that topic. These frames contain information about stereotypical events and objects.

One such stereotypical situation, for example, would be the wedding mentioned above. A reader would have certain expectations associated with such an event. These expectations—the information filling the slots to the reader's wedding-event frame—would serve as the inferential information necessary to make sense of a story about a wedding. One slot might be for color of the bridal dress—white for Americans, red for Indians. This stereotypical knowledge would enhance the reader's "default reasoning," which provides an able reader with the ability to supply information not explicitly mentioned in the text. For a computer to succeed at such a reading task, it must be capable of understanding such stereotypical situations and must supply missing information.

Researchers at Yale, largely in association with Schank, have enlarged upon Minsky's work on frames. Schank called his framelike structures scripts (Schank & Abelson 1977).

Parallel Processing

Traditionally, our understanding of language processing has been that it is serial in nature: One step occurs, followed by the next, then the third, and so on until meaning is achieved. In the field of reading, this conceptualization has been most widely represented in recent years in the work of Gough. His 1972 model of the reading process proceeded in a step-by-step fashion from the visual system through various processing stages to the vocal output system.

In the development of computer models for language processing, this serial approach (or related hierarchical approaches that were serial in nature but in which certain steps in the series were more dominant than others) could be modeled within existing concepts of programming that were themselves serial in nature. The serial models of language, in other words, are convenient for programming purposes.

In addition, the serial models pictured each step of the language process as relatively autonomous. The results of prior steps would influence later steps. Syntactic analysis, for example, might precede semantic analysis, feeding its input into the semantic analyzer and then move back to analyze new inputs from perception. Once again, the autonomy of each step of the process lent itself to programming models. The model for each step could be programmed separately. Then the step modules could be linked together to form a serial chain.

While the serial models of language processing may be convenient for contemporary programming techniques, "convenient processing assumptions lead to problems in building models for cognition" (Waltz & Pollack 1985, p. 52). A variety of research indicators suggest that cognitive processing does not occur in a sequential series of steps. Rather, the various language subsystems appear to process simultaneously, in parallel fashion. Rather than each subsystem's receiving information, processing it, then feeding it to the next sub-system, processing appears to be interactive. Information is constantly being transferred back and forth between the various subsystems.

Also, rather than syntax being the dominant, controlling aspect of understanding language (as has been the assumption of most linguistics research in the past), semantics—the search for meaning—appears to play the controlling role (Schank, Goldman, Rieger, & Riesbeck 1973; Riesbeck & Schank 1976).

CHALLENGES TO COGNITIVE SCIENCE

The contemporary analogy between computer operations and cognitive oper-ations appears to be a useful tool for both psychologists investigating cognition and computer scientists investigating artificial intelligence. As noted above, not all would agree that the tool is appropriate for modeling human thought processes. Searle (1984), for instance, argued from a philosophical position against the cognitive scientists' viewpoint. He suggested that every new tech-nological innovation, from the catapult to the telephone, has been used in such a manner, and he predicted that the computer metaphor for human cognition will die out within the next few years.

Yet the vast majority of contemporary psychologists see the computer as an appropriate model. The question of whether this relationship is merely analogical, however, remains open. Is human thought simply the result of complex "programming" of our neurons? Is our consciousness—our sense of ourselves as sentient beings—simply the result of neuron electrochemical discharges?

John von Neumann, one of the early pioneers in work with computers, accepted the concept of a close correspondence between neuron functioning and the functions of digital computers:

> The neuron is an organ which accepts and emits definite physical entities, the pulses. Upon receipt of pulses in certain combinations and synchronisms it will be stimulated to emit pulses of its own, otherwise it will not. . . . This is clearly the description of the functioning of an organ in a digital machine, and of the way in which the role and function of a digital organ has to be characterized. It therefore justifies [my] original assertion, that a nervous system has a *prima facie* digital character. (1958, pp. 43-44)

The "reductionist" takes this belief several steps further, asserting that our minds and "souls"—our sense of consciousness—are *nothing* but the result of complex neuronal interactions. For the reductionist, all that exists of us is physical. We have no metaphysical components—no "souls" in the traditional Judeo-Christian sense of the word. Everything in the universe—including all life and all thought—can be reduced by science to laws of physics. The popular science writer Carl Sagan introduced his best-selling book *Dragons of Eden* (1977) with the words "My fundamental premise about the brain is that its workings—what we sometimes call 'mind'—are a consequence of its anatomy and physiology and nothing more" (p. 7).

From what, then, does consciousness arise? Dawkins (1981), in an exposition of a reductionist approach to the concept of "mind," claims that this question is "the most profound mystery facing modern biology" (p. 141). Note that he chose the field of biology as most promising in dealing with the issue, not theology, philosophy, or psychology. Dawkins suggested that the ability to simulate future events—to deal with "what if" thinking—was a successful evolutionary trait that resulted in subjective consciousness. Nothing metaphysical is involved.

Hofstadter and Dennett's fascinating book *The Mind's I* (1981) presents a variety of essays and short stories on the topic of computers and consciousness. They point out some weaknesses in the reductionist viewpoint. They also make the point that such a philosophy is dangerous socially: "The way we respond to our fellow human beings is dependent on the way we conceptualize them in our theoretical formulations" (p. 41). If man is simply a machine, can we not then treat him as disposable and ultimately meaningless? Immanuel Kant (1724-1804), in his philosophical proof for the existence of God, had warned of a similar problem and its threat to morality: If there were no God, we would have to invent Him simply to maintain a basis for morality and social justice.

On the other hand, as computers become more complex, will they achieve subjective consciousness? Turing's foundational article "Computing Machinery and Intelligence" (1950), in which he proposed the Turing test for machine intelligence discussed above, dealt with the question "Can machines think?" Turing criticized the question as ambiguous and rephrased it in terms of operational behavior: Can a computer exhibit humanlike thought under given circumstances?

Advocates of holistic instruction in reading and language arts suggest that language processes cannot be taught by breaking the processes down into component parts (that is, subskills), because the mind's dealings with language have no component parts: Language is learned as a whole. Advocates of subskill instruction in language argue just the opposite: Language operation can be broken down into subskills, and teaching occurs most effectively in rule-by-rule fashion. Language is learned by mentally organizing the host of complex rules into a coherent system.

The rationalist understanding of the human mind had its start in the philosophy of Socrates (ca. 469 B.C.-399 B.C.) and Plato (ca. 427 B.C.-347 B.C.), who thought of wisdom as the ability to think in terms of rules—definitions and principles. Much of Western philosophy was founded on their arguments that important decisions (such as social and political decisions) must be based on rulelike principles rather than on intuitive hunches. A society governed by philosophers—lovers of wisdom—who understood these principles would be the ideal society.

Platonic rationalism was questioned from the start, even by Plato's student Aristotle (384 B.C.-322 B.C.), who suggested that true wisdom must be based at least in part on intuition, which in turn has its basis in experience. As natural science developed, however, it became apparent that Plato's ideas were valuable foundations for organization of knowledge of the world into objective laws. Galileo (1564-1642), for example, asserted that planetary and stellar movements proceeded according to a specific pattern.

René Descartes (1596-1650) suggested that this rational approach, the analysis of a problem into its components and the rules relating to those components, could be used to solve any problem. For example, knowledge of the world and apropriate actions to take in it could be deduced logically from asking oneself how a perfectly rational and good God would create His world and desire His created beings to act.

Blaise Pascal (1623-1662) disputed Cartesian rationalism, arguing that humans could not reason logically from first principles to completely understand ethics or science. Instead, he argued in the tradition of holistic philosophy that mankind must trust to its experiences and its intuitions to discover truth. A mathematician himself, Pascal admitted that "the mathematical mind"—rationalism—has its limits.

> . . . because the principles are not known to us in the same [explicitly defined] way, and because it would be an endless matter to undertake it. We must see the matter at once, at one glance, and not by a process of reasoning, at least to a certain degree. . . . The heart has its reasons, which reason does not know. (Pascal 1938 trans., pp. 10, 98)

The seventeenth and eighteenth centuries found the rationalist Gottfried Wilhelm von Leibniz (1646-1716) posed against the empiricist David Hume (1711-1776). Hume argued that, rather than attempting to ground our ethical decisions on principles, we must trust to natural moral feelings. Kant attempted to synthesize aspects of both Leibniz's and Hume's ideas, suggesting that it is impossible to know God's mind so as to rationally develop clear principles of science and of conduct. Nevertheless, the mind does operate rationally. Mental concepts are in fact systems of rules.

The German philosopher, Edmund Husserl (1859-1938), elaborated on Kant's picture of concepts as rules to suggest that concepts are actually hierarchies of rules and subrules. A car, for example, might be identified by a particular rule: If it has an engine, tires, and a seat for the driver, it is a car. The rule for recognizing a car would contain subrules for recognizing engines, tires, and driver's seats.

One of the fundamental commitments of Husserl's philosophical approach, called phenomenology (1913), was to freedom from presuppositions, from constructions whose existence was beyond the realm of experience. Nothing can be taken for granted. Husserl was convinced that philosophy must be an absolute science, a self-standing system that can precisely describe the whole of human experience in terms of clear concepts and principles. He distinguished his phenomenological approach from the approaches of other philosophers who, he said, based their views of the world on prior assumptions rather than on close observation of the world.

A variety of twentieth-century philosophers have disputed attempts to describe the mind in a rational way. Human knowledge, they have asserted, is not simply knowing facts and the rules that relate those facts. They have suggested that humans understand their world through "knowing how" rather than "knowing that" (Dreyfus & Dreyfus 1986, p. 4).

Maurice Merleau-Ponty, for example, has suggested that human perception and understanding are based on our ability to learn flexible styles of behavior, not systems of rules. One easily transfers knowledge of driving different kinds of vehicles because of this flexibility, not because of learned rule systems.

Merleau-Ponty, an associate of the existentialist Jean-Paul Sartre and Simone de Beauvoir, wrote in reaction to the Cartesian, mechanistic tradition. He argued that the human mind is not constituted of a purely rational knowledge of the world. (Rationalists such as Descartes, Leibniz, and Spinoza had argued that knowledge of the world must be derived from pure reasoning, without appeal to empirical observation.) Human knowledge instead has its roots in active involvement with the world.

Much of Merleau-Ponty's (1964) work involved an effort to establish an alternative both to Cartesian rationalism and to empiricism in the tradition of Locke, Berkeley, Hume, and John Stuart Mill. The empiricist tradition has opposed rationalism with its arguments that knowledge is based on experience rather than reasoning.

Merleau-Ponty criticized both views for presupposing an objective world as the basis for knowledge. There is no absolute truth. He argued that the true basis of knowledge is not an objectively knowable world, but instead the living experience itself, in which objects come to exist for us. A vital part of that living experience involves our bodies that perceive and behave. We are able to experience other objects only through analogical reasoning based on our own bodily experiences. The body has a meaning-giving existence. Without it, objects outside the body have no meaning. Consciousness and perception, then, cannot exist without a body, in Merleau-Ponty's original viewpoint. A machine, no matter how complex, is incapable of either.

Martin Heidegger (1889-1976), though originally a student of Husserl, has also asserted that conceptual understandings are based on experiences rather than on internalized rule systems. One understands what a car is because it is a part of the cultural experience in which one grows up and with which one becomes familiar.

Contemporary Critiques of Cognitive Science

Dreyfus and Dreyfus (1986) admit that computer modeling of cognition has achieved significant success to date. They note, however, that achievements have fallen far short of early expectations and argue that future advances will be even more limited, due to erroneous assumptions that lie at the heart of cognitive psychology. They offer a five-step model of development of expertise, from novice to expert, to illustrate their arguments.

Novices in any skill depend upon being taught precise rules. In order to avoid initial confusions, these rules are portrayed as "context-free." That is, the rules are to be applied no matter what else is happening. The exceptions to the rules—and there are always exceptions—are not mentioned. For example, a novice automobile driver learning to operate a manual-transmission car is told to shift into second gear when the car reaches a certain speed. No mention is made of the many complicating factors, such as traffic density, movement of other cars in the area, or anticipated stops.

Similarly, beginning readers are usually presented invariant phonics patterns during initial word recognition instruction in basal reading lessons. Children are taught the short *a* sound, then drilled on words in which every *a* is short—no long sounds and no *r*-controlled sounds. They read sentences and short stories in which vocabulary is controlled so that the children only see sight words and words in which phonics patterns match those patterns already taught.

Whole-language advocates, on the other hand, argue that such controlled vocabulary is artificially limiting for students, and they use techniques such as Language Experience Approach stories, children's trade books in shared book lessons, and sustained silent reading, none of which controls vocabulary. The 1972 edition of the Scott Foresman basal series, a project directed in large measure by a leading psycholinguistic whole-language advocate, Kenneth Goodman, was an attempt to introduce uncontrolled, natural vocabulary into the basal-using classroom. It was decidedly unpopular.

In like fashion, a new reading teacher is generally taught a simplistic, rule-oriented approach dealing with individual differences. The teacher might be told, "Teach to weaknesses. Find skill areas with which the child is having difficulty and provide additional instruction and practice." Or, in a whole-language situation, the teacher might be told, "Find books in which the child is interested. Read to him and allow him to read." These general principles may be accepted as all-encompassing rules of practice by novice teachers, without recognition of the many variables that could affect the effectiveness of their implementation.

As the novices obtain expertise with real situations, they first learn more sophisticated rule systems. They also begin to recognize the limits of a context-free perspective and begin to make decisions based on situational elements that are not precisely specifiable in terms of meaningful rules. For example, a novice driver might use the situational engine sounds of a car to determine gear shifting. A chess player learns to recognize overextended positions. This learning is derived not from rules but from experiences that allow the learner to recognize the similarities of new situations to prior examples.

Intuitive decision making is situational. Understanding takes place effortlessly through seeing similarities to previous experiences. The experienced reading specialist, for example, depends far more on a broad range of prior experiences with disabled readers to make diagnoses than on a step-by-step decision-making pattern. Weisberg (1984) found that novice reading specialists, trained to follow a specified diagnostic pattern, were more likely to suggest similar diagnoses than were experienced specialists. Experience leads to a greater reliance on intuition than on rules.

Stage 5 experts, according to Dreyfus and Dreyfus, have achieved a skill level that is so much a part of them that they are not aware of the skill involved. They do not experience themselves as consciously and deliberately performing. They simply perform. The expert car driver, for example, does not "think about" driving but simply drives. An expert teacher does not "think about" explaining a particular comprehension problem—she or he simply explains it. "When things are proceeding normally, experts don't solve problems and don't make decisions. They do what normally works" (Dreyfus & Dreyfus 1986, pp. 30-31).

Experience-based understandings are founded in the expert's broad repertoire of situational knowledge. It has been estimated that a chess master can distinguish 50,000 types of positions. Automobile drivers, teachers, and medical doctors can probably do the same in their respective areas of expertise. The mind apparently can store vast numbers of such typical situations, which can be instantaneously accessed, with the corresponding decision, action, or tactic.

Dreyfus and Dreyfus were quick to point out that this expert performance is not necessarily nonreflective. When time permits, experts do deliberate before acting. This deliberation, however, is not a step-by-step problem solving but a critical analysis of their intuitions. The chess player, for example, might choose an overall strategy, but accumulating evidence for or against that strategy must be weighed appropriately. Also, in any given situation there will be some differences between it and prior situations experienced by the expert. These disturbing differences are contemplated with the goal of reducing the sense of uneasiness.

So the debate among philosophers and psychologists continues. If indeed criticisms of the rule-governed approach to modeling cognition are valid—if Dreyfus and Dreyfus are correct—the cognitive movement will fail in its objective of developing a computer that can understand natural language in a fashion parallel to that of human beings. The past rate of achievement in artificial intelligence cannot be sustained, and even now has slowed considerably. "Artificial intelligence cannot be extended indefinitely to wide and wider domains and more and more sophisticated skills with increasingly positive results" (Dreyfus & Dreyfus 1986, p. 41). Russell (1983) has quoted Hubert Dreyfus as stating, "I don't think computers will ever be able to understand a simple children's story of the sort that any four-year-old can understand" (p. 7).

SOURCES OF INFORMATION

WINOGRAD, TERRY. 1984. "Computer Software for Working with Language." *Scientific American* 251, no. 3 (September): 130-145.
    This article serves as an excellent introduction to the history of natural language research with computers. Winograd discusses the key difficulties facing students of computer-based natural language, and he summarizes progress in four major strands of natural language research and development, including machine translation, word-processing, and question-answering systems.

DREYFUS, HUBERT L., AND STUART E. DREYFUS. 1986. *Mind over Machine.* New York: Free Press.
    The authors take a strong stand against rule-based approaches to studying and imitating human cognition. This text is one of the most powerful arguments that artificial intelligence approaches to natural language will achieve little in the future. Dreyfus and Dreyfus also present a nontechnical overview of the controversy between rationalists and empiricists in Western philosophy, a controversy of crucial importance to present-day psychological and artificial intelligence research.

SCHANK, ROGER, AND LARRY HUNTER. 1985. "The Quest to Understand Thinking." *BYTE* 10, no. 4 (April): 143-158.
    Schank's ideas on the structure of memory in memory organization packets (MOPs) and the relation of background knowledge to language comprehension are explained. Schank also justifies the use of computers to aid in understanding cognition, including cognition involved in learning how to read. The authors include a discussion of the importance of artificial intelligence research to reading education, concluding, "Perhaps AI's most promising applications are in education—helping to teach people how to read, remember, and think based on a fundamental knowledge of those processes" (p. 155).

COMMERCIAL SOFTWARE

Bank Street Filer
    Scholastic, Inc.
    PO Box 7502
    2931 E. McCarty St.
    Jefferson City, MO 65102
    Apple II series
DBASE II
    Ashton-Tate
    Jefferson Blvd.
    Culver City, CA 90230
    CP/M, IBM-PC

Lotus 1-2-3
    Lotus Development Corporation
    First St.
    Cambridge, MA 02142
    IBM-PC and others
PFS: File
    Scholastic
    Apple II series

13

INTELLIGENT COMPUTER-ASSISTED
INSTRUCTION

Intelligent-computer-assisted instruction (ICAI) results from an attempt to relate research findings in cognitive psychology and artificial intelligence to instructional applications. It is referred to by a variety of names, including intelligent tutoring systems, instructional expert systems, and pedagogical natural language. In order to appropriately understand ICAI, a clear comprehension of the structure and function of traditional CAI is vital. In addition, an understanding of the function of knowledge bases and production rules (explained in terms of expert systems in Chs. 14 and 15 of this volume) is useful.

This chapter is primarily concerned with the components of typical ICAI systems, and the first major section deals with the three key components that characterize such systems: the domain, curriculum, and aptitude components. The second major section deals with some examples of ICAI systems: the reader should refer to sources listed at the end of the chapter for more detailed lists and descriptions of such examples. The final section of the chapter discusses advantages and disadvantages of ICAI for instruction, including the outlook for future developments.

The goal of ICAI is the development of computer programs that can perform many of the instructional functions performed by expert human tutors. These functions can include diagnosis of student difficulties in performing tasks designated by the instructional objectives. If equipped with a natural language front end (see Chapters 11 and 12 of this volume), the program might be able to converse intelligently with the student users in order to lead them to an understanding of the instructional topic. It might provide learning exercises appropriate to the learners' needs, using their inputs to determine whether they understand.

Work on the development of computer-based tutors is of crucial importance because of the significant educational consequences of individualized tutoring. Bloom (1984), for example, compared private tutoring by human teachers with classroom instruction. He found that 98 percent of the individually tutored students performed better than students taught in a classroom setting. Poorer students benefited the most.

Traditional CAI is based on either a linear or a branched structure. In linear structures, information is presented to the student and elicited from the student in unvarying order. The program works from point A (assumption of lack of understanding of digraphs, for example) to point B (mastery of digraphs) in the same sequential fashion for all users. The only individualization available involves the speed of presentation: Users may proceed at a rate that seems best to them.

Branched CAI structures allow for increased individualization of program content. Based on student needs, for example, the program might provide more or fewer problems for practice. Failure to understand a first presentation of a concept might lead to a branch to another presentation.

Contemporary ICAI programs may appear to function similarly to branched CAI. The basic difference between the two involves the complexity of processes that underlie the branching. In ICAI, there are no rigid sequences of frames presented, the teaching is learner-oriented, and error detection is more sophisticated (Tennyson & Christensen 1986). In CAI, the program branches according to a precisely predetermined series of branching rules called IF . . . THEN statements. The program itself has no true "knowledge" of the content. It merely functions according to a predetermined flowchart-like sequence. For example, it branches according to rules such as the following:

IF the student scores equal to or greater than 12 correct THEN go on to the next lesson.

IF the student answers this question incorrectly THEN repeat the instructional presentation.

The program might be quite complex and effective in meeting the specific needs of students. It will not, however, "think" about the instructional setting in any meaningful way. In addition, in complex subject and skill areas such as reading, the difficulty involved in specifying all possible instructional branches is prohibitive.

An ICAI program might make identical decisions about the student's needs and supply identical instruction. A major difference lies in how those decisions are made. Rather than being made on the basis of unvarying IF . . . THEN programming, the decision making is carried out on the basis of a model of student thinking developed through an analysis of the student's mistakes or in reaction to student questions.

COMPONENTS OF AN ICAI SYSTEM

Lesgold's (1985) suggestion that ICAI knowledge bases be structured in three layers presents one version of the basic components: domain, curriculum, and aptitude. Each component is composed of production rules dealing with its specific aspect of the teaching process. ICAI is in part distinguished from CAI by the separation of these layers into discrete modules of information.

Domain Knowledge

The domain knowledge layer (sometimes called the expert module or knowledge base) contains the concepts to be taught by the program. The concepts are arranged in an interlinking network. The organization of the network should mirror the organization of knowledge in the mind of an expert on the network topic—the structure of the discipline, so to speak.

The kind of information contained in the domain knowledge varies with the domain in question. A program such as SCHOLAR (Carbonell 1970), for example, designed to teach South American geography, contains a large body of facts about the countries, capitals, languages, peoples, and products of South America.

A second type of domain knowledge may be required to manipulate the facts through inferencing and problem solving. In an electronics problem-solving program such as SOPHIE (Brown, Burton, & de Kleer 1982), such procedural knowledge is coded into a set of rules that describe what to do and when to do it.

The domain knowledge layer may contain information on systematically incorrect methods that students use in answering questions and solving problems. Knowledge of error patterns in reasoning is crucial if the system is to make comments on or to criticize student performance.

Curriculum Knowledge

The curriculum layer (Sleeman & Brown 1982 called this the "list of teaching operations"; also sometimes called the tutorial module) contains the pedagogical information of vital importance to the presentation of domain concepts to the learner. A crucial failing of many past educational ventures (such as many originating in the post-Sputnik era) has been that novices have been taught content from the perspective of the expert—according to the discipline's structure as perceived by experts.

Novices must be taught as novices. The domain must be split into reasonable components that are then taught in the order in which experts acquire their expertise, not according to the pattern by which established experts view their discipline. Fundamental pedagogical concepts involved in teaching the targeted concept or skill—such as what prerequisite concepts must be learned before a goal concept can be taught—are programmed in the curriculum layer.

Aptitude Knowledge

Lesgold (1985) calls his third layer the aptitude, or metacognitive, layer. The purpose of this knowledge system is to match the course of instruction to the needs of each individual learner. As Stevens, Collins, and Goldin (1982) have noted, a good human tutor does not march inexorably through predetermined material at a predetermined pace. Instead, a tutor probes the student about many aspects of the knowledge domain and responds in a variety of ways to the student's misconceptions. The aptitude layer deals with issues of student ability and achievement. It might slow down or speed up the pace of instruction as needed.

The aptitude layer might diagnose skill needs or conceptual difficulties or learning strategy failures and prescribe supplemental instruction. Sleeman and Brown (1982) divided this layer into two components: a student model that evaluates student needs and a series of means-ends guidance rules (sometimes called the student interface module) that relate the stored curricular strategies to the student model.

Student model. The term *student model* is particularly fitting because it clearly identifies the function of this layer as constructing an internal "model" of the student's strengths and weaknesses by inferring from students' responses to problems. The thinking that is carried out is the heart of the program. In contrast with this, for example, the heart of traditional CAI is usually considered to be its logically presented sequence of frames of information and questions. As such, conventional CAI is sometimes called frame-based CAI (Carbonell 1970).

The ICAI student model is constructed on the basis of decisions made by the system about the student's knowledge, skills, and systematic errors. Researchers have experimented with a variety of approaches in developing the internal student model—the computer's understanding of the student.

Goldstein (1982), for example, pictured the student model as a subset of the domain of expert knowledge. If the expert's knowledge is pictured as a network, with every node of the network a particular skill or concept, the student model would consist of the parts of the network that have been mastered. Goldstein called this the overlay method. If the student model is deficient in any skills or concepts, the student is given instruction in those topics.

Early ICAI systems such as SCHOLAR and SOPHIE constructed the student model by the overlay method. When the system determined that a specific subset of information was known by the student, that subset was marked in system memory as "known."

Soloway, Woolf, Rubin, and Barth (1981) approached development of the student model from a different perspective, that of variant reasoning strategies between student and expert. The system attempts to find a pattern from incorrect responses of the student in order to identify the student's incorrect, or buggy (from the term *bug*, a programming error) strategy. Various incorrect strategies are included in the knowledge base as models of buggy strategies.

Burton and Brown (1982) applied this bug model, or perturbation model, procedure in their development of an arithmetic game in which student strategies employed to play the game were compared with the strategies of experts. In BUGGY and DEBUGGY, student misconceptions were diagnosed by the system on the basis of systematically erroneous answers to questions and problems. Burton and Brown attempted to construct models of student misconceptions that are able to predict not only whether an answer will be correct "but the exact digits of the incorrect answer on a novel problem" (Burton 1982, p. 160).

Greeno (1985) used this basic model in an algebra tutorial, though student-expert differences were conceived in terms of knowledge rather than of strategies. An example of such expert knowledge is the general rule that if a variable (A or B, for example) appears more than once in a rule, all of its occurrences have the same value (as in $(A \times (B + C) < = > (A \times B + (A \times C)$; A times (B plus C) does not equal (A times B) plus (A times C)).

Development of an accurate student model is essential, for the curriculum layer of the system draws on that information as it decides on the content and methods of instruction. Construction of the student model is difficult for several reasons. Students are generally unaware of what they know and do not know. Information must be acquired implicitly, based on student responses to questions and problems rather than based explicitly on direct self-evaluation questions.

In addition, ICAI systems do not have access to all knowledge sources available to human teachers. A considerable amount of a teacher's understanding of his or her students is based on visual input inaccessible to the computer: observation of student attention and inattention, nods and frowns, and so forth.

Developers of the WHY system analyzed tutorials carried out by human teachers on the topic of the causes of rainfall. They isolated some 16 common bugs in students' understanding of rainfall (Stevens, Collins, & Goldin 1982). For example, some students had the "sponge pattern, absorption-by-expansion" bug. They thought that the air mass over a body of water was like a giant sponge that expanded to absorb moisture and later squeezed it out over land. A human teacher discovering such a bug in the student reasoning would point out that air temperature is the operant variable in allowing absorption of water into the air mass, not volume of the air mass.

Only when the student model has been created and skill/concept faults or buggy strategies have been identified can the teaching component of the system be brought into play. Stevens, Collins, and Goldin (1982) analyzed tutorial dialogues between students and human teachers and found that such tutors spend a good part of their time diagnosing conceptual bugs from errors elicited from students in the dialogues.

Teaching module.   Severe technical obstacles appear to stand in the way of ICAI development in areas such as reading and language arts. ICAI has been most successful in areas where the subject matter is well defined and fairly simple in terms of complexity. The BUGGY domain of simple subtraction skills offers a good example. In most reading and language arts skills, where ambiguities and subtleties are commonplace, ICAI development will be incalculably more difficult.

Woolf and McDonald (1984) developed a sophisticated instructional delivery system that can make decisions at several stages to refine the tutorial to meet the needs of the learner. The first decision level handles the choice between display of the introductory material and provision of a tutoring strategy. Later decisions are made between questioning the learner and presentation of simplified material. The system also decides which topics are appropriate for presentation and questioning. This tutorial system is based on a comprehensive student model.

Brown, Burton, and de Kleer (1982) noted that the teaching module must be programmed with an understanding of the circumstances under which to intervene in instruction. Discontinuous flow of information interrupts learning and decreases motivation to learn. If systematic instruction is interrupted whenever the ICAI system diagnoses a need, learning will be hampered. Decisions to intervene must be based on the relative importance of the student's faulty reasoning at any given point in the instructional sequence.

EXAMPLES OF ICAI SYSTEMS

Comprehensive ICAI systems require a tremendous amount of financing for research, development, and field-testing. To date, no ICAI system has been constructed for teaching reading or language arts skills. Systems have been developed for a variety of other subject areas, and several other projects are in early stages of development (see Figure 13-1). For the most part, existing ICAI systems were built as laboratory experiments. Few have been used extensively with students (Woolf & McDonald 1985).

SCHOLAR

SCHOLAR, the first ICAI system (Carbonell 1970), was developed at the Bolt, Beranek, and Newman research center to teach South American geography. It was equipped with a simple parser to allow students to input questions,

System Name	Subject	References
LMS	Algebraic equations	Sleeman and Smith, 1981
SOPHIE	Debugging electronic circuits	Brown, Burton, and Bell, 1975; Brown, Burton, and de Kleer, 1982
GUIDON	Medical diagnosis	Clancey, 1982
SCHOLAR	South American geography	Carbonell, 1970
WHY	Causes of rainfall	Stevens, Collins, and Goldin, 1982
WEST	Game tutor for teaching algebraic expressions	Burton and Brown, 1982
WUSOR	Game tutor for problem-solving	Goldstein, 1982
BUGGY	Arithmetic	Burton, 1982

FIGURE 13-1. Listing of Key Experimental ICAI Systems

as long as the questions corresponded to a built-in list of question types. SCHOLAR was also able to present its output in short sentences. The system was designed to stimulate a Socratic dialogue by eliciting responses from students, identifying errors, and presenting correct information to the students for revision of their errors.

Information within SCHOLAR's data base was arranged in a semantic network so that the system could search the data to answer questions such as "Is Buenos Aires in Argentina?" with a "Yes" and "Is Argentina in Buenos Aires?" with "No, Buenos Aires is in Argentina" (Barr & Feigenbaum 1982).

Carbonell* presented the following dialogue as an example of SCHOLAR's capabilities. The student's responses are preceded and followed by asterisks.

```
WHAT IS CHILE?
*A COUNTRY*
THAT'S FINE.
SELECT AN ALTERNATIVE FROM THE LIST:
    214000.
    800300.
     49883.
     63690.
```

*From J. R. Carbonell, "AI in CAI: An Artificial Intelligence Approach to Computer-Assisted Instruction," in *IEEE Transactions on Man-Machine Systems* (December 1970), pp. 190–202. © Copyright 1970 by IEEE.

```
     FOR THE QUESTION:
     APPROX WHAT IS THE AREA OF CHILE?
*800300*
YOUR ANSWER IS INCORRECT.
THE CORRECT ANSWER IS: 214000.
*WHAT IS THE AREA OF BRAZIL?*
THE AREA OF BRAZIL IS APPROX 3600000. SQUARE MILES.
```

In a traditional computer-assisted instructional program, anticipated replies and questions would be coded exactly in memory, as in

```
PRINT "The area of Brazil is approx 3600000. square
     miles."
```

In SCHOLAR, information was stored in a structured data base from which the system could draw facts when relevant. Carbonell (1970, p. 194) gave the following example for part of the Argentina network of information within the data base.

```
(CAPITAL (I1)
  BUENOS/AIRES)
(CITIES (13)
  PRINCIPAL NIL ($L BUENOS/AIRES CORDOBA ROSARIO
  MENDOZA LA/PLATA TUCUMAN)))
```

Within the limits of the program, SCHOLAR could understand questions about the information stored in its semantic network and create questions and replies of its own, phrasing them in sentence form.

SOPHIE

ICAI systems that followed SCHOLAR allowed less openness to student-initiated interruptions than did SCHOLAR. SOPHIE (SOPHisticated Instructional Environment) taught students troubleshooting of electronic equipment. It too was developed at Bolt, Beranek, and Newman, and attempted to simulate goal-oriented Socratic dialogue. A malfunctioning piece of equipment was presented to students, who then formed hypotheses about the causes of the problem. SOPHIE evaluated the hypotheses and helped students understand any faults in their troubleshooting techniques. In this way, students learned problem-solving skills by active involvement rather than by direct instruction.

SOPHIE's natural language processor was designed to minimize the frustration that arises when students must try several ways to express an idea before the system understands. The parser could ignore words or phrases it did not understand and try to make sense from the remainder. In order to guard against misunderstandings, it responded to questions in full sentences to indicate what question was being answered.

BUGGY

BUGGY, still another Bolt, Beranek, and Newman system, was an important departure from the typical view of student arithmetic errors as caused by carelessness. BUGGY looked for systematic faults in students' problem-solving behaviors. Later versions of the program were capable of isolating over 100 faulty subprocedures in students' subtraction skills.

ADVANTAGES AND DISADVANTAGES OF ICAI

One of the major problems of ICAI implementation is the cost of system development (Swigger 1985). The research needed for study of expert and novice knowledge and strategies is labor-intensive. The resulting information must then be programmed, and comprehensive field-testing is required.

To date, most interest in ICAI development has come from the military and business communities, where training costs are high and inadequate results have serious consequences. The U.S. Air Force, for example, is engaged in a large-scale research project where cognitive task analysis is being applied to technical learning in over 100 apprenticeship occupations (Gott 1986; Lajoie 1986).

The development of tutoring systems will require intensive research and modeling of skill and concept development activities, as well as a refined approach to theory of instruction. Precise understanding of a target topic is a requirement in the development of an ICAI program. In most aspects of instruction, such precision is unavailable from the body of research literature.

Construction of ICAI systems will require a major investment of research time and effort for cognitive task analyses and learning analyses in the subject-area domains (Ohlsson 1986). The advances coming from such research will provide valuable new insights, not only to educators but to cognitive scientists as well (Greeno 1985). The ICAI requirement for explicitness will lead to clarification in usable form of theoretical ideas about the subject and the learning situation.

Development of educational technology can enhance understanding of cognition in a variety of ways. For example, in order to study learning, one must have a learning activity to study. Obviously, a computer system designed to give instruction in a subject area provides these learning activities as a focus for study. Additionally, the ICAI systems allow a far greater control over the learning situation and greater opportunities for data collection than in more traditional learning environments.

Another important way in which ICAI technology will improve understanding of cognition involves the empirical feedback available from ICAI systems on strengths and weaknesses of the cognitive understanding of the skills or concept learning activities. This feedback is highly specific and enables researchers to determine the accuracy of cognitive task analyses of complex tasks such as reading. If the system breaks down or is ineffective, researchers will be forced to recognize that their understanding of the learning situation in the student model is awry. As Schank and Hunter (1985) have stated, "Programming forces us to be explicit, and being explicit forces us to confront the problems with our theories" (p. 143).

Another limitation of contemporary systems, a limitation that will continue to exist for the foreseeable future, is topic limitations. Because of the complexity involved in detailing a knowledge base for a single topic, systems designed today must be limited in scope (Dede 1986). Many computer-based tutors must be created, each handling only a small part of the overall curriculum.

While a superficial examination of the research literature on ICAI may lead readers to suppose that tremendous advances will occur in the near-term future, a closer study leads to some pessimism in this regard. The theory and design of ICAI systems have outpaced actual system development. While an ICAI system properly is composed of discrete but interacting levels, as discussed above, in practice these levels are often more theory than reality. Further, many systems described in the literature are not operative. The descriptions are based on theory rather than on demonstrable development.

Additional research is necessary to improve the natural language communication between computer and learner. While menu systems and exact-match (see Ch. 11 of this volume) human-computer interfaces can be used effectively in some cases, an ability to provide natural language instructional dialogue is a key goal. This problem proved a far greater challenge than expected 20 years ago. Dede, Zodhiates, and Thompson (1985) have reported that some ICAI researchers have given up on development of natural language input devices ("Natural language is dead," p. 89) and are searching for alternative input modes.

SOURCES OF INFORMATION

Sleeman, D., and J. S. Brown. 1982. *Intelligent Tutoring Systems*. New York: Academic Press.
    This is a comprehensive collection of articles describing the theory underlying development of ICAI systems. A wide variety of early ICAI systems are described as well, with detailed examples of the kind of instruction and dialogue offered by each.

14

EXPERT SYSTEMS

The purpose of this chapter is to describe decision-making expert systems and discuss their implications for education, especially reading diagnosis and prescription. The chapter begins with a detailed description of how a reading-diagnostic expert system might operate to aid classroom teachers. Then advantages and limitations of expert systems for educational use are discussed. The chapter concludes with a discussion of pragmatic concerns in the construction of educational expert systems, including the issues of obtaining and organizing expert knowledge and of using an expert system shell to carry out the mechanical operations of decision making.

Tomás, a fourth grader, had been having trouble keeping up with the other children in the class in reading. His teacher, Mrs. Tomczak, had kept track of Tomás's lack of progress with great concern and had spent extra time helping him. Finally, in early December, she decided that some outside help was necessary. She sat down at her microcomputer and typed her name and the password that allowed her to access the school's administrative software.

`How can I help you?`

the computer printed on its monitor.

`I would like to do a reading diagnosis of a student`

Mrs. Tomczak typed in.

At this point, the computer scanned the sentence Mrs. Tomczak had typed. It used a text parser to analyze the input into its grammatical components. Then those components were compared with words in an internal dictionary, a list of words built into the software, to identify the sentence's words and to build an interpretation of their probable meaning.

The words *reading diagnosis* and *student* were most readily recognizable in terms of the possible functions that the computer knew it could perform. To doublecheck its understanding of the teacher's meaning, it asked the following.

> Would you like to use my reading diagnosis/prescription program to analyze the progress of a student? (Y/N)

Mrs. Tomczak replied Y.

Immediately the computer's opening program accessed RD2P, a special "expert system" program designed to aid classroom teachers in diagnosing and prescribing for reading problems. The opening statement briefly explained the function of the expert system and asked for identification of the student.

> READING DISABILITIES—DIAGNOSIS AND PRESCRIPTION RD2P
> The function of this program is to guide teachers to an understanding of the possible problems underlying a particular student's reading difficulties.
> Operation:
> You will be asked some questions concerning your observations of the student's classroom performance. On the basis of an analysis of your input, and taking into account the student's cumulative records, RD2P will suggest possible interpretations of the student's reading problems and will offer suggestions for materials and methods.
>
> What are the student's first and last names?
> _____

Mrs. Tomczak typed in, "Tomás Hernandez."

The monitor screen immediately displayed a menu page—a listing of possible avenues of exploration—of possible reading problems:

> Have you noticed any of the following problems with Tomás? If so, use the up or down arrow keys to move

```
the cursor to each problem noticed, and press the
carriage return key.

The student has difficulty pronouncing unfamiliar
    words during oral reading.
The student does not understand readings.
The student does not complete reading drill assign-
    ments.
The student does not satisfactorily read stories
    assigned.
The student is scoring poorly on vocabulary tests.
The student is doing poorly in the reading of con-
    tent area subjects (e.g., science, social stud-
    ies, literature).
The student is demonstrating a poor attitude toward
    reading.
```

Simultaneously with presentation of this menu page, the computer begins to search the school's cumulative record on Tomás. Mrs. Tomczak's microcomputer is connected by telephone line to the school system's central data base that contains the complete test results, background information, grades, and teacher evaluations of all students in the system.

The RD2P expert system immediately begins to analyze Tomás's records in order to target possible problems that Mrs. Tomczak can consider:

1. A preliminary check on the student's intelligence scores indicates that IQ and aptitude testing results were consistently within the first standard deviation above the mean, suggesting an average to slightly above average achievement potential. The program decides to assign a low priority to the possibility that Tomás would benefit from a slower pace of instruction (often called "adapted reading instruction").

2. The computer notices that the child has a Hispanic background and immediately hypothesizes that ethnic, socioeconomic, and linguistic differences could be playing a role in Tomás's reading problem. Further investigation of background information, however, indicates that the family does not fit the profile for such problem sources. Both the parents are college graduates, English is the only language spoken in the home, and parental concern for the child's education seems high—the parents have regularly attended the school's parent-teacher conference days. In addition, Tomás has not displayed the weaknesses in verbal aptitude typical of students who have linguistic background problems.

3. Student reading achievement records are checked carefully and compared with achievement in other skill areas. Tomás had tested somewhat low on a reading achievement test administered halfway through his first grade year, but the end-of-year testing had indicated a slightly higher than average ability. In the next two years, Tomás had scored average or slightly above

average. Computer analysis of the standardized testing indicates no high-priority potential areas of difficulty.

4. Records indicate that Mrs. Webb, Tomás's second grade teacher, had consulted the reading specialist and the RD2P system regarding his reading ability. The final conclusion had been that Tomás had some motivational problems, but no satisfactory solution had been reported at the time. RD2P assigns a high priority to the possibility that Tomás's present problems are motivational in nature.

On the basis of this information, RD2P checks the identity of the boy's third grade teacher. It was Mr. Tegrini. There was no indication of reading difficulty during the third grade year. Noticing that both teachers suggesting a reading problem had been female, RD2P assigns a moderate priority to the possibility that Tomás functions better with male teachers.

In the meantime, Mrs. Tomczak had identified the following concerns from the menu page displayed to her:

```
The student does not understand readings.
The student does not satisfactorily read stories
    assigned.
The student is doing poorly in the reading of con-
    tent-area subjects (e.g., science, social stud-
    ies, literature).
The student is demonstrating a poor attitude toward
    reading.
```

A computer analysis of these items suggests that all are compatible with the high-priority hypotheses assigned on the basis of the student's records. As a result, an even higher probability is assigned to the motivation hypothesis, and the computer decides to follow up on that issue with additional questions.

```
How would you rate the following statement:
    Tomás's reading problems are due to motiva-
    tional problems.

    1. I am confident this statement is true.
    2. This statement is possibly true.
    3. I am not sure that this statement is true.
    4. This statement is possibly false.
    5. I am confident this statement is false.

(For preliminary information on motivational prob-
    lems, press Function Key 4.)

(Choose 1-5.)
```

A press of function key 4 would cause the computer to list characteristic behaviors of fourth grade children with motivational problems. Mrs. Tomczak, however, presses the 2 key, indicating some degree of assurance that motivation is the root of Tomás's problem. The computer continues this line of attack with a series of questions:

How long has Tomás been displaying these behaviors?
How often does Tomás fail to satisfactorily complete his story reading assignments?
Does Tomás show any indication that he reads on his own at home?
Has Tomás indicated any hostility toward his parents?
Does Tomás appear to have a healthy attitude toward his mother?
How well has Tomás been getting along with the other children in the class?
Has Tomás made any overt comments about his attitudes toward reading?
Has Tomás indicated any hostility to you personally?
Does Tomás appear to read stories assigned to him as classwork?
What are Tomás's hobbies? Does he have any particular interests?

Mrs. Tomczak is requested to give a confidence rating for several of her answers. As she inputs each answer, the computer adjusts the probability level of its preliminary diagnoses about motivational derivations of the reading problem. Finally the computer is ready to print its diagnosis and prescription.

RD2P DIAGNOSTIC REPORT
Student: Tomás Hernandez
Teacher: L. Tomczak
Date of consultation: 12/3/88
Summary of Diagnosis:
Tomás's reading problem is probably a short-term motivational difficulty. It is almost certainly true that his attitude is not due to an active dislike for reading. It is probably true that reading is not sufficiently positively reinforcing for completion of all assignments.
Tomás is reading on-level for a fourth grader. It is

probably not true that the present difficulties
have affected his reading achievement.
Press Function Key 8 for a summary of procedures
used in completing this diagnosis.

Pressing function key 8 would allow the teacher to print out in hard copy
the exact reasoning used by RD2P in developing its diagnosis. All the tentative
hypotheses, with both preliminary and final probability weighting, would be
printed, with the reasons for acceptance or rejection.

Prescription:
1. Consult with Mrs. Webb, Tomás's second grade
   teacher, who also had a motivational problem
   with Tomás. Press Function Key 1 for a list of
   prescriptive suggestions provided by RD2P at
   that time. There are no records on-line that
   indicate whether the suggestions were applied
   or how effective they were.
2. There are no Reading Interest Inventory results
   available that are recent enough to have bearing
   on this case. Press Function Key 2 for results of
   a Reading Interest Inventory administered to
   Tomás two years ago.
3. Your indication that Tomás is interested in science fiction movies can be used to promote interest in reading. The school librarian can be
   consulted for a list of popular science fiction
   novels appropriate for fourth graders. Local
   bookstores usually carry paperbacks designed as
   spin-offs of popular recent science fiction
   movies.
4. Administer a Reading Interest Inventory to Tomás
   to determine hobbies and interests. An on-line
   inventory designed for fourth graders may be
   accessed using filename RII-11D. Results will
   be analyzed automatically and a list of suggested reading materials will be provided.
   Press Function Key 7 if you wish to have an inventory printed out in hard copy.
5. Have you considered decreasing the amount of
   emphasis on basal reading materials in favor of
   more real-life materials for your classroom?
   Directed Reading Activities and other types of

lesson plans may be constructed for the following real-life reading materials:

Newspapers
Children's magazines
Sports Magazines

6. Results of this year's on-line Reading Interest
Inventories for fourth graders in this school
system are summarized in filename RI-11G. Press
Function Key 3 for a list of the ten favorite
books for fourth grade boys. Press Function Key 4
for a list of the ten favorite hobbies/
activities for fourth grade boys.
7. Press Function Key 5 for a summary of research on
motivation and interests of middle grade youngsters and a list of suggested readings from the
school system's professional library.

Note that the computer has received insufficient substantiation for one of its
original hypotheses, that Tomás's motivational problem was related to the sex
of his teachers. The possibility is not mentioned to the teacher in order to
avoid overloading her with information, but she can investigate the computer's
logic by pressing function key 8.

On the other hand, the computer has been convinced to a significant
degree that the problem is actually motivational in nature: It uses the words
probably and *probably true* in the diagnostic summary to indicate the high degree
of substantiation to the teacher. The computer is convinced to an even higher
degree that Tomás's motivational problem is not hard-core, and indicates this
by the words *almost certainly true* in the diagnostic summary.

Prescription items 4 to 6 are part of the standard RD2P response to all
diagnoses of middle grade youngsters indicating motivation as the primary
problem involved in reading difficulties. The use of the function keys to
request additional optional information is another device to avoid overloading
the teacher with information—she need request only what she wants.

WHAT IS AN EXPERT SYSTEM?

RD2P is an expert system. While much of the research in artificial intelligence
is theoretical at present, since the late 1970s a variety of program systems
based on AI principles have achieved more practical status. The most obvious

practical application at present is the "expert system," a software system designed to imitate the reasoning of a human expert in a given content topic.

Expert systems, "computer-based consultation" systems, are designed as advisers. They are one example of a particular variety of AI software known as knowledge-based, rule-based, or production rule systems. These systems combine the content-area knowledge and decision-making ability of an expert with the user's understanding and knowledge of particular circumstances. The end result involves the system in making decisions about the circumstances, decisions that are then suggested to the user. In the RD2P example above, Mrs. Tomczak provided the key information about Tomás's particular circumstances. RD2P accessed background information and made the diagnostic/prescriptive decisions.

MYCIN is one of the best-known early expert systems. Designed by the Stanford University Heuristic Programming Project, MYCIN consulted with physicians to diagnose infectious diseases (Buchanan & Shortliffe 1984). It first asked the user questions about the patient's symptoms. A complex hierarchy of rules about infectious diseases, their causes and cures, was then used to deduce relationships, to exclude certain possible diagnoses, and to include others. MYCIN then concluded with statements as to possible treatments. As of 1977, MYCIN's diagnoses were in 72 percent agreement with the diagnoses of professional medical experts (Nau 1983).

Expert systems can be developed in almost any topic area in which decision-making expertise is involved. DENDRAL made decisions about the molecular structure of unknown molecules on the basis of spectroscopic analysis. Its success (Buchanan & Feigenbaum 1978) was instrumental in directing artificial intelligence researchers toward investigating limited domains, in contrast with earlier work that had sought to develop powerful, general-purpose programs for problem solving. PROSPECTOR helped geologists in analysis of mineral exploration problems (Duda, Gaschnig, & Hart 1979). CASNET performed medical diagnoses, primarily in the area of glaucoma (Weiss, Kulkowski, Amarel, & Safir 1978).

Within the field of education, applications of expert systems have been limited. Interest among artificial intelligence researchers has instead been directed toward development of systems that model the human mind in, for example, reading comprehension processes (Schank 1982b). Interest in ICAI—intelligent computer-assisted instruction (Carbonell 1970)—has focused on development of AI programs that have the background knowledge, dialogue capabilities, and inductive power of human tutors in specific topic areas.

The RD2P system described in the example involving Mrs. Tomczak and Tomás is a hypothetical description of what may come about in the near future. Any reading-diagnostic expert systems possible in the near future will involve significantly less power (Balajthy 1986d). For example, systems will not have a text parser to understand inputs of natural language. All teacher inputs will be strictly structured, probably in multiple-choice formats.

LIMITATIONS AND ADVANTAGES OF EXPERT SYSTEMS

As educators consider the construction of expert systems, they must consider the planned functions of the programs in relation to the task demands. While expert systems offer many possibilities for education's future, present realities hamper their effectiveness, especially in terms of development and maintenance of the knowledge base and the interface with teacher-users.

Limitations

1. Construction of an expert system can take from 10 to 25 man-years and can cost from $1 to $2 million. Even if such large sums of money were available for education, the expertise necessary for such development is presently in much demand from high-paying industrial and military sources. It seems unlikely that educational applications will soon receive high priorities for development.

2. The field of education is labor-intensive. That is, there are many human teachers who have been "sufficiently" trained to meet society's qualifications for the position. In reading, for example, most schools are staffed with personnel capable of carrying out necessary reading diagnoses. In addition, teacher salaries are low. There is less call for computerized consultation systems than there would be in, for example, a highly specialized field where there are few trained experts who demand high salaries.

3. Educational decisions are often based on a complex set of factors, many of which may be debated by experts. In reading, for example, the role of neurological factors is uncertain. Remedial therapy is often prescribed according to philosophical presuppositions of the expert—for instance, in holistic versus subskill approaches. Even if all cognitive issues were settled and exact, the affective influences on education are of vital concern. An expert system designed to deal with these varying issues must be extremely complex to be worthwhile.

In artificial intelligence circles, a problem-solving domain such as reading diagnosis is characterized as "wide and shallow" knowledge (Basden 1984). That is, there is a wide range of potentially relevant factors. No one can claim absolute expertise in the knowledge domain, as there is limited agreement about which factors are relevant. Domains such as reading and economics are wide and shallow. "Deep and narrow" domains have agreed-upon expertise, and the relevant factors lie within narrow bounds, as in many aspects of the physical sciences and engineering. Most expert systems have been targeted to these latter domains.

The fact that reading diagnosis is a wide and shallow domain does not automatically eliminate the potential for expert systems. Since human knowledge, the decisions of reading specialists, is itself not 100 percent accurate (see Ch. 4 of this volume), the expert system need merely achieve a higher degree of accuracy than the typical human. And, as Basden (1984, p. 70) noted, "The scales are tipped in favour of the expert system by our capacity for forgetting the vital fact."

4. Because education is not so highly specialized as many other professions, expert systems must be designed to play an educational role as well as a decision-making role. That is, a consultative system on reading difficulties designed for classroom teacher use must not only diagnose and prescribe. It must also be capable of training teachers (or of referring teachers to training materials) in how to apply the prescriptions.

There is no doubt that teaching is more highly specialized than in the past. Many schools have reading specialists, learning disabilities specialists, writing specialists, English as a second language teachers, bilingual teachers, special education teachers, and so forth.

Nonetheless, the vast majority of teachers in any school are generalists— classroom teachers who must deal with a wide variety of different types of students. Even the specialists must deal with a great variety of problems. Consider the wide assortment of reading problems, for example, or the variety of special education needs.

As a result, mere diagnosis accompanied by briefly outlined prescriptions is insufficient feedback to teachers. Techniques must be described in detail and concrete examples given if teachers are to benefit from use of the system. Sources of relevant teaching materials ought to be listed as well.

5. Design of the human-machine interface must be carried out with recognition of the necessity for user-friendliness. Teachers, as well as professionals in most other areas, do not have the time to learn complex software operations. A typical teacher might use a reading diagnostic expert system perhaps several times a year. If each time a complex set of documentation must be studied in order to use the system, few teachers will be enthusiastic about it.

The most useful interface would involve natural language comprehension on the part of the computer. At present, however, such systems are limited and extremely expensive. The natural language front end for MYCIN uses a limited subset of English—the technical terminology of the medical profession—to enhance its user-friendliness. Doctors working in the area of diagnosis use precise terminology in stereotyped ways. For example, they might use *acute* for *short-term* and *chronic* for *long-term*. This precision of language allows the front end to understand medical "natural" language— which is actually a small subset of the English language.

Advantages

1. An expert system allows an organization to place untrained staff in key decision-making positions. Because of the enormous complexity of the educational process, teachers often must make decisions in areas about which they have received little or no training. Is a student suffering from an emotional problem? Does a student have a specific learning deficit? Are there reading skills that the student lacks? Does a special student need certain kinds of help?

A teacher could use an expert system to deal with each of these issues. The system could be designed to obtain information from the teacher, structure the teacher's thinking about the problem, and provide specific ideas for solution of any problems diagnosed.

2. Barr and Feigenbaum (1982) note that there is a "combinatorial explosion in the solution search space" in many of the problems facing professionals. The number of solutions and the complexity of each solution are outpacing the ability of professionals to keep up with their field.

Educational research has proved to be no exception to this information explosion. Johns (1982) has indicated that as many reading research studies were carried out in the decade from 1971 to 1980 as in all other decades combined since the beginning of reading research in the 1880s.

Despite the tremendously increased knowledge base, however, teacher training remains much the same. Professors of education are hard-pressed simply to cover the basics of educational methodology during the few education courses required of undergraduate teaching majors. Lack of funding and inadequate salaries in the field of education have further hindered teacher training. Most teachers in the field have received only a minimum of training in the area of reading, and even certified reading specialists often feel inadequately trained in the face of the complexities of reading disabilities. Edmund Burke Huey, one of the formative thinkers in the early years of the scientific study of reading processes, summed up the task thus: "Problem enough, for a life's work, to learn how we read" (1908).

The "computer revolution" in education offers a solution to dealing with the overwhelming amount of information available today. While attention in the mass media has generally focused on instructional applications of microcomputers (that is, using computers to teach children directly), the fact is that educators have known since the 1960s that, at best, computers have limited instructional advantages over human instructors. Indeed, even many educators are unaware that the "cutting edge" of educational technology has rejected the tutorial and drill-and-practice software in favor of using computers as tools to enhance meaningful activities such as writing (for example, word-processing programs) and researching (data-base programs).

Roger Schank, director of the artificial intelligence program at Yale University, has suggested that AI programming has the potential to release human beings from the burdens of overwhelming technical demands. His analysis of the medical profession (1984) suggested that general practitioners, like teachers, are no longer able to keep pace with the expanding knowledge base of their field. Expert diagnostic systems free doctors from mechanical and rote memory tasks to provide services that only humans can provide:

> With computers taking over the technical aspects of a profession, the human aspects will remain. Teachers and doctors will be prized for how well they deliver the human aspects of their service. The technical aspects, ever enlarging in the modern world, will be under their control instead of overwhelming them. (p. 234)

3. An expert system can bring the best and most expensive expertise to bear on a problem. Imagine, for example, an expert system that combined the diagnostic perspectives of several nationally known reading experts. Such a system might well be designed to analyze a problem from a variety of viewpoints, offering the teacher-user several alternatives, each based on a different model of the reading process or a different philosophy of instruction.

One viewpoint, for instance, might be the holistic approaches advocated by Goodman (1986) and his colleagues. Another approach might take the subskill orientation used by basal reading series. Still another viewpoint might suggest remedies based on psychoanalytic findings (Bettelheim & Zevan 1982).

4. Expert systems can be designed so as not to overlook remote possibilities. Neurological research, for example, is not well known to most reading specialists. Only a small percentage of the population of reading problems may be affected by these lesser-known causative factors. In an early article discussing the possibilities of computer applications to medical diagnosis, Ledley and Lusted (1959) noted that the most frequent type of diagnostic error was an error of omission, in which the diagnostician failed to consider all possibilities. A comprehensive diagnostic system can be prepared to help in such cases.

5. A properly designed expert system can be easily updated as new knowledge becomes available. Direct programming changes in the knowledge base can be made with the help of programmers. A more flexible approach has been demonstrated by Stanford University's TEIRESIAS system (Davis 1984), designed to update expert systems such as the medical diagnostic program MYCIN.

The basic approach used by TEIRESIAS is to provide a subject-area expert with output containing known errors, based on the information within the existing knowledge base. The expert is then asked to pinpoint missing or incorrect information causing the errors, information that is known to human experts but that is incorrectly incorporated or missing from the knowledge base.

Once the needed information has been pinpointed, TEIRESIAS is capable of helping the human expert (who is probably not familiar with expert system programming or internal operations) add the information to the knowledge base.

6. Expert systems can be used for teaching purposes. Imagine, for example, a reading specialist being trained in diagnosis. A reading diagnostic expert system could be used as a teaching device, especially if the system could clearly explain its decisions and arrange simulated diagnostic experiences for the learner (see Ch. 4 of this volume). GUIDON is a program that uses MYCIN's medical knowledge for teaching purposes (Clancey 1979).

7. Finally, and perhaps most important, the construction of an expert system within a given field of expertise can be an important experience for the field. "The actual codification of knowledge within the area of expertise can be

a valuable and insightful exercise for new ideas as to how to teach that area of expertise" (Barr & Feigenbaum 1982, v. 2, pp. 79-80).

Too often, fields of expertise within education suffer from a lack of comprehensive organization. Thinking can be sloppy. Ideas and relationships between those ideas have not been carefully formulated. Research has not been closely analyzed.

The construction of an expert system—or of competing expert systems—must of necessity raise questions about the field of expertise. What are the ultimate goals of the diagnostics? What are the logical substages involved in achievement of the final diagnosis? What actual evidence does the field have for the components of the knowledge network within the expert system? "Systematically writing production rules in their own area of interest generally appears a most enlightening exercise for students or even for professionals" (Lagrange & Renaud 1985, p. 43).

An effective project for the design and construction of an expert system must accurately document each of the information nodes within the system, as well as each of the cause-and-effect rules that link those nodes. Of necessity, in the preliminary construction the validity of many nodes and linkages will be dubious. The resulting system will be, to some extent, a "flying-by-the-seat-of-your-pants" operation simply because the field provides no substantive research evidence at important steps.

One immediate outcome of the construction of such a system would be the pinpointing of areas where additional research is needed. An expert system project would benefit greatly from being paired with empirical researchers within the expertise field who could carry out research in these areas. Certainly the construction of a field's first expert system will raise more questions than it answers—but the ultimate outcome would be to greatly strengthen the field in its understanding.

TRANSFER OF EXPERTISE

A key difficulty in the construction of a knowledge-based system involves what is called transfer of expertise (or "expertise modeling" or "knowledge acquisition")—the task of acquiring knowledge from human subject-area experts and arranging it in a way that is analyzable by computers. The arrangement of knowledge in the mind is highly complex, to the point where psychologists do not yet understand how humans use their knowledge to draw conclusions. As a result, most creators of knowledge-based systems do not attempt to model the human decision-making process. Instead, they attempt to design their systems so as to achieve the same outcomes, to draw the same conclusions as human experts would. The internal processes differ, but the external outcomes are, it is hoped, similar.

Transfer of knowledge from the human expert to the computer is a complex area of study. For example, consider the computer scientist who approaches a reading specialist and says, "Tell me all that you know about reading diagnosis." What would be the result? The specialist might describe the foundational general principles of diagnosis. Then she or he might describe the typical diagnostic procedures and some tests that are often used. She or he would probably talk about the purposes of diagnosis, as well as the relationship between diagnosis and prescription.

In whatever way the reading specialist answered, however, the results would not be a minutely detailed, step-by-step, logical progression from a concretely defined beginning point to the series of possible conclusions, with every intermediate pathway clearly defined. Barr and Feigenbaum (1982) note that human experts "insist on 'talking about' what they do rather than 'dumping' what they know, as computers do" (v. 2, p. 80). Human experts, whether in reading or in any other field, simply do not think like computers.

What Must an Expert System Know?

Creators of knowledge-based systems must gather a variety of types of knowledge. Each bit must then be sorted and arranged into a workable system (Barr & Feigenbaum 1982, v. 2; Negoita 1985).

Theory about the domain.   An expert's theory involves the foundational approach to thinking about the subject area and to solving problems within it. Different experts within the same subject area can have dramatically different theories, and as a result the problem-solving outcomes will be different.

How does fluent reading occur? What processes are involved, and how can those processes be learned? These questions must be answered before a coherent decision-making system can be arranged. Within the field of reading, for example, the division between advocates of a holistic, process orientation toward reading and language arts and advocates of a subskill approach has led to significantly different theories of reading instruction and reading disability. Similarly, the design for an expert system based on a theory involving neurological bases for reading difficulties would be different from a system based on educational and environmental bases.

Facts about the domain.   These facts are also called domain knowledge. They include the following: "Students with reading problems often have motivational problems." "Vocabulary weaknesses can lead to comprehension problems." "A low IQ is often associated with low reading scores."

Rules or procedures.   These are "hard and fast," involving invariant procedures. Barr and Feigenbaum (1982, v. 2, p. 81) give as an example the rule "Always unplug the [TV] set before you stick a screwdriver into the back." For reading diagnostics, rules might be "Always compare diagnostic test subscores for relatively high or relatively low scores" and "Always request date of test administration."

Heuristics.   These are helpful strategies for solving problems in the knowledge domain. Examples are "If motivation is poor, investigate high-interest activities for the appropriate age group" and "If phonetic analysis subscore is low, suggest administration of an individual phonics criterion test."

Points of expert disagreement.   Even if the experts upon whose knowledge the system is constructed are in agreement as to basic domain theories, there will still be points of disagreement within the system. A comprehensive expert system must be aware of these disagreements and of their implications in the problem-solving process.

On identifying a weakness in word recognition ability in a young adolescent, for instance, one expert might recommend that special attention be paid to phonetic analysis and structural analysis skills. Another expert might disagree, pointing to the youngster's age as an indication that such lower-level skill work would be self-defeatingly dull. The second expert might suggest work on contextual analysis, with a major emphasis on meaningful comprehension.

A useful expert system would consider both possibilities in the light of any additional evidence. Depending on the weighting of the various factors connected with the decision, one or both of the prescriptions could be reported to the teacher-user.

Explanation of Reasoning

An additional vital component of an expert system is its ability to communicate its reasoning procedures to a user. Just as human experts are capable of explaining and justifying their reasoning, the computer system should be able to clearly explain the steps involved in making decisions.

These explanations are useful for two important reasons. First, few teacher-users will be satisfied with a "black box" approach to reasoning in which, as if by magic, an unexplained answer to their problems suddenly appears. Professionals need some justification for the advice they are given in a manner suitable to their needs, or else they will not trust that advice (Coombs & Alty 1984).

Second, without the ability to look into the reasoning processes of the expert system, subject-area experts will not be able to spot inconsistencies, inaccuracies, or missing rules and information. No expert system can be seen as the "last word" in any domain of knowledge. Just as human experts must keep up-to-date in their specialty areas, the expert system will need constant updating. Also, especially during construction and initial field-testing, there will be many additions and corrections to the system.

Capability of Learning

As noted above, expert systems require many modifications both during and after their initial development. The expert system must be kept up-to-date on new findings from the content domain. In all probability users will want to see the system's capabilities expanded in a variety of directions after the system has been put into use.

Simpler expert systems do not have the capability of independent learning. That is, modifications of and additions to their knowledge bases and their production rules must be carried out by programmers who actually modify the code or the knowledge base files.

Newer and more complex systems actually have the capability of learning "on their own." New data, for instance, could be "automatically" fed into the knowledge base from its source. A knowledge base can be programmed to ask questions of its users and to learn from experience.

The MYCIN bacteriological diagnostic system, for instance, can be used in conjunction with a service subsystem known as TEIRESIAS, to pinpoint inaccurate or insufficient knowledge areas and to correct them (Davis 1984). If an expert-user notices that MYCIN has reached an incorrect diagnosis, the question-answering system TEIRESIAS is activated to determine which facts or rules were involved. If expert-users decide that certain facts or rules need to be changed, TEIRESIAS allows them to make those changes, even if the users do not know progamming.

ORGANIZATION OF KNOWLEDGE

The process of constructing a knowledge base, a collection of facts about the subject-area domain, and of building the inference procedures necessary in order to interpret the facts, is called knowledge engineering. Negoita (1985) suggests that there are three basic problems to be faced by the knowledge engineer.

First is knowledge representation—how can information be represented and organized in structures that can be processed by computers? For example, how can our knowledge of diagnostic procedures for word-structure analysis skills be organized so that the computer can "think" about such diagnoses in a way similar to the thinking of a human reading specialist?

Second is inference generation—how can the knowledge structures be used to make inferences and draw conclusions about specific cases related to the domain? How is the computer's "thinking" actually carried out when applied to the structural analysis problems of a particular child?

Third is knowledge acquisition—how can human knowledge be translated into computer-usable representations? This is the problem of "transfer of expertise" discussed earlier, the problem involving the transfer of knowledge from texts and human experts into abstract representations necessary for computer processing.

In an effort to deal with these problems, most researchers in expert systems have used a production rule approach to representation of knowledge. A production rule is similar to an IF-THEN arrangement in programming. Antecedents have their consequents. Causes have their effects.

1. IF A is true, THEN B is true.
2. IF A is false, THEN B is false.
3. IF Mark is tall, THEN Mark is heavy.
4. IF Mark is not-tall, THEN Mark is not-heavy.
5. IF Susan has good word recognition skills, THEN Susan has good general reading ability.
6. IF Susan has not-good word recognition skills, THEN Susan has not-good general reading ability.

Notice that when we come to apply the production rule system to real-life examples, as in rules 3-6 above, serious problems occur. Real-life rules of thought rarely involve totally true or totally false criteria. This leads to an imporant issue—the role of what is called the certainty factor or fuzzy knowledge. For the sake of clarity of explanation, however, this issue will be considered somewhat later.

For the moment, the realization that a proposition's TRUE-FALSE value is rarely absolute can lead to rephrasing the propositions listed above in the following manner:

1. A is true *implies* B is true.
2. A is false *implies* B is false.
3. Mark is tall *implies* Mark is heavy.
4. Mark is not-tall *implies* Mark is not-heavy.
5. Susan has good word recognition skills *implies* Susan has good general reading ability.
6. Susan has not-good word recognition skills *implies* Susan has not-good general reading ability.

A knowledge base consists of a set of such production rules in conjunction with the set of the variables contained in those rules—each of the variables being associated with a value that can vary. The variables in the production rules above would include A, B, HEIGHT (tall and not-tall are the values of this variable), WEIGHT (heavy and not-heavy are the values), WORD RECOGNITION ABILITY (good and not-good), and COMPREHENSION ABILITY (good and not-good).

In addition to production rules, a knowledge base contains two other types of knowledge: propositions and frames (Negoita 1985). A proposition is simply a statement that states the value of a variable:

HEIGHT of Mark is not-tall.

The value of the variable HEIGHT is "not-tall." A more exact proposition, in which the value of the variable HEIGHT would be specified more exactly, might be

HEIGHT of Mark is 5′9″.

Some other possible propositions might be

WORD RECOGNITION ABILITY of Susan is good.
WORD RECOGNITION ABILITY of Susan is not-good.

More exact phrasings of the same propositions might be

WORD RECOGNITION ABILITY of Susan is 83rd percentile.
WORD RECOGNITION ABILITY of Susan is 14th percentile.

Frames are organizational devices that link associated knowledge about a variable. Some researchers have suggested that frame-based knowledge systems are actually models of human memory organization (Minsky 1975; Nilsson 1980). Most conceptualizations of frames involve a different frame for different objects, with associated slots that contain information relevant to that object.

For example, a frame about a student's reading ability might include slots for the variables WORD RECOGNITION ABILITY, VOCABULARY ABILITY, COMPREHENSION ABILITY, and so forth. For a particular student (for example, Susan), each slot would be filled with a particular value:

Susan

WORD RECOGNITION ABILITY is 83rd percentile

VOCABULARY ABILITY is 54th percentile

COMPREHENSION ABILITY is 67th percentile

The three basic types of knowledge in an expert system—production rules, propositions, and frames—are linked in an intricate web, or network. The internal state of this network is constantly changing, depending on information fed into the system by the user.

For example, consider a teacher who consults a reading diagnostic expert system concerning a student with learning problems. The system might be programmed first to determine basic standardized testing information about the student. It places this information in slots within its "standardized test results" frame, such as the following:

1. STUDENT NAME
   2. TOTAL READING ABILITY

3. READING COMPREHENSION ABILITY
4. READING VOCABULARY ABILITY

Each of the four variables listed above would be an empty slot within the frame. In order to begin filling those empty slots with specific information, the computer could ask the student's name for slot 1, then:

What was Mark's test score on total reading?

The teacher replies,

9th grade.

This input becomes a proposition relating to the variable TOTAL READING ABILITY, to the effect:

TOTAL READING ABILITY of Mark is 9.

If this is the only standardized test score available for the student, the expert system might be programmed to make some inferences in order to complete the frame of standardized test information about Mark. These inferences would be phrased as production rules such as the following:

IF TOTAL READING ABILITY is known
and
IF READING COMPREHENSION ABILITY is not known

THEN READING COMPREHENSION ABILITY implies equal-
ity to TOTAL READING ABILITY

Since the conditions of the production rule—the two IF clauses—are met in this case, the production rule would be carried out. This process is called instantiation. Of course, the rules above are artificially simplified for their use here as examples.

Once this preliminary production rule has been instantiated, other production rules contingent upon its instantiation could be carried out—instantiated in their own right. For example, another production rule might read:

IF READING COMPREHENSION ABILITY is equal to or
greater than 9
and
IF MOTIVATION LEVEL is poor

THEN make assignments from among the following high
interest books—

The teacher could be referred to a list of reading material suitable for the student.

Each instantiation of a production rule within the expert system would change the internal state of his network of inferences. It would in turn cause the instantiation of other production rules, ultimately leading to the final decisions made by the system. "Any rule instantiation is a chain reaction, or ripple effect, in which the state of the inference network triggers instantiation of a certain rule that in turn triggers the instantiation of another rule and so on" (Negoita 1985, p. 26).

TOOLS FOR BUILDING EXPERT SYSTEMS

Until the 1980s, artificial intelligence software was developed almost exclusively by direct use of LISP. LISP is a programming language that is better suited to artificial intelligence applications than more familiar languages such as FORTRAN and Pascal.

Researchers have recently developed a variety of tools that are designed to facilitate development of AI software and of expert systems in particular. Some require no knowledge of programming at all, though this does not mean that someone totally unfamiliar with the structure of expert systems can sit down and easily construct one. While technical programming knowledge may not be necessary, it is vital to clearly understand the concepts underlying expert system construction, structure of knowledge and of the decision-making process, and transfer of expertise.

In order to understand how these AI tools operate, it is important to understand the difference between a rule-based knowledge system (such as an expert system) and a traditional computer program such as one might construct using FORTRAN or Pascal. In a traditional program (sometimes called an algorithmic program, or an ordinary applications program) the programmer writes down a series of steps that will solve a particular problem. The computer does not "understand" the problem in the sense that it does not have any actual knowledge of the content area, the domain, associated with the problem. For example, if the problem involves making a decision on scheduling a student for a remedial reading class, the computer does not "understand" the concepts of remedial reading or of scheduling in any way. It simply follows a prestructured sequence of operations to determine whether the child should be scheduled: Do this, do this, do that, and finally do that.

In an expert system, the computer does "understand"—it has "intelligence" in the domain of remedial reading and scheduling. This intelligence is, of course, different from human intelligence. Negoita (1985) defines intelligence as "the internalization of a model of the external milieu" (p. 31). An expert system has an internal model of reality—the reality of the domain—and it bases its decision making on the facts and rules in that model. "Their logic processes are state-driven rather than hard-coded," said Heines (1983, p. 65). As with any model of reality, this internalization is simplified—perhaps even simpleminded, if the programming is inadequate.

Unlike the traditional algorithmic program that consists of hard-coded procedures, the typical expert system has two separate components, a collection of facts and rules about a content domain (such as reading, medicine, auto mechanics, or whatever) and a way of making inferences and drawing conclusions about that domain. The first is usually called a knowledge base (or a data structure). The second is usually called the inference engine (or an inference system or control strategy or control structure).

The knowledge base contains the basic data about the domain or slots for data that the user must provide (for example, the student's comprehension and vocabulary scores, in a reading diagnostic expert system). It also contains the rules—the production rules—that tell how the data for a problem can be manipulated in order to solve the problem.

The inference engine makes decisions as to how to use the problem-solving knowledge in the knowledge base. It selects the best rule for each substep of the decision-making process from the collection of rules in the knowledge base. The inference engine has metaknowledge—knowledge about the structure and control of knowledge within its knowledge base—that allows it to choose most efficiently and effectively. This metaknowledge is in the form of metarules, rules that direct the inference engine in its selection of rules from the knowledge base.

Expert-system building systems are designed to facilitate the construction of expert systems in new content domains. The expert-system building system can be arranged in a variety of ways, but the major responsibility of the person who is constructing the new system is that of knowledge engineering—developing the knowledge base of facts and rules and entering it into the computer according to specified procedures so that the inference engine can deal with it. The inference engine is already developed and performs its task automatically. The expert-system building system allows the same inference engine to be used for a variety of different knowledge bases.

After the MYCIN infectious disease diagnostic system was developed, researchers used its inference engine, its basic reasoning mechanism, to develop other decision-making systems. The inference engine was called EMYCIN (for Empty MYCIN), a title descriptive of the fact that it was the MYCIN program emptied of all its domain knowledge about infectious diseases (van Melle, Shortliffe, & Buchanan 1984). EMYCIN has been used as the foundational decision-making engine for a variety of domain-specific expert systems, including PUFF, which diagnoses breathing disorders (Smith & Clayton 1984).

Expert-system building systems have been in use for only a short time, and there have been few applications to education. Chapter 15 details use of expert-system building systems for educational decision-making purposes.

SOURCES OF INFORMATION

LIEBOWITZ, JAY. 1985. "Evaluation of Expert Systems: An Approach and Case Study." In *Proceedings of the Second Conference on Artificial Intelligence Applications*, pp. 564-571. Washington, DC: IEEE Computer Society Press.
Liebowitz surveys the software evaluation literature. He presents and discusses criteria for evaluating expert systems: ability to update, ease of use, hardware issues, cost-effectiveness, understandability of input and output, and quality of decisions, advice, and performance. This article is of practical importance to anyone considering building or buying an expert system.

BUCHANAN, BRUCE G., AND EDWARD H. SHORTLIFFE. 1984. *Rule-Based Expert Systems: The MYCIN Experiments of the Stanford Heuristic Programming Project*. Reading, MA: Addison-Wesley.
This book contains a collection of key articles describing Stanford University's comprehensive research project centered on the MYCIN expert system described above. The book gives clear insight into the complexities of computer-based decision making and is a resource for those interested in the background of expert system development.

BARR, AVRON, AND EDWARD A. FEIGENBAUM. 1982. *Handbook of Artificial Intelligence*. 3 vols. Los Altos, CA: William Kaufmann.
This is an encyclopedia of research and development in all areas of artificial intelligence, including natural language, expert systems, and intelligent computer-assisted instruction. The books serve as a moderately technical introduction to the various topics, and comprehensive lists of references are included. Major systems are described in detail. For instance, in the expert system category the following systems are described: MYCIN, TEIRESIAS, DENDRAL, MACSYMA, SRI, PROSPECTOR, CASNET, INTERNIST, IRIS, and EXPERT.

15

CONSTRUCTION OF AN EXPERT SYSTEM

The development of the first commercial expert-system building systems (also called knowledge systems or expert system shells) for microcomputers in the mid-1980s allowed construction of expert systems without time-consuming programming tasks. A domain expert, such as a reading specialist, can use an expert system shell to construct a reading diagnostic expert system. No knowledge of LISP or any other programming language is required.

Anyone building an expert system must still have a clear understanding of its function and operation. But expert system shells are designed to be as user-friendly as possible to the domain expert attempting to build a decision-making program. The user-friendliness of the shells, however, limits their flexibility, so that a system constructed on the basis of one of these expert system shells has inevitable limitations.

The present chapter describes the components of a typical expert system shell and outlines procedures necessary for construction of a reading diagnostic expert system. Emphasis is placed on the actual construction of the decision-making system rather than on the complexities of "knowledge engineering"—the difficulties involved in deciding just what the reading field knows about diagnosis and how to arrange that knowledge in a logical form. The relationship of knowledge engineering to the field of reading diagnosis is discussed in Chapter 4 of this volume.

In order to improve clarity, the present chapter uses a specific example of a reading diagnostic expert system under development, the *Reading Disability Diagnosis and Prescription* system (RD2P). This expert system uses the *Insight Knowledge System* as its expert system shell. *Insight* is one of a variety of expert system shells that can be purchased as the foundational decision-making mechanisms for construction of an expert system (Wilson & Welsh 1986; Welsh & Wilson 1986).

BASIC COMPONENTS

As described in Chapter 14, an expert system typically has two major components, an inference engine and a knowledge base. The inference engine is the part of the system that operates on the knowledge base, carrying out the rule-based inference operations according to a prescribed sequence. It formulates the questions to be asked of the user and draws conclusions from the user's input and from information contained in the knowledge base.

The knowledge base is composed of several types of information, structured according to a rule system and written in accordance with a knowledge base construction language. In the *Insight Knowledge System*, for example, the knowledge base is constructed according to the rules of PRL (Production Rule Language), a simple language employing a great deal of natural English for its components.

In order to explain how an expert system is constructed, an actual example will be used, though some of the discussion below presents a simplified view of its makeup in order to avoid bogging down in petty details that require irrelevant explanations and can vary from system to system. Development of RD2P was begun in 1985. It is a prototype expert system for the diagnosis of and prescription for reading disabilities. There were two major purposes in its construction:

1. The program is a tool for the training of reading specialists.
2. The program is a pilot for the development of a comprehensive consultative system for use by classroom teachers who are dealing with reading-disabled students.

There is an important difference between the knowledge engineering involved in constructing an expert system based on a shell and more conventional programming (such as that in the CARA reading diagnostic consultation program; see Ch. 4 of this volume). In using an expert system shell, the system developer is not required to describe each step of actual computer operation. Instead, the developer must exactly specify the facts and relationships between facts involved in the decision-making process in the domain field. This process of specification is known as knowledge engineering.

The computer operation is handled by the shell program. This generic control structure relieves the developer of the need to specify exact problem-solving algorithms. The control structure, or inference engine, is usable with a wide variety of knowledge bases. In the *Insight Knowledge System*, the inference engine is called *Insight*.

The two key components of a knowledge base in *Insight* are production rules and goals. Production rules contain the primary representation of knowledge within the system. They specify the cause-and-effect relationships that interrelate the information within a subject domain such as reading diagnosis.

Goals are the conclusions that can be drawn by the expert system. They are based both on the information provided to the system by the user, such as a teacher consulting the system, and on the production rules specified by the knowledge engineer who developed the diagnostic system.

Production Rules

One aspect of the effectiveness of a knowledge system lies in the ease with which knowledge of the decision-making process can be represented. Production rules function to make this representation more user-friendly.

Production rules model cause-effect relationships using IF . . . THEN . . . statements. For example, the following rule is a simplification of an RD2P production rule that specifies one path through which the system might conclude that a specific student is a developmental reader.

```
RULE    Developmental diagnosis—comprehension
IF    Comprehension  subtest  grade  equivalent
    score >= grade level
AND    Comprehension  subtest  grade  equivalent
    score >= reading potential
THEN    The student is developmental in comprehen-
    sion.
```

Essentially, this rule states that

1. IF the grade equivalent score on a comprehension subtest is greater than or equal to the student's grade level,
2. AND if that test score is also greater than or equal to the student's reading potential (an estimate based on an intelligence test),
3. THEN the student is assigned the classification of "developmental" (that is, average—not needing supplemental help) in the subskill of comprehension.

This rule serves as an example of a production rule. It is, however, a simplification of an actual production rule for a variety of reasons. For one, there is no specification as to how the scores, such as reading potential, are obtained by the system. Also, the "greater than or equal to" component needs further specification. Teachers would probably want to classify as developmental those students who are an insignificant amount below grade level on a standardized score.

PRL, the language used to construct an *Insight* production rule network, does not require a specific ordering of rules. New rules may be added to the network at any time, as new knowledge becomes available or as field-testing suggests modifications. The typical PRL rule consists of several parts, or statements:

1. The name of the rule, signified by the term RULE placed at the left margin, as shown in the example above.
2. The supporting condition for the rule, signified by the term IF. As in the example, a rule may have more than one supporting condition, in which case those conditions following the first are preceded by the term AND.
3. The conclusion, signified by the term THEN. A rule may have more than one conclusion, in which case those conclusions following the first are preceded by the term AND. All conclusions can in turn become supporting conditions for other rules deeper within the knowledge network.

In addition to these three required components, a rule may have other optional parts:

4. The confidence statement, to be explained below.
5. An alternative conclusion statement, signified by the term ELSE. This statement follows the THEN conclusion statement in those situations where, if the conclusion statement is not verified, another set of conclusions can be drawn.

Goal Statements

One difficulty faced by designers of expert systems has had to do with development of outcome goals. In a complex system, the number of possible outcomes—the goals or final decisions—can be enormous. A truly complete reading diagnostic system, for example, would contain a mind-boggling variety of possible diagnostic and prescriptive outcomes. In order to choose among these possible outcomes for a particular student, the system requires a correspondingly enormous amount of information about that student. This information must be provided by the user in response to questions generated by the system.

For example, consider a situation in which a reading specialist wants a detailed analysis of test and observational data on a student who is possibly reading-disabled. The system would generate a series of questions to draw out this data. RD2P questions include the following requests for test information:

```
What is the student's IQ score?
What is the student's phonetic analysis subscore?
What is the student's reading rate?
What is the student's inferential comprehension
    subscore?
```

Only after the specialist had responded to all these requests for information would the expert system be able to draw conclusions as to specific diagnoses. This would be a time-consuming task for the reading specialist, considering the amount of time necessary to administer the testing. In terms of teacher-time effectiveness, this is not always a beneficial route to take.

Suppose, on the other hand, that the reading specialist recognized that the student's problem was one of comprehension. Her or his requirement of the expert system would be to peform an analysis of the student's abilities and needs within that particular subskill area. Without some method of specifying needs, the specialist would again be forced to respond to a tremendous number of computer queries, few of which would be directly related to the need at hand.

One approach to solving this problem is to require the knowledge engineer to develop a goal system that forms a foundation for the knowledge base of production rules. In essence, the knowledge base is constructed backward from these goals, through the network of production rules, to the questions asked of the user. *Insight* structures this goal system according to a traditional outline format.

For example, at one point in the RD2P knowledge network, the set of outcome goals involves the series of possible diagnoses below.

1. The student requires decoding remediation.
2. The student requires vocabulary remediation.
3. The student requires comprehension remediation.

At the beginning of an RD2P session, the teacher-user is presented with a more complex version of this sample list. If the specific need is already known, as in the example above of a reading specialist consulting RD2P concerning a student with comprehension problems, that need can be specified. Only the queries relevant to that need will be presented to the user.

The actual set of goal statements is more complex than that listed above, however, so *Insight* allows for more than one level within the set of goal statements. Lower levels within the goal hierarchy, called subgoals, are specified in outline format:

1. The student requires decoding remediation.
    1.1. The student requires general decoding remediation.
    1.2. The student requires phonetic analysis remediation.
        1.2.1. The student requires word division remediation.
        1.2.2. The student requires word blending remediation.
    1.3 The student requires structural analysis remediation.
2. The student requires vocabulary remediation.
3. The student requires comprehension remediation.
    3.1 The student requires literal comprehension remediation.
    3.2 The student requires inferential comprehension remediation.

The greater the depth of subgoals possible within a shell system such as *Insight*, the more complexity is allowed the program builder. For example, a goal such as 1.2.1 may be labeled as "three deep" within the hierarchy. The *Insight* system allows a maximum "depth" of 48—a depth rarely achieved in any actual system.

Relation of Production Rules to Goal Statements

The task of the inference engine, or control structure, is to verify a goal statement. The structure does this by finding the rules that contain supporting statements that result in the goal conclusion. A goal statement may be concluded in more than one possible way. For example, consider the general goal statement below:

> THEN   The student should be referred to a reading
>   specialist.

There will be a variety of paths leading to its conclusion, since there are a variety of different supporting conditions for such a goal statement.

On the other hand, consider a more specific goal:

> THEN   The student should receive remedial work in
>   phonetic analysis.

There would probably be fewer paths leading to this goal. A path is a condition that arises when the concluding statement of one rule references another rule by becoming one of the supporting statements in the second rule. Paths leading to the conclusion of a goal statement may be as short as one rule or may be extremely long, with many contributing rules. The only limit on path length is the limit of memory resources within the computer hardware.

Confidence Levels

The thoughtful reader may have noticed a critical weakness in our description of expert system shells: that when a human expert draws a conclusion, that conclusion is rarely an all-or-nothing affair. There is usually some degree of confidence associated with it. Without a provision for such an expression of confidence level in their statements and conclusions, expert systems could be used in a limited number of decision-making situations.

For example, consider the sample rule from the RD2P knowledge base cited earlier, a THEN statement:

> THEN   The student is developmental in comprehen-
>   sion.

This conclusion cannot be considered a 100 percent certainty by any teacher. A variety of factors could have led the computer to have drawn an incorrect conclusion, even assuming that the production rules within the knowledge base are accurate. No test, for example, is 100 percent reliable.

As another example, consider the first of the supporting conditions to the production rule given above:

> IF   Comprehension subtest grade equivalent
>   score >= grade level.

This condition assumes the accuracy of the test on which the grade equivalent score is based. The second supporting condition,

> AND   Comprehension subtest grade equivalent
>   score >= reading potential,

includes that assumption, as well as the assumption that the IQ test on which the reading potential score is based is accurate. As all teachers realize, such assumptions are unwarranted. Tests, especially the group tests administered in schools, have built-in error factors. Their results cannot be supposed to be completely accurate.

Expert system shells do, however, make provision for varying levels of confidence in the decisions made. The use of uncertain knowledge in reasoning, called fuzzy knowledge by artificial intelligence researchers, is one of the truly innovative developments of AI work.

Confidence levels in the *Insight* system, for example, are stated using the term *confidence* in conjunction with the rule's concluding statement. The use of the term *confidence* requires a numerical value between 0 and 100. 0 signifies that the conclusion is completely false. 100 signifies that the conclusion is completely true. A confidence level of 75 might signify "probably true," 50 might signify "unsure," and 25 "probably false." Omitting the confidence level in a conclusion statement indicates that the confidence level is 100. Thus, the sample rule might actually look like the following in the knowledge base, indicating a reasonably high confidence in the conclusion:

> RULE   Developmental   diagnosis—comprehen-
>   sion
> IF   Comprehension subtest grade equiv-
>   alent score >= grade level
> AND   Comprehension subtest grade equiv-
>   alent score >= reading potential
> THEN   The student is developmental in com-
>   prehension
> CONFIDENCE 85

As defined earlier, a path is a condition that arises when the concluding

THEN statement of one rule references another rule by becoming one of the supporting statements in the second rule. When the concluding statement of the first rule has a confidence level of less than 100, if the second rule is verified by the inference engine, it also will have less than 100 percent confidence.

The *Insight* system deals with this problem by multiplying the confidence level of the supporting statement by the confidence level of the concluding statement to develop a confidence statement for the specific instantiation of the rule. If in the developmental diagnosis—comprehension example cited above, the confidence level of the first supporting statement is 90 and the confidence level of the second supporting statement is 80, *Insight* will choose the lower of the two levels. This will be multiplied against the level of the concluding statement, 85:

.80 * .85 = .68

The final confidence level of the rule would be 68. Note that the longer the pathway, the more uncertainty would be likely to accumulate. Since there would come a point at which conclusions would be so uncertain as to be practically guesswork, the knowledge engineer must assign a threshold level, the lowest acceptable level of confidence for which *Insight* is allowed to reach a conclusion. For example, the knowledge engineer might specify:

THRESHOLD = 40

If the confidence level of a pathway—the series of supporting statements and conclusions—fell below 40, *Insight* would dismiss that pathway as improbable.

In addition to confidence levels specified within the system by the knowledge engineer, teacher-users are asked to specify a confidence level as part of their answer to questions asked of them by the knowledge base. In response to the question

The student has an attentional problem?

the teacher-user might be asked to assign a confidence level with one of the following values:

```
CONFIDENT IT IS TRUE     =      100
POSSSIBLY TRUE           =       75
NOT SURE                 =       50
POSSIBLY FALSE           =       25
CONFIDENT IT IS FALSE    =        0
```

Queries and Data Types

The *Insight* system allows for input of three data types. Each type of information is handled in a slightly different way. The user provides this information in response to queries from the knowledge base.

Factual information. The user is required to decide whether a statement is true or false. The example given above, "The student has an attentional problem?," would request the user to assign a confidence value of 0 (that is, confident it is false), 25, 50, 75, or 100 (that is, confident it is true).

Value information. The user is required to provide a numeric reply in response to a question. For example:

```
What is the student's phonetic analysis subtest
    score?
```

Insight is capable of comparing this numeric input with other input or with numeric values within the knowledge system. A supporting statement of a rule might state:

```
IF phonetic analysis subtest score <= 3
THEN student requires phonetic analysis remedia-
    tion.
```

In this example, the knowledge system is capable of analyzing the user's input to find whether it is less than or equal to 3.

Set information. The user is required to choose from a list of possible responses provided by the knowledge system. An item or an attribute must be identified. If an item from the list cannot be identified, the user can press the UNKNOWN function key. In a set information question, choice of one item indicates that the other items are not true.

A designer using the *Insight* system must work within a limited framework in designing requests for information from the user. This requires a great deal of foresight in some instances. A slight change of wording in factual information queries, for instance, may dramatically change the confidence level users assign to the statement. Inadvertently leaving out some possibilities in the set information queries will lead to confusion on the part of the user and result in inability to proceed with the analysis. In addition, *Insight* is incapable of handling sets of information in which more than one item choice can be made.

Another serious limitation of the *Insight* system involves its inability to perform arithmetic operations on numerical input. For example, in reading diagnosis, remedial levels are generally determined as being two or more grade levels below expectancy potential levels. In order to determine the remedial level cutoff for a student, a knowledge system can query the user for the student's expectancy potential level, which might be 6 (for sixth grade). If the system were capable of performing an arithmetic operation, it could simply subtract 2 from 6 to get 4 as the possible remedial level. *Insight* is not able to do this. The user is required to perform the operation and to type the new number.

Expansion of Information

An important part of the function of an expert system, in addition to expert analysis and problem solving, is the provision of expert information. For example, the simple conclusion that a student requires remediation in phonetic analysis may be helpful to a teacher-user of the system. If the analysis stops there, however, the teacher is left with the question "What kind of remedial activities are appropriate to improve phonetic analysis abilities at this student's grade level?"

An expert system can be programmed to provide such information at appropriate points within the analysis. *Insight* allows for two types of expanded information, an automatic and an optional provision.

The automatic information function, accessed with the command DIS-PLAY, provides a screen page of information at any point within the program without a request from the user. This allows the system designer to provide needed information.

The optional information function, accessed with the command EXPAND, allows the user to request additional information at any point within the program. The press of a function key yields the screen page display of information.

Conclusions and Report Function

When the knowledge base reaches a final goal or conclusion to the problem at hand, the conclusion is presented to the user. In *Insight* the conclusion display includes all the intermediate and final conclusions resulting from the session. In those cases where *Insight* cannot reach a conclusion, the message "Insufficient information to reach a conclusion" is displayed. This would occur when a specified threshold confidence level has not been reached.

As noted in Chapter 14, the capability of an expert system to explain its reasoning is of vital importance. Users will place little confidence in a "black box" approach to decision making. With the *Insight* system, the conclusion display offers a report option that can be printed out either on the monitor or in hard copy.

This report traces the path of reasoning used by the knowledge system and also includes the user's inputs. The rules accessed during the session are displayed with explanatory comments, such as "In order to find out if . . . ," "By using the rule . . . ," and "It is necessary to find out if . . . ." The report function serves not only to explain the system's analysis to the user but also to provide important feedback to the knowledge engineer during construction of the system.

CONCLUSIONS

Construction of expert systems in government and industry has dramatically increased with the development of expert system shells such as *Insight*. Even with the aid of shells, however, the construction of diagnostic expert systems in education is a tremendous task. Decision making in reading diagnosis, for example, is a highly complex affair if carried out in a rule-based fashion, with hundreds of rules for a truly complete set of conclusions. While prototype systems such as RD2P have been under development and limited field-testing, effective and efficient artificial intelligence systems will require major funding for research and development.

SOURCES OF INFORMATION

WILSON, BRENT G., AND JACK R. WELSH. 1986. "Small Knowledge-Based Systems in Education and Training: Something New Under the Sun." *Educational Technology* 26, no. 11 (November): 7-13.
  The authors briefly review the purpose and function of expert systems, and discuss their impressive development costs. A list of commercially available expert system shells, with their publishers, is provided.

GILMORE, JOHN F., AND KURT PULASKI. 1985. "A Survey of Expert System Tools." In *Proceedings of the Second Conference on Artificial Intelligence Applications*, pp. 498-502. Washington, DC: IEEE Computer Society Press.
  This article contains a comparison of eight of the more popular expert system tools, most of which are designed for mainframe computers or minicomputers. They are ART, Knowledge Craft, KES II, Rule Master, Duck, KEE, M1, and S1.

NEGOITA, CONTANTIN VIRGIL. 1985. *Expert Systems and Fuzzy Systems*. Reading, MA: Benjamin/Cummings.
  This is a technical introduction to expert systems, with a particular emphasis on fuzzy knowledge and probability reasoning in relation to computer-based decision making.

WATERMAN, DONALD A. 1986. *A Guide to Expert Systems*. Reading, MA: Addison-Wesley.
  Waterman provides a clear and comprehensive introduction to and explanation of expert systems. A special strength of the book is the extensive attention paid to expert system tools. He deals with issues such as choosing an expert system tool, acquiring knowledge from an expert, and common pitfalls in development of an expert system. An extensive descriptive catalog of expert systems and expert system tools is included.

COMMERCIAL SOFTWARE

Insight Knowledge System
    Level 5 Research, Inc.
    4980 South A-1-A
    Melbourne Beach, FL 32951
    IBM-PC

REFERENCES

ADDAMS, SHAY. 1985. "If yr comptr cn rd this . . ." *Computer Entertainment* (August): 24-27, 76-77.

AHL, DAVID H. (ED). 1978. *Basic Computer Games*. Morristown, NJ: Creative Computing Press.

ALDERMAN, DONALD L., LOLA RHEA APPEL, AND RICHARD T. MURPHY. 1978. "PLATO and TICCIT: An Evaluation of CAI in the Community College." *Educational Technology* 18, no. 4 (April): 40-46.

ALEXANDER, CLARA. 1984. *Microcomputers and Teaching Reading in College*. Research Monograph Series Report no. 8. New York: Instructional Resource Center, City University of New York.

ALLEN, JONATHAN. 1976. "Synthesis of Speech from Unrestricted Text." *Proceedings of the IEEE* 64, no. 4 (April): 433-442.

ALLEN, JONATHAN. 1981. "Linguistic-Based Algorithms Offer Practical Text-to-Speech Systems." *Speech Technology* 1, no. 1 (Fall): 12-16.

ALLEN, ROACH VAN. 1976. *Language Experiences in Communication*. Boston: Houghton Mifflin.

ALVERMANN, DONNA E. 1985. "Effects of Interactive Video and Refutation Text on Reading Comprehension." Paper presented at the College Reading Association, Pittsburgh, October.

AMERICAN PSYCHIATRIC ASSOCIATION. 1980. *Diagnostic and Statistical Manual of Mental Disorders*. 3rd ed. Washington, DC: American Psychiatric Association.

ANDERSON, RICHARD C., AND W. BARRY BIDDLE. 1975. "On Asking People Questions About What They Are Reading." In *The Psychology of Learning and Motivation*, vol. 9, ed. Gordon H. Bower, pp. 90-132. New York: Academic Press.

ANDERSON, RICHARD C., JEAN OSBORN, AND ROBERT J. TIERNEY. 1984. *Learning to Read in American Schools*. Hillsdale, NJ: Lawrence Erlbaum.

ANDERSON, RICHARD C., AND P. DAVID PEARSON. 1984. "A Schema-Theoretic View of Basic Processes in Reading." In *Handbook of Reading Research*, ed. P. David Pearson, pp. 255-292. New York: Longman.

ANDERSON, THOMAS H. 1980. "Study Strategies and Adjunct Aids." In *Theoretical Issues in Reading Comprehension*, ed. Rand J. Spiro, Bertram C. Bruce, and William F. Brewer, pp. 483-502. Hillsdale, NJ: Lawrence Erlbaum.

ANDERSON, THOMAS H., RICHARD C. ANDERSON, BRUCE R. DALGAARD, EDWARD J. WIETECHA, W. BARRY BIDDLE, DONALD W. PADEN, H. RICHARD SMOCK, STEPHEN M. ALESSI, JOHN R. SURBER, AND LAURA L. KLEMT. 1974. "A Computer Based Study Management System." *Educational Psychologist* 11, no. 1: 36-45.

ANDERSON-INMAN, LYNNE. 1987. "The Reading-Writing Connection: Classroom Applications for the Computer." *The Computing Teacher* 14, no. 6 (March): 15-18.

ARONIS, JOHN M., AND SANDRA KATZ. 1984. "RICHARD: An Interactive Computer Program for Rhetorical Invention." *Educational Technology* 14, no. 11 (November): 26-30.

ATHEY, IRENE. 1983. "Language Development Factors Related to Reading Development." *Journal of Educational Research* 76, no. 4 (March/April), 197-203.

ATKINSON, RICHARD C. 1967. "Reading Instruction Under Computer Control." *American School Board Journal* 155, no. 3 (September): 316-317.

ATKINSON, RICHARD C. 1968a. "The Role of the Computer in Teaching Initial Reading." *Childhood Education* 44, no. 7 (March): 464-470.

ATKINSON, RICHARD C. 1968b. "Computerized Instruction and the Learning Process." *American Psychologist* 23, no. 4 (April): 225-239.

ATKINSON, RICHARD C. 1969. "Computer-Assisted Learning in Action." In *Proceedings of the National Academy of Sciences* 63, no. 3 (July): 588-594.

ATKINSON, RICHARD C., AND JOHN D. FLETCHER. 1972. "Teaching Children to Read with a Computer." *The Reading Teacher* 25, no. 4 (January): 319-327.

ATKINSON, RICHARD C., AND DUNCAN N. HANSEN. 1966. "Computer-Assisted Instruction in Initial Reading: The Stanford Project." *Reading Research Quarterly* 2, no. 1 (Fall): 5-25.

BAKER, LINDA, AND ANN L. BROWN. 1984. "Metacognitive Skills and Reading." In *Handbook of Reading Research* ed. P. David Pearson, pp. 353-387. New York: Longman.

BALAJTHY, ERNEST. 1982. "The Relationship of Training in Self-Generated Questioning with Passage Difficulty and Immediate and Delayed Retention." Doctoral dissertation, Rutgers University.

BALAJTHY, ERNEST. 1984a. "Evaluation of Models of the Reading Process." Paper presented at the International Reading Association, Atlanta, May.

BALAJTHY, ERNEST. 1984b. "Reinforcement and Drill by Microcomputer." *The Reading Teacher* 37, no. 6 (February): 490-495.

BALAJTHY, ERNEST. 1985. "Artificial Intelligence and the Teaching of Reading and Writing by Computers." *Journal of Reading* 29, no. 1 (October): 23-33.

BALAJTHY, ERNEST. 1986a. *Microcomputers in Reading and Language Arts.* Englewood Cliffs, NJ: Prentice Hall.

BALAJTHY, ERNEST. 1986b. "Microcomputers in Reading and Language Arts: A Syllabus." In *Preparation of Teachers for Microcomputer Instruction in Reading and Language Arts*, ed. Ernest Balajthy, pp. 58-66. Newark, DE: Special Interest Group on Microcomputers in Reading, International Reading Association.

BALAJTHY, ERNEST. 1986c. "The Relationship of Training in Self-Generated Questioning with Passage Difficulty and Immediate and Delayed Retention." In *Learners, Teachers, & Researchers*, 35th Yearbook of the National Reading Conference, ed. Jerome A. Niles and Rosary V. Lalik, pp. 41-46. Rochester, NY: National Reading Conference.

BALAJTHY, ERNEST. 1986d. "Expert Systems: A Challenge for the Reading Profession." Paper presented at the International Reading Association, Philadelphia, April. [ERIC Document Reproduction no. ED 268 485]

BALAJTHY, ERNEST. In press, a. "Software Review: *Computer Assisted Reading Assessment.*" *Micro Missive.*

BALAJTHY, ERNEST. In press, b. "Implications of Artificial Intelligence Research for Human-Computer Interaction in Reading Instruction." In *Computers and Reading: Issues for Theory and Practice*, ed. David Reinking. New York: Teachers College Press.

BALAJTHY, ERNEST. In press, c. "Computer-Based Feedback for Editing in the Early Grades." In *Writing with Computers in the Early Grades*, ed. James L. Hoot and Steven B. Silvern. Reading, MA: Addison-Wesley.

BALAJTHY, ERNEST, LINDA BACON, AND PATRICIA HASBY. 1985. "Introduction to Computers and Introduction to Word Processing: Integrating Content Area Coursework into College Reading/Study Skills Curricula Using Microcomputers." Paper presented at the City University of New York Conference on Microcomputers and Basic Skills in College, New York, November.

BALAJTHY, ERNEST, LINDA BACON, AND PATRICIA HASBY. In press. "Comparison of Computer-Based and Traditional Practice Exercises for Development of Content Area Vocabulary at the College Level." In *Proceedings of the Eighth National Educational Computing Conference.* New York: Association for Computing Machinery.

BALAJTHY, ERNEST, ROBERT MCKEVENY, AND LORI LACITIGNOLA. 1986. "Teaching Students Revision Skills Using Microcomputers." *Reading Instruction Journal* 29, no. 3 (Spring/Summer): 27-30.

BALAJTHY, ERNEST, ROBERT MCKEVENY, AND LORI LACITIGNOLA. 1986-1987. "Microcomputers and the Improvement of Revision Skills." *The Computing Teacher* 14, no. 4 (December/January): 28-31.

BALLAND, JOHN C., WILLIAM D. TAYLOR, JAMES CANELOS, FRANCIS DWYER, AND PATTI BAKER. 1985. "Is the Self-Paced Instructional Program, via Microcomputer-Based Instruction, the Most Effective Method of Addressing Individual Learning Differences?" *ECTJ: Educational Communication and Technology Journal* 33, no. 3 (Fall): 185-198.

BANGERT-DROWNS, ROBERT L., JAMES A. KULIK, AND CHEN-LIN C. KULIK. 1985. "The Effectiveness of Computer-Based Education in Secondary Schools." *Journal of Computer-Based Instruction* 12, no. 3 (Summer): 59-68.

BARDWELL, REBECCA. 1981. "Feedback: How Does It Function?" *Journal of Experimental Education* 50, no. 1 (Fall): 4-9.

BARR, AVRON, AND EDWARD A. FEIGENBAUM. 1982. *The Handbook of Artificial Intelligence.* 3 vols. Los Altos, CA: William Kaufmann.

BASDEN, ANDREW. 1984. "On the Application of Expert Systems." In *Developments of Expert Systems*, ed. M. J. Coombs, pp. 59-75. London: Academic Press.

BEAN, JOHN C. 1983. "Computerized Word-Processing as an Aid to Revision." *College Composition and Communication* 34, no. 2 (May): 146-148.

BEAUGRANDE, ROBERT DE. 1981. "Design Criteria for Process Models of Reading." *Reading Research Quarterly* 16, no. 2: 261-315.

BEAULIEU, JOHN E. 1985. "A Study of the Effects of Selected Feedback Delay Intervals upon Retention of Science Material in a Computer Assisted Instructional Task with Junior High School Students." Doctoral dissertation, University of Oregon. [*Dissertation Abstracts* 46, no. 7 (1986), p. 1872a. Order no. DA 852 0697]

BECKER, HENRY J. 1982. *Microcomputers in the Classroom—Dreams and Realities.* Report no. 319. Baltimore: Center for the Social Organization of Schools, Johns Hopkins University.

BECKER, HENRY JAY. 1983a. *School Uses of Microcomputers: Reports from a National Survey.* Issue no. 1. Baltimore: Center for Social Organization of Schools, Johns Hopkins University.

BECKER, HENRY JAY. 1983b. "School Uses of Microcomputers: Report #1 from a National Survey." *Journal of Computers in Mathematics and Science Teaching* 3, no. 1 (Fall): 29-33.

BECKER, HENRY JAY. 1985a. *How Schools Use Microcomputers: Summary of the First National Survey.* Baltimore: Center for Social Organization of Schools, Johns Hopkins University.

BECKER, HENRY JAY. 1985b. "National School Uses of Microcomputers Survey: Review of Past and Promise of Future Data." Paper presented at American Educational Research Association, Chicago, April.

BECKER, HENRY JAY. 1986. "Equity in School Computer Use: National Data and Neglected Considerations." Paper presented at the American Educational Research Association, San Francisco, April.

BEREITER, CARL, AND MARLENE SCARDAMALIA. 1984. "Learning About Writing from Reading." *Written Communication* 1, no. 2 (April): 163-188.

BETTELHEIM, BRUNO, AND KAREN ZEVAN. 1982. *On Learning to Read: The Child's Fascination with Meaning.* New York: Knopf.

BETTS, EMMETT A. 1946. *Foundations of Reading Instruction.* New York: American Book Co.

BIRKHEAD, EVAN. 1986. "Technology Update: Installed Base of LANs Will Skyrocket During 1986-1987 School Year." *T.H.E. Journal* 13, no. 9 (May): 12-13.

BLANCHARD, JAY S. 1984. "U.S. Armed Services Computer Assisted Literacy Efforts." *Journal of Reading* 28, no. 3 (December): 262-265.

BLANCHARD, JAY S. 1985. *Computer-Based Reading Assessment Instrument* [manual]. Dubuque, IA: Kendall/Hunt.

BLANCHARD, JAY S. 1987. "Microcomputer-Based Reading Assessment." Paper presented at the International Reading Association, Anaheim, CA, May.

BLIXEN, KAREN. 1980. *Out of Africa*. London: Folio Society. [Originally published 1937]

BLOHM, PAUL J. 1982a. "Computer-Aided Glossing and Facilitated Learning in Prose Recall." *New Inquiries in Reading Research and Instruction*, 31st Yearbook of the National Reading Conference, ed. Jerome A. Niles and Larry A. Harris, pp. 24-28. Rochester, NY: National Reading Conference.

BLOHM, PAUL J. 1982b. "I Use the Computer to ADVANCE Advances in Comprehension-Strategy Research." Paper presented at the Symposium on Factors Related to Reading Performance, Milwaukee, WI, June. [ERIC Documentation Reproduction Service ED 216-330]

BLOHM, PAUL J., AND H. CUSTER WHITESIDE. 1986. "Effect of Color Highlighting and Decision Type for Improving Learners' Recall of Text on the Microcomputer." *International Journal of Instructional Media* 13, no. 1 (Spring): 19-26.

BLOOM, BENJAMIN S. 1984. "The 2 Sigma Problem: The Search for Methods of Group Instruction as Effective as One-to-One Tutoring." *Educational Researcher* 13, no. 6 (June/July): 4-16.

BOBROW, DANIEL G. 1968. "Natural Language Input for a Computer Problem-Solving System." In *Semantic Information Processing*, ed. Marvin Minsky, pp. 146-226. Cambridge, MA: MIT Press.

BORK, ALFRED. 1984a. "Computer Futures for Education." *Creative Computing* 10, no. 11 (November): 178-180.

BORK, ALFRED. 1984b. "Computers and Information Technology as a Learning Aid." In *Computers and Education: Policy Problems and Experiences*, ed. J. C. M. M. Moonen and H. E. Wuite-Harmsma, pp. 77-90. Amsterdam: North-Holland.

BORK, ALFRED. 1985. *Personal Computers in Education*. New York: Harper & Row.

BOSCO, JAMES. 1986. "An Analysis of Evaluations of Interactive Video." *Educational Technology* 26, no. 5 (May): 7-17.

BRACEY, GERALD W. 1982. "Computers in Education: What the Research Shows." *Electronic Learning* 2, no. 3 (November/December): 51-54.

BRACEY, JERRY. 1985. "Another Viewpoint on SAT Programs." *Electronic Learning* 4, no. 7 (April): 32.

BRADEY, PHILIP. 1986. "Computer Simulations and Reading Instruction." *The Computing Teacher* 14, no. 2 (October): 34-36.

BRILLIANTINE, LANCE R. 1985. "Design and Selection Guide to Local Area Networks." *Administrative Management* 46, no. 10 (October): 34-37.

BROWN, ANN L., JOSEPH C. CAMPIONE, AND CRAIG R. BARCLAY. 1979. "Training Self-Checking Routines for Estimating Test Readiness: Generalization from List Learning to Prose Recall." *Child Development* 50, no. 2 (June): 501-512.

BROWN, ANN L., JOSEPH C. CAMPIONE, AND JEANNE D. DAY. 1981. *Learning to Learn: On Training Students to Learn from Text*. Technical Report no. 89. Urbana: Center for the Study of Reading, University of Illinois.

BROWN, ANN L., AND JEANNE D. DAY. 1983. "Macrorules for Summarizing Texts: The Development of Expertise." *Journal of Verbal Learning and Verbal Behavior* 22, no. 1 (February): pp. 1-14.

BROWN, JAMES W. 1986. "Some Motivational Issues in Computer-Based Instruction." *Educational Technology* 26, no. 4 (April): 27-29.

BROWN, JOHN SEELY. 1983. "Learning by Doing Revisited for Electronic Learning Environments. "In *The Future of Electronic Learning*, ed. Mary Alice White, pp. 13-32. Hillsdale, NJ: Lawrence Erlbaum.

BROWN, JOHN SEELY, RICHARD R. BURTON, AND ALAN G. BELL. 1975. "SOPHIE: A Step Toward Creating a Reactive Learning Environment." *International Journal of Man-Machine Studies* 7, no. 5 (September): 675-696.

BROWN, JOHN SEELY, RICHARD R. BURTON, AND JOHAN DE KLEER. 1982. "Pedagogical Natural Language, and Knowledge Engineering Techniques in SOPHIE I, II, and III." In *Intelligent Tutoring Systems*, ed. D. Sleeman and J. S. Brown, pp. 227-282. New York: Academic Press.

BROWN, JOHN SEELY, AND KURT VAN LEHN. 1980. "Repair Theory." *Cognitive Science* 4, no. 4 (October-December): 379-426.

BRUCKERT, ED. 1984. "A New Text-to-Speech Product Produces Dynamic Human-Quality Voice." *Speech Technology* 2, no. 2 (January-February): 114-119.

BUCHANAN, BRUCE G., AND EDWARD A. FEIGENBAUM. 1978. "DENDRAL and Meta-DENDRAL: Their Application Dimension." *Journal of Artificial Intelligence* 11: 5-24.

BUCHANAN, BRUCE G., AND EDWARD H. SHORTLIFFE. 1984. *Rule-Based Expert Systems: The MYCIN Experiments of the Stanford Heuristic Programming Project.* Reading, MA: Addison-Wesley.

BURNETT, J. DALE D., AND LARRY MILLER. 1984. "Computer-Assisted Learning and Reading: Developing the Product or Fostering the Process." *Computer Education* 8, no. 1 (April): 145-150.

BURNS, HUGH. 1984a. "Recollections of First-Generation Computer-Assisted Prewriting." In *The Computer in Composition Instruction: A Writer's Tool,* ed. William Wresch, pp. 15-33. Urbana, IL: National Council of Teachers of English.

BURNS, HUGH. 1984b. "The Challenge for Computer-Assisted Rhetoric." *Computers and the Humanities* 18, no. 3/4 (July): 173-182.

BURNS, PATRICIA KNIGHT, AND WILLIAM C. BOZEMAN. 1981. "Computer-Assisted Instruction and Math Achievement: Is There a Relationship?" *Educational Technology* 21, no. 10 (October): 32-39.

BURTON, RICHARD R. 1982. "Diagnosing Bugs in a Simple Procedural Skill." In *Intelligent Tutoring Systems,* ed. D. Sleeman and J. S. Brown, pp. 157-184. New York: Academic Press.

BURTON, RICHARD R., AND JOHN SEELY BROWN. 1982. "An Investigation of Computer Coaching for Information Learning Activities." In *Intelligent Tutoring Systems,* ed. D. Sleeman and J. S. Brown, pp. 79-98. New York: Academic Press.

CALKINS, LUCY MCCORMICK. 1986. *The Art of Teaching Writing.* Portsmouth, NH: Heinemann.

CALVERT, E. J., AND R. C. WESTFALL. 1982. "A Comparison of Conventional and Automated Administration of Raven's Standard Progressive Matrices." *International Journal of Man-Machine Studies* 17, no. 3 (October): 305-310.

CARBONELL, JAIME R. 1970. "AI in CAI: An Artificial-Intelligence Approach to Computer-Assisted Instruction." *IEEE Transactions on Man-Machine Systems* 11, no. 4 (December): 190-202.

CARMODY, STEVEN, WALTER GROSS, THEODOR H. NELSON, DAVID RICE, AND ANDRIES VAN DAM. 1969. "A Hypertext Editing System for the /360." In *Pertinent Concepts in Computer Graphics,* ed. M. Faiman and J. Nievergelt, pp. 291-330. Urbana: University of Illinois Press.

CALVIN, CLAUDIA S., E. D. CAVIN, AND J. J. LAGOWKSI. 1981. "The Effect of CAI on the Attitudes of College Students Towards Computers and Chemistry." *Journal of Research in Science Teaching* 18, no. 4 (July): 329-333.

CHAMBERS, J. 1987. "Interactive Video: A Genuine or Imagined Potential." *British Journal of Educational Technology* 18, no. 1 (January): 21-24.

CHEN, PETER PIN-SHAN. 1986. "The Compact Disk ROM: How It Works." *IEEE Spectrum* 23, no. 4 (April): 44-49.

CHOMSKY, CAROL. 1986. "Media in Reading Instruction." Abstract of presentation at American Educational Research Association, San Francisco, April.

CLANCEY, WILLIAM J. 1979. "Dialogue Management for Rule-Based Tutorials." In *Proceedings of the International Joint Conference on Artificial Intelligence,* vol. 6, pp. 155-161. Los Altos, CA: William Kaufmann.

CLANCEY, WILLIAM J. 1982. "Tutoring Roles for Guiding a Case Method Dialogue." In *Intelligent Tutoring Systems,* ed. D. Sleeman and J. S. Brown, pp. 201-226. New York: Academic Press.

CLARK, RICHARD E. 1982. "Antagonism Between Achievement and Enjoyment ATI Studies." *Educational Psychologist* 17, no. 2 (Spring): 92-101.

CLARK, RICHARD E. 1983. "Reconsidering Research from Media." *Review of Educational Research* 53, no. 4 (Winter): 445-459.

CLARK, RICHARD E., AND STUART LEONARD. 1985. "Computer Research Confounding." Paper presented at American Educational Research Association, Chicago, March.

CLEMENT, FRANK J. 1981. "Affective Considerations in Computer-Based Education." *Educational Technology* 21, no. 4 (April): 28-32.

COLBY, KENNETH MARK, SYLVIA WEBER, AND FRANKLIN DENNIS HILF. 1971. "Artificial Paranoia." *Artificial Intelligence* 2, no. 1 (Spring): 1-25.

COLLIER, RICHARD M. 1983. "The Word Processor and Revision Strategies." *College Composition and Communication* 34, no. 2 (May): 149-155.

COLLINS, CARMEN. 1984. *Read, Write, Reflect.* Englewood Cliffs, NJ: Prentice Hall.

COOMBS, MIKE, AND JIM ALTY. 1984. "Expert Systems: An Alternative Paradigm." In *Developments in Expert Systems*, ed. M. J. Coombs, pp. 135-157. London: Academic Books.

CULBERTSON, JACK A., AND LUVERN L. CUNNINGHAM (EDS.). 1986. *Microcomputers and Education: Eighty-fifth Yearbook of the National Society for the Study of Education*, Part 1. Chicago: University of Chicago Press.

CUSHMAN, WILLIAM F. 1986. "Reading from Microfiche, a VDT, and the Printed Page: Subjective Fatigue and Performance." *Human Factors* 28, no. 1 (February): 63-74.

DAIUTE, COLETTE. 1986. "Physical and Cognitive Factors in Revising: Insights from Studies with Computers." *Research in the Teaching of English* 20, no. 2 (May): 141-159.

DAIUTE, COLETTE A. 1982. "Computers and Writing." Paper presented at Computing and Writing Consortia of the Metropolitan School Study Council, Columbia University, New York, July.

DAIUTE, COLETTE A. 1983. "The Computer as Stylus and Audience." *College Composition and Communication* 34, no. 2 (May): 134-145.

DANIEL, DANNY B. In press. "The Construct of Legibility in the Reading Environment of a Microcomputer." In *Computers and Reading: Issues for Theory and Practice*, ed. David Reinking. New York: Teachers College Press.

DAVIDOVE, ERIC A. "Design and Production of Interactive Videodisc Programming." *Educational Technology* 26, no. 8 (August): 7-14.

DAVIES, IVOR K., AND HAROLD G. SHANE. 1986. "Educational Implications of Microelectronic Networks." In *Microcomputers and Education*, 85th Yearbook of the National Society for the Study of Education, Part I, ed. Jack A. Culbertson and Luvern L. Cunningham, pp. 1-21. Chicago: University of Chicago Press.

DAVIS, FREDERICK B. (ED.). 1971. *The Literature of Research in Reading with Emphasis on Models.* New Brunswick, NJ: Graduate School of Education, Rutgers University.

DAVIS, FREDERICK B. 1972. "Psychometric Research on Comprehension in Reading." *Reading Research Quarterly* 7, no. 4 (Summer): 628-678.

DAVIS, RANDALL. 1984. "Interactive Transfer of Expertise." In *Rule-Based Expert Systems*, ed. Bruce G. Buchanan and Edward H. Shortliffe, pp. 171-208. Reading, MA: Addison-Wesley.

DAVY, JOHN. 1984. "Mindstorms in the Lamplight." In *The Computer in Education: A Critical Perspective*, ed. Douglas Sloan, pp. 11-20. New York: Teachers College Press.

DAWKINS, RICHARD. 1981. "Selfish Genes and Selfish Memes." In *The Mind's I*, ed. Douglas R. Hofstadter and Daniel C. Dennett, pp. 124-144. New York: Bantam Books. [Excerpted from Richard Dawkins, *The Selfish Gene.* London: Oxford University Press, 1976]

DEDE, CHRISTOPHER. 1986. "A Review and Synthesis of Recent Research in Intelligent Computer-Assisted Instruction." *International Journal of Man-Machine Studies* 24, no. 4 (April): 329-353.

DEDE, CHRISTOPHER J., PHILIP P. ZODHIATES, AND CHARLES L. THOMPSON. 1985. "Intelligent Computer-Assisted Instruction: A Review and Assessment of ICAI Research and Its Potential for Education." Newton, MA: Educational Technology Center.

DICKINSON, DAVID K. 1985. "Young Children's Collaborative Writing at the Computer." Paper presented at American Educational Research Association, Chicago, March.

DICKSON, WAYNE, AND MIKE RAYMOND. 1984. *The Language Arts Computer Book: A How-to Guide for Teachers.* Reston, VA: Reston Publishing.

DOUGLAS, ELI, AND DEBORAH G. BRYANT. 1985. "Implementing Computer-Assisted Instruction: The Garland Way." *T.H.E. Journal* 13, no. 2 (September): 86-91.

DOYLE, CLAIRE. 1983. "Writing and Reading Instruction Using the Microcomputer." *T.H.E. Journal* 1, no. 1 (September): 144-145.

DREYER, LOIS G., ANN E. BOEHM, AND BARBARA SANDBERG. 1984. "Computer-Assisted Reading Remediation: A Three-Way Interaction." Paper presented at the National Reading Conference, St. Petersburg, FL, December.

DREYFUS, HUBERT L., AND STUART E. DREYFUS. 1984. "Putting Computers in Their Proper Place: Analysis vs. Intuition in the Classroom." *Teachers College Record* 85, no. 4 (Summer): 578-601.

DREYFUS, HUBERT L., AND STUART E. DREYFUS. 1986. *Mind over Machine*. New York: Free Press.

DUDA, RICHARD, JOHN GASCHNIG, AND PETER HART. 1979. "Model Design in the PROSPECTOR Consultant System for Mineral Exploration." In *Expert Systems in the Micro Electronic Age*, ed. Donald Michie, pp. 153-167. Edinburgh: Edinburgh University Press.

DUDLEY, ART. 1983. "Integrated Learning Systems." *Electronic Learning* 5, no. 6 (February): 72-76.

DUNN, RITA, AND KENNETH DUNN. 1978. *Teaching Students Through Their Learning Styles: A Practical Approach*. Reston, VA: Reston Publishing.

DURKIN, DOLORES. 1978-1979. "What Classroom Observations Reveal About Reading Comprehension Instruction." *Reading Research Quarterly* 14, no. 4 (Summer): 481-533.

DWECK, CAROL S., AND JANINE BEMPECHAT. 1983. "Children's Theories of Intelligence: Consequence for Learning." In *Learning and Motivation in the Classroom*, ed. Scott G. Paris, Gary M. Olson, and Harold W. Stevenson, pp. 239-258. Hillsdale, NJ: Lawrence Erlbaum.

EASTMAN, SUSAN TYLER. 1984. "Videotex in Middle School: Accommodating Computers and Printouts in Learning Information Processing Skills." Paper presented at International Communication Association, San Francisco, May. [ERIC Document Reproduction no. 248 870]

EDUCATIONAL PRODUCTS INFORMATION EXCHANGE. 1986. "VDTs and Their Impact on Users." *MICROgram* 4, no. 9 (June): 1-4.

EDUCATIONAL TESTING SERVICE. 1984. *The ETS Evaluation of Writing to Read*. Princeton, NJ: Educational Testing Service.

EDWARDS, JUDITH, SHIRLEY NORTON, SANDRA TAYLOR, MARTHA WEISS, AND RALPH DUSSELDORP. 1975. "How Effective is CAI? A Review of the Research." *Educational Leadership* 33, no. 2 (November):147-153.

ELLIOT, PAUL, AND RICHARD VIDEBECK. 1973. "Reading Comprehension Materials for High School Equivalency Students on the PLATO IV Computer-Based Education System." *Educational Technology* 13, no. 9 (September): 20-22.

ELSER, LESLIE. 1985. "Can Kids Outgrow Word Processing Programs?" *Classroom Computer Learning* 5, no. 5 (February): 52-55.

ENGLEBERT, DOUGLAS C., AND WILLIAM K. ENGLISH. 1968. "A Research Center for Augmenting Human Intellect." *Joint Computer Conference* 33, no. 1 (Fall): 395-410.

EPSTEIN, WILLIAM. 1967. "Some Conditions of the Influence of Syntactical Structure on Learning: Grammatical Transformation, Learning Instruction, and Chunking." *Journal of Verbal Learning and Verbal Behavior* 6, no. 3 (June): 415-419.

EYSENCK, H. J. 1978. "An Exercise in Mega-Silliness." *American Psychologist* 33, no. 5 (May): 517.

FEELEY, JOAN, AND SHELLEY WEPNER. 1986. "Rate Improvement in College: The Computer vs. Traditional Print." Paper presented at the College Reading Association, Knoxville, TN, October.

FEINER, STEVEN, SANDOR NAGY, AND ANDRIES VAN DAM. 1982. "An Experimental System for Creating and Presenting Interactive Graphical Documents." *ACM Transactions on Graphics* 1, no. 1 (January): 59-77.

FISHER, GLENN. 1983. "Where CAI Is Effective: A Summary of the Research." *Electronic Learning* 3, no. 3 (November-December): 82-84.

FLAVELL, JOHN H. 1979. "Metacognition and Cognitive Monitoring—A New Era of Cognitive-Developmental Inquiry." *American Psychologist*, 34, no. 10 (October): 906-911.

FLEMING, MALCOLM L., AND W. HOWARD LEVIE. 1978. *Instructional Message Design: Principles from the Behavioral Sciences*. Englewood Cliffs, NJ: Educational Technology Publications.

FLETCHER, J. D., AND R. C. ATKINSON. 1972. "Evaluation of the Stanford CAI Program in Initial Reading." *Journal of Educational Psychology* 63, no. 6 (December): 597-602.

FRASE, LAWRENCE T. In press. "Computer Analysis of Written Materials." In *Computers and Reading: Issues for Theory and Practice*, ed. David Reinking. New York: Teachers College Press.

FRASE, LAWRENCE T., AND MARY DIEL. 1986. "UNIX Writer's Workbench: Software for Streamlined Communication." *T.H.E. Journal* 14, no. 3 (October): 74-78.

FRASE, LAWRENCE T., NINA H. MACDONALD, PATRICIA S. GINGRICH, STACEY A. KEENAN, AND JAMES L. COLLYMORE. 1981. "Computer Aids for Text Assessment and Writing Instruction." *National Society for Programmed Instruction Journal* 20, no. 9 (November): 21-24.

FULLAN, MICHAEL. 1982. *The Meaning of Educational Change.* New York: Teachers College Press.

FULLAN, MICHAEL. 1985. "Change Processes and Strategies at the Local Level." *Elementary School Journal* 85, no. 3 (January): 391-421.

GAMBRELL, LINDA B., VIRGINIA N. BRADLEY, AND ELAINE M. MCLAUGHLIN. 1985. "Young Children's Comprehension and Recall of Computer Screen Displayed Text." Paper presented at the College Reading Association, Pittsburgh, October.

GARHART, CASEY, AND MICHAEL HANNAFIN. 1986. "The Accuracy of Cognitive Monitoring During Computer-Based Instruction." *Journal of Computer-Based Instruction* 13, no. 3 (Summer): 88-93.

GARRETT, NORMAN A. 1984. "Using Compuserve to Facilitate Co-Writing." In *Microcomputers in Educational Conference: Literacy Plus,* ed. Ruth A. Camuse, pp. 158-162. Rockville, MD: Computer Science Press.

GAY, GERALDINE. 1986. "Interaction of Learner Control and Prior Understanding in Computer-Assisted Video Instruction." *Journal of Educational Psychology* 78, no. 3 (June): 225-227.

GELLNER, E. A. 1964. "Model (Theoretical Model)." In *A Dictionary of the Social Sciences,* ed. Julius Gould and William L. Kolb, p. 435. New York: Free Press.

GENISHI, CELIA, PAMELA MCCOLLUM, AND ELIZABETH STAND. 1985. "Research Currents: The Interactional Richness of Children's Computer Use." *Language Arts* 62, no. 5 (September): 526-532.

GIL, DORON, ETHELYN HUFFMEYER, JOEL VAN ROEKEL, AND ANNETTE WEINSHANK. 1979. *Clinical Problem-Solving in Reading: Theory and Research.* Research Series no. 45. East Lansing: Institute for Research on Teaching, Michigan State University.

GILMAN, DAVID ALAN. 1969. "The Effect of Feedback on Learners' Certainty of Response and Attitude Toward Instruction in a Computer-Assisted Instruction Program for Teaching Science Concepts." *Journal of Research in Science Teaching* 6, no. 2: 171-184.

GILMORE, JOHN F., AND KURT PULASKI. 1985. "A Survey of Expert System Tools." In *Proceedings of the Second Conference on Artificial Intelligence Applications,* pp. 408-502. Washington, DC: IEEE Computer Society Press.

GLEASON, GERALD T. 1981. "Microcomputers in Education: The State of the Art." *Educational Technology* 21, no. 3 (March): 7-18.

GLOSSBRENNER, ALFRED. 1985. *The Complete Handbook of Personal Computer Communication: Everything You Need to Go Online with the World.* New York: St. Martin's Press.

GOLDSTEIN, IRA P. 1982. "The Genetic Graph: A Representation for the Evolution of Procedural Knowledge." In *Intelligent Tutoring Systems,* ed. D. Sleeman and J. S. Brown, pp. 51-78. New York: Academic Press.

GOODMAN, KENNETH. 1967. "Reading: A Psycholinguistic Guessing Game." *Journal of the Reading Specialist* 6, no. 4 (May): 126-135.

GOODMAN, KENNETH. 1976. "Behind the Eye: What Happens in Reading.: In *Theoretical Models and Processes of Reading,* 2nd ed., ed. Harry Singer and Robert B. Ruddell, pp. 470-496. Newark, DE: International Reading Association.

GOODMAN, KENNETH S. 1986. *What's Whole in Whole Language?* Portsmouth, NH: Heinemann.

GOTT, SHERRIE P. 1986. "Utility of Cognitive Task Analysis for Examining Complex Technical Skills." Paper presented at the American Educational Research Association, San Francisco, April.

GOUGH, PHILIP B. 1972. "One Second of Reading." In *Language by Ear and by Eye,* ed. James F. Kavanagh and Ignatius G. Mattingly, pp. 331-358. Cambridge, MA: MIT Press.

GRAVES, DONALD H. 1976. "Let's Get Rid of the Welfare Mess in the Teaching of Writing." *Language Arts* 53, no. 6 (September): 645-651.

GRAVES, DONALD. 1983. *Writing: Teachers and Children at Work.* Portsmouth, NH: Heinemann.

GREEN, BERT F., ALICE K. WOLF, CAROL CHOMSKY, AND KENNETH LAUGHERY. 1963. "Baseball: An Automatic Question Answerer." In *Computers and Thought,* ed. Edward A.

Feigenbaum and Julian Feldman, pp. 207-216. Malabar, FL: Robert E. Krieger. [Reprinted New York: McGraw-Hill, 1981]

GREENE, BETH G., AND DAVID B. PISONI. In press. "Perception of Synthetic Speech by Adults and Children: Research on Processing Voice Output from Text-to-Speech Systems." In *The Vocally Impaired*, vol. 2, ed. L. E. Bernstein. New York: Academic Press.

GREENE, BETH G., JOHN S. LOGAN, AND DAVID B. PISONI. 1986. "Perception of Synthetic Speech Produced Automatically by Rule: Intelligibility of Eight Text-to-Speech Systems." *Behavior Research Methods, Instruments, and Computers* 18, no. 2 (April): 100-107.

GREENO, JAMES G. 1985. "Advancing Cognitive Science Through Development of Advanced Instructional Systems." Paper presented at American Educational Research Association, Chicago, April.

GREENWOOD, CHARLES R., JOSEPH C. DELQUADRI, AND R. VANCE HALL. 1984. "Opportunity to Respond and Student Academic Performance." In *Focus on Behavior Analysis in Education*, ed. William L. Heward, pp. 58-88. Westerville, OH: Charles Merrill.

GRESSARD, CLARICE, AND BRENDA H. LOYD. 1985. "Age and Staff Development Experience with Computers as Factors Affecting Teacher Attitudes Towards Computers." *School Science and Mathematics* 85, no. 3 (March): 203-209.

GRUBB, RALPH E. 1977. "Student Control: Exploration in CAI." In *Computers and Communication: Implications for Education*, ed. Robert J. Seidel and Martin Rubin, pp. 237-244. New York: Academic Press.

GUNTON, COLIN E. 1985. *Enlightenment and Alienation*. Grand Rapids, MI: William B. Eerdmans.

GUSKEY, THOMAS R. 1986. "Staff Development and the Process of Teacher Change." *Educational Researcher* 15, no. 5 (May): 5-12.

HAAS, CHRISTINA, AND JOHN R. HAYES. 1986. "What Did I Just Say? Reading Problems in Writing with the Machine." *Research in the Teaching of English* 20, no. 1 (February): 22-35.

HAGUE, SALLY, AND NANCY CHILDERS. 1986. "Micros and Reading: What Do Secondary Reading Teachers Say?" Paper presented at the College Reading Association, Knoxville, TN, October.

HAMBLETON, RONALD K., AND HARIHARAN SWAMINATHAN. 1985. *Item Response Theory: Principles and Applications*. Boston: Kluwer Nijhoff.

HANNAFIN, MICHAEL J. 1985. "Empirical Issues in the Study of Computer-Assisted Interactive Video." *ECTJ: Educational Communications and Technology Journal* 33, no. 4 (Winter): 235-247.

HANSEN, CRAIG, AND LANCE WILCOX. 1984. "Adapting Microcomputers for Use in College Composition Courses." Paper presented at the meeting of the Delaware Valley Writing Council, Villanova, PA, February. [ERIC Document Reproduction no. ED 247 609]

HARRIS, CAROLYN, DeMEYER, ROBERT SANDACCA, AND BEVERLY HUNTER. 1985. "Evaluation of the TSC Dolphin Computer Assisted Instructional System in the Chapter 1 Program of the District of Columbia Public Schools." Report no. 85-9. Alexandria, VA: Human Resources Research Organization.

HARSTE, JEROME C., VIRGINIA A. WOODWARD, AND CAROLYN L. BURKE. 1984. *Language Stories & Literacy Lessons*. Portsmouth, NH: Heinemann.

HARTLEY, JAMES. 1982. "Designing Instructional Text." In *The Technology of Text*, ed. David H. Jonassen, pp. 193-214. Englewood Cliffs, NJ: Educational Technology Publications.

HARTLEY, SUSAN STRAIT. 1977. "Meta-Analysis of the Effects of Individually Paced Instruction in Mathematics." Doctoral dissertation, University of Colorado. [*Dissertation Abstracts*, 38, no. 7 (1978), p. 4003-A. Order no. 77-29, 926]

HASHIMOTO, IRWIN. 1985. "Structured Heuristic Procedures: Their Limitations." *College Composition and Communication* 36, no. 1 (February): 73-81.

HAWKINS, JAN. 1983. "Learning LOGO Together: The Social Context." Technical Report no. 13. New York: Center for Children and Technology, Bank Street College of Education.

HAWKINS, JAN. 1984. "Computers and Girls: Rethinking the Issues." Technical Report no. 24. New York: Center for Children and Technology, Bank Street College of Education.

HAWKINS, JAN, AND KAREN SHEINGOLD. 1986. "The Beginning of a Story: Computers and the Organization of Learning in Classrooms." In *Microcomputers and Education*, 85th Yearbook of the National Society for the Study of Education, Part I, ed. Jack A.

Culbertson and Luvern L. Cunningham, pp. 40-58. Chicago: University of Chicago Press.

HAWKINS, JAN, KAREN SHEINGOLD, MARYL GEARHART, AND CHANA BERGER. 1982. "Microcomputers in Schools: Impact on the Social Life of Elementary Classrooms." *Journal of Applied Developmental Psychology* 3, no. 4 (October-December): 361-373.

HAYNES, JACQUELINE A., BARBARA A. KAPINUS, DAVID MALOUF, AND CHARLES MAC-ARTHUR. 1984. "An Investigation of Disabled Readers' Perceived Mastery of Word Meanings Using Microcomputer and Traditional Practice Techniques." Paper presented at the National Reading Conference, St. Petersburg Beach, FL, December.

HEINES, JESSE M. 1983. "Basic Concepts in Knowledge-Based Systems." *Machine-Mediated Learning* 1, no. 1 (April): 65-95.

HEPPNER, FRANK H., JOHN G. T. ANDERSON, ALAN E. FARSTRUP, AND NELSON H. WEIDERMAN. 1985. "Reading Performance on a Standardized Test Is Better From Print than from Computer Display." *Journal of Reading* 28, no. 4 (January): 321-325.

HISCOX, MICHAEL D., AND SUZANNE B. HISCOX. 1986. "The Potential of OD-ROM in Education." *TechTrends* 31, no. 3 (April): 14-19.

HOFFMAN, KAAREN I., AND GEORGE D. LUNDBERG. 1976. "A Comparison of Computer-Monitored Group Tests with Paper-and-Pencil Tests." *Educational and Psychological Measurement* 36, no. 4 (Winter): 791-809.

HOFFMAN, PAUL E. 1986. "Book Reviews—CD ROM: The New Papyrus." *Byte* 11, no. 10 (October): 65-68.

HOFSTADTER, DOUGLAS R., AND DANIEL C. DENNETT. (EDS.) 1981. *The Mind's I.* New York: Bantam.

HOLZMAN, THOMAS G., AND ROBERT GLASER. 1977. "Developing a Computer Literacy in Children, Some Observations and Suggestions." *Educational Technology* 17, no. 8 (August): 5-11.

HOUGHTON MIFFLIN. 1981. Reading Skills: 3-8. Hanover, NH: Houghton Mifflin.

HOUSE, ARTHUR S., CARL E. WILLIAMS, MICHAEL H. L. HECKER, AND K. D. KRYTER. 1965. "Articulation-Testing Methods: Consonantal Differentiation with a Closed-Response Set." *Journal of the Acoustical Society of America* 37, no. 1 (January): 158-166.

HOWE, SAMUEL. 1984. "Interactive Video." *Instructor* 93, no. 5 (January): 108-110.

HOYLE, ERIC. 1983. "Computers and Education: A Solution in Search of a Problem?" In *World Yearbook of Education 1982/83: Computers and Education*, ed. Jacquetta Megarry, David R. F. Walker, Stanley Nisbett, and Eric Hoyle, pp. 55-69. New York: Nichols Publishing.

HSU, TSE-CHI. 1986. "Developments in Microcomputer Applications to Testing." Paper presented at American Educational Research Association, San Francisco, April.

HSU, TSE-CHI, AND ANTHONY J. NITKO. 1983. "Microcomputer Testing Software Teachers Can Use." *Educational Measurement: Issues and Practice* 2, no. 3 (Winter): 15-30.

HUEY, EDMUND BURKE. 1908. *The Psychology and Pedagogy of Reading.* New York: Macmillan. [Republished Cambridge, MA: MIT Press, 1968]

HUSSERL, EDMUND. 1931. *Ideas: General Introduction to Pure Phenomenology.* Trans. W. R. Boyce Gibson. New York: Collier Books. [German original published in 1913]

JACKSON, GREGG B. 1980. "Methods for Integrative Reviews." *Review of Educational Research* 50, no. 3 (Fall): 438-460.

JACKSON, GREGORY A., AND TERRENCE E. DEAL. 1985. "Technology, Learning Environments, and Tomorrow's Schools." *Peabody Journal of Education* 62, no. 2 (Winter): 93-113.

JAMISON, DEAN N., PATRICK SUPPES, AND STUART WELLS. 1974. "Effectiveness of Alternative Instructional Media." *Review of Educational Research* 44, no. 1 (Winter): 1-67.

JANDREAU, STEVEN M., STEVEN J. MUNCER, AND THOMAS G. BEVER. 1986. "Improving the Readability of Text with Automatic Phrase-Sensitive Formating." *British Journal of Educational Technology* 17, no. 1 (May): 128-133.

JARCHOW, ELAINE, AND JANEY MONTGOMERY. 1985. "Dare to Use Adventure Games in the Language Arts Classroom." *English Journal* 74, no. 2 (February): 104-106.

JENKINS, TRACIE M., AND ELIZABETH J. DANKERT. 1981. "Results of a Three Month PLATO Trial in Terms of Utilization and Student Attitudes." *Educational Technology* 21, no. 3 (March): 44-47.

JENSEN, KAREN, AND GEORGE E. HEIDORN. 1984. "First Aid to Authors: The IBM EPISTLE Text-Critiquing System." In *Digest of Papers: Spring Compcon 84, 28th IEEE Computer Society International Conference*, pp. 462-464. Los Alamitos, CA: IEEE Computer Society Press.

JOHNS, J. L. 1982. "Research in Reading: A Century of Inquiry." In *Summary of Investigations Related to Reading, July 1, 1980, to June 30, 1981*, ed. Samuel Weintraub, Helen K. Smith, Gus P. Plessas, Nancy L. Roser, Walter R. Hill, and Michael W. Kibby, pp. v-ix. Newark, DE: International Reading Association.

JOHNS, JERRY L. 1981. *Advanced Reading Inventory*. Dubuque, IA: William C. Brown.

JONES, GARY L., AND KENNETH D. KEITH. 1983. "Computer Clinical Simulations in Health Sciences." *Journal of Computer-Based Instruction* 9, no. 3 (Winter): 108-114.

JONES, MARLENE. 1984. "Expert Systems: Their Potential Roles Within Special Education." *Peabody Journal of Education* 62, no. 1 (Fall): 52-66.

KAMIL, MICHAEL L. 1982. "Technology and Reading: A Review of Research and Instruction." In *New Inquiries in Reading Research and Instruction*, 31st Yearbook of the National Reading Conference, ed. Jerome A. Niles and Larry A. Harris, pp. 251-260. Rochester, NY: National Reading Conference.

KAPLAN, GADI. 1986. "IEEE Publications on Disk." *IEEE Spectrum* 23, no. 4 (April): 45.

KEEFE, JAMES W. 1979. "Learning Styles: An Overview." In *Student Learning Styles*, pp. 156-163. Reston, VA: NASSP Publications.

KENNEDY, MARY LYNCH. 1980. "Reading and Writing: Interrelated Skills of Literacy on the College Level." *Reading World* 20, no. 2 (December): 131-141.

KINDMAN-KOFFLER, BETTE. 1984-1985. "Artificial Intelligence: Improving Software Through Research." *The Reading Instruction Journal* 28, no. 2 (Winter): 21-23.

KLARE, GEORGE R., WILLIAM H. NICHOLS, AND EMIR H. SHUFORD. 1957. "The Relationship of Typographic Arrangement to the Learning of Technical Training Material." *Journal of Applied Psychology* 41, no. 1 (February): 41-45.

KOCH, KENNETH. 1970. *Wishes, Lies and Dreams*. New York: Vintage Books.

KOETKE, WALTER. 1984. "Computers, Children and Learning: One Complete Iteration." *Creative Computing* 10, no. 11 (November): 163-169.

KOLODNER, JANET L. 1984. "Towards an Understanding of the Role of Experience in the Evolution from Novice to Expert." In *Developments in Expert Systems*, ed. M. J. Coombs, pp. 95-116. London: Academic Press.

KRUK, RICHARD S., AND PAUL MUTER. 1984. "Reading of Continuous Text on Video Screens." *Human Factors* 26, no. 3 (June): 339-346.

KUHN, THOMAS S. 1962. *The Structure of Scientific Revolutions*. Chicago: University of Chicago Press.

KULHAVY, RAYMOND W., AND RICHARD C. ANDERSON. 1972. "Delay-Retention Effect with Multiple-Choice Tests." *Journal of Educational Psychology* 63, no. 5 (October): 505-512.

KULIK, CHEN-LIN, AND JAMES A. KULIK. 1986. "Effectiveness of Computer-Based Education in Colleges." *AEDS Journal* 19, no. 2-3 (Winter-Spring): 81-108.

KULIK, CHEN-LIN, JAMES A. KULIK, AND BARBARA J. SCHWALB. 1986. "The Effectiveness of Computer-Based Adult Education: A Meta-Analysis." *Journal of Educational Computing Research* 2, no. 2: 235-252.

KULIK, JAMES A., ROBERT L. BANGERT, AND GEORGE W. WILLIAMS. 1983. "Effects of Computer-Based Teaching on Secondary School Students." *Journal of Educational Psychology* 75, no. 1 (February): 19-26.

KULIK, JAMES A., CHEN-LIN KULIK, AND ROBERT L. BANGERT-DROWNS. 1985a. "Effects of Computer-Based Education in Elementary Schools." *Computers in Human Behavior* 1, no. 1 (Winter): 59-74.

KULIK, JAMES A., CHEN-LIN KULIK, AND ROBERT L. BANGERT-DROWNS. 1985b. "The Importance of Outcome Studies: A Reply to Clark." *Journal of Educational Computing Research* 1, no. 4 (April): 381-387.

KULIK, JAMES A., CHEN-LIN C. KULIK, AND PETER A. COHEN. 1980. "Effectiveness of Computer-Based College Teaching: A Meta-Analysis of Findings." *Review of Educational Research* 50, no. 4 (Winter): 525-544.

LABERGE, DAVID, AND S. JAY SAMUELS. 1974. "Toward a Theory of Automatic Information Processing in Reading." *Cognitive Psychology* 6, no. 2 (April): 293-323.

LAGRANGE, MARIE-SALOME, AND MONIQUE RENAUD. 1985. "Intelligent Knowledge-Based Systems in Archaeology: A Computerized Simulation of Reasoning by Means of an Expert System." *Computers and Humanities* 19, no. 1 (January-March): 37-49.

LAJOIE, SUSANNE P. 1986. "Cognitive Task Analysis: Implications for Intelligent Tutor Development." Paper presented at the American Educational Research Association, San Francisco, April.

LAKE, DANIEL T. 1986. "Telecommunications from the Classroom." *The Computing Teacher* 13, no. 7 (April): 43-46.

L'ALLIER, JAMES JOSEPH. 1980. "An Evaluation Study of a Computer-Based Lesson That Adjusts Reading Level by Monitoring On-Task Reader Characteristics." Doctoral dissertation, University of Minnesota. [*Dissertation Abstracts*, 41, no. 7 (1981), p. 2914-A. Order no. 81-02, 111]

LAMBERT, STEVE, AND SUZANNE ROPIEQUET. (EDS.) 1986. *CD ROM: The New Papyrus*. Redmond, WA: Microsoft Press.

LASOFF, EDWARD MARVIN. 1981. "The Effects of Feedback in Both Computer-Assisted Instruction and Programmed Instruction on Achievement and Attitude." Doctoral dissertation, University of Miami. [*Dissertation Abstracts*, 42, no. 4 (1982), p. 1553-A. Order no. 81-21, 115]

LEDLEY, ROBERT, AND LEE B. LUSTED. 1959. "Reasoning Foundations of Medical Diagnosis." *Science* 130, no. 3366 (July 3): 9-21.

LEINHARDT, GAEA, NAOMI ZIGMOND, AND WILLIAM W. COOLEY. 1981. "Reading Instruction and Its Effects." *American Educational Research Journal* 18, no. 3 (Fall): 343-361.

LESGOLD, ALAN N. 1983. "A Rationale for Computer-Based Reading Instruction." In *Classroom Computers and Cognitive Science*, ed. Alex Cherry Wilkinson, pp. 167-182. New York: Academic Press.

LESGOLD, ALAN M. 1985. "Critical Research Issues in the Implementation of the Next Generation of Educational Technology." Paper presented at American Educational Research Association, Chicago, April.

LESGOLD, ALAN M., AND CHARLES A. PERFETTI. 1981. *Interactive Processes in Reading*. Hillsdale, NJ: Lawrence Erlbaum.

LEVIN, HENRY M., AND GAIL R. MEISTER. "Computers in the Balance: Weighing Costs and Effectiveness." Report from Institute for Research on Educational Finance and Governance, Stanford University. Cited in Richard Alan Smith, "Learning from Media—A Controversy," *AEDS Monitor* 24, no. 1 & 2 (July/August 1985): 6, 24.

LEVINE, JANE. 1963. "Let's Debate Programmed Instruction." *The Reading Teacher* 16, no. 6 (March): 337-341.

LICHTMAN, DAVID. 1979. "Survey of Educators' Attitudes Towards Computers." *Creative Computing* 5, no. 1 (January): 48-50.

LIEBOWITZ, JAY. 1985. "Evaluation of Expert Systems: An Approach and Case Study." In *Proceedings of the Second Conference on Artificial Intelligence Applications*, pp. 564-571. Washington, DC: IEEE Computer Society Press.

LINDSAY, E. JAY, AND STEPHEN R. ROGERS. 1982. "Evaluation Study of Dolphin Mathematics, Reading, and Language Arts." Report no. 3. Hanover, NH: TSC.

LINN, MARCIA C. 1985. "The Cognitive Consequences of Programming Instruction in Classrooms." *Educational Researcher* 14, no. 5 (May): 14-16, 25-29.

LITTLEJOHN, TINA, RHONDA P. ROSS, AND PAUL V. GUMP. 1984. "Using Microcomputers in Elementary Schools: Implementation Issues." Paper presented at American Educational Research Association, New Orleans, April.

LORD, FREDERIC M. 1980. *Applications of Item Response Theory to Practical Testing Problems*. Hillsdale, NJ: Lawrence Erlbaum.

LORTIE, DAN C. 1975. *Schoolteacher: A Sociological Study*. Chicago: University of Chicago Press.

LOYD, BRENDA H., AND CLARICE GRESSARD. 1984. "The Effects of Sex, Age, and Computer Experience on Computer Attitudes." *AEDS Journal* 18, no. 2 (Winter): 67-77.

LOYD, BRENDA H., DOUGLAS E. LOYD, AND CLARICE GRESSARD. 1986. "Computer Attitudes: Differing Perspectives by Gender and Amount of Computer Experience." Paper presented at the American Educational Research Association, San Francisco, April.

LUCE, PAUL A., TIMOTHY C. FEUSTAL, AND DAVID B. PISONI. 1983. "Capacity Demands in Short-Term Memory for Synthetic and Natural Speech." *Human Factors* 25, no. 1 (February): 17-32.

LUEHRMANN, ARTHUR. 1985. "School of the Future = School of the Past: Adopting Micro-computers in Ways That Will and Won't Work." *Peabody Journal of Education* 62, no. 2 (Winter): 42-51.

MALONE, THOMAS W. 1981. "Toward a Theory of Intrinsically Motivating Instruction." *Cognitive Science* 5, no. 4 (October-December): 333-369.

MARKMAN, ELLEN M. 1979. "Realizing That You Don't Understand: Elementary School Children's Awareness of Inconsistencies." *Child Development*, 50, no. 3 (September): 643-655.

MARTIN, CHARLES E., MICHAEL A. MARTIN, AND D. G. O'BRIEN. 1984. "Spawning Ideas for Writing in the Content Areas." *Reading World* 24, no. 2 (December): 11-15.

MASON, GEORGE E. 1980. "Computerized Reading Instruction: A Review." *Educational Technology* 20, no. 10 (October): 18-22.

MASON, GEORGE E. 1986. "The Printout: The New Speaking Programs." *Reading Teacher* 39, no. 6 (February): 618-620.

MASON, GEORGE E., JAY S. BLANCHARD, AND DANNY B. DANIEL. 1983. *Computer Applications in Reading*, 2nd ed. Newark, DE: International Reading Association.

MAYER, RICHARD E. 1980. "Elaboration Techniques That Increase the Meaningfulness of Technical Text: An Experimental Test of the Learning Strategy Hypothesis." *Journal of Educational Psychology* 72, no. 6 (December): 770-784.

McBRIDE, JAMES R., AND JOHN T. MARTIN. 1983. "Reliability and Validity of Adaptive Ability Tests in a Military Setting." In *New Horizons in Testing*, ed. David J. Weiss, pp. 224-237. New York: Academic Press.

McCARTHY, JOHN. 1968. "Programs with Common Sense." In *Semantic Information Processing*, ed. Marvin Minsky, pp. 403-418. Cambridge, MA: MIT Press.

McCLINTOCK, ROBERT. 1986. "Into the Starting Gate: On Computing and the Curriculum." CC&T Technical Report no. 4. New York: Department of Communication, Computing, and Technology in Education, Teachers College, Columbia University.

McCOMBS, BARBARA L. 1985. "Instructor and Group Process Roles in Computer-Based Training." *ECTJ: Educational Communication and Technology Journal* 33, no. 3 (Fall): 159-168.

McCONKIE, GEORGE W., AND DAVID ZOLA. In press. "Two Examples of Computer-Based Research on Reading: Eye Movement Monitoring and Computer Aided Reading." In *Computers and Reading: Issues for Theory and Practice*, ed. David Reinking. New York: Teachers College Press.

McKENNA, MICHAEL. 1986a. "CARA: New Tool for Reading Assessment." *The Computing Teacher* 13, no. 5 (February): 16-19.

McKENNA, MICHAEL. 1986b. *CARA Manual*. Dubuque, IA: Kendall Hunt.

McKINLEY, ROBERT L., AND MARK D. RECKASE. 1984. "Implementing an Adaptive Testing Program in an Instructional Program Environment." Paper presented at American Educational Research Association, New Orleans, April.

McNINCH, GEORGE H., MARY B. CREAMER, AND GARY L. SHAFFER. 1985. "The Microcomputer Versus the Controlled Reader for the Presentation of Tachistoscopic Reading." Paper presented at the College Reading Association, Pittsburgh, October.

MERLEAU-PONTY, MAURICE. 1964. *The Primacy of Perception and Other Essays on Phenomenological Psychology*, ed. James E. Edie. Evanston, IL: Northwestern University Press.

MERRILL, M. DAVID. 1980. "Learner Control in Computer Based Learning." *Computers and Education* 4, no. 2: 77-95.

MICHAEL, G., AND M. SLIGER. 1976. *LARS Instructor's Manual*. Urbana: Computer-Based Education Laboratory, University of Illinois.

MICHAELS, SARAH. 1986. "The Computer as a Dependent Variable." Paper presented at the American Educational Research Association, San Francisco, April.

MILLER, ELWOOD E., AND MARY LOUIS MOSLEY (EDS.) 1985. *Educational Media and Technology Yearbook, 1985*. Vol. 11. Littleton, CO: Libraries Unlimited.

MILLER, L. A. 1981. "Natural Language Programming: Styles, Strategies and Contrasts." *IBM Systems Journal* 20, no. 2: 184-215.

MILLER, LARRY. 1985. "Computers and Writing: A Theoretical Perspective." *McGill Journal of Education* 20, no. 1 (Winter): 19-28.

MILLER, LARRY. 1987. "What Does the Reading Field Have to Say to Software Publishers?" Paper presented at the International Reading Association, Anaheim, CA, May.

MILLER, LARRY. In press. "Computers and the Language Arts: Publishing Without Perishing." *Canadian Journal of Language Arts.*

MILLER, LARRY, AND J. DALE BURNETT. 1986a. "The Puzzler: Reading Strategy Lessons in a Computer-Based Mode." *Reading-Canada-Lecture* 3, no. 1: 36-48.

MILLER, LARRY, AND J. DALE BURNETT. 1986b. "Theoretical Considerations in Selecting Language Arts Software." *Computing Education* 10, no. 1: 159-165.

MINSKY, MARVIN. 1975. "A Framework for Representing Knowledge." In *The Psychology of Computer Vision,* ed. Patrick Henry Winston, pp. 211-277. New York: McGraw-Hill.

MODLA, GINGER. 1986. "IBM's *Write to Read* Program." *Micro Missive* 4, no. 3 (April): 4-7.

MODLA, VIRGINIA B. 1986. "Microcomputers in Reading and Language Arts: A Syllabus." In *Preparation of Teachers for Microcomputer Instruction in Reading and Language Arts,* ed. Ernest Balajthy, pp. 35-41. Newark, DE: Special Interest Group on Microcomputers in Reading, International Reading Association.

MOFFET, JAMES, AND BETTY JANE WAGNER. 1983. *Student-Centered Language Arts and Reading: K-13.* 3rd ed. Boston: Houghton Mifflin.

MULLINS, CAROLYN J. 1985. "The SAT: Cramming with Your Computer." *Electronic Learning* 4, no. 7 (April): 31-35, 79.

MUNCER, S. J., B. S. GORMAN, S. GORMAN, AND D. BIBEL. 1986. "Right Is Wrong: An Examination of the Effect of Right Justification on Reading." *British Journal of Educational Technology* 17, no. 1 (January): 5-10.

NAU, DANA S. 1983. "Expert Computer Systems." *Computer* 16, no. 2 (February): 63-85.

NEGOITA, CONTANTIN VIRGIL. 1985. *Expert Systems and Fuzzy Systems.* Reading, MA: Benjamin/Cummings.

NEWELL, ALLEN. 1962. "Some Problems of Basic Organization in Problem-Solving Programs." In *Self-Organizing Systems,* ed. Marshall C. Yovits, George T. Jacobi, and Gordon D. Goldstein, pp. 393-423. Washington, DC: Spartan Books.

NEWELL, ALLEN. 1973. "Production Systems: Models of Control Structures." In *Visual Information Processing,* ed. William G. Chase, pp. 463-526. New York: Academic Press.

NEWELL, ALLEN, AND H. A. SIMON. 1963. "GPS, a Program That Simulates Human Thought." In *Computers and Thought,* ed. Edward A. Feigenbaum and Julian Feldman, pp. 279-293. New York: McGraw-Hill.

NEWMAN, JUDITH M. 1984. "Online: Reading, Writing and Computers." *Language Arts* 61, no. 7 (November): 758-763.

NILSSON, NILS J. 1980. *Principles of Artificial Intelligence.* Palo Alto, CA: Tioga.

NIST, SHERRIE L., AND RUTH C. SABOL. 1984. "Disparities Among Reading, Writing, and Oral Language: A Look at Underprepared College Students." *Reading World* 24, no. 2 (December): 96-104.

NORTON, DONNA E. 1985. *The Effective Teaching of Language Arts,* 2nd ed. Columbus, OH: Charles E. Merrill.

NUSBAUM, HOWARD C., AND DAVID B. PISONI. 1985. "Constraints on the Perception of Synthetic Speech Generated by Rule." *Behavior Research Methods, Instruments, and Computers* 17, no. 2 (April): 235-242.

OBERTINO, PRISCILLA. 1974. "The PLATO Reading Project." *Educational Technology* 14, no. 2 (February): 8-13.

O'CONNOR, MARY ANN, AND FRANK J. MOORE. 1986. "Applications: CD-ROM Goes to Work: Education." *CD-ROM Review* 1, no. 1: 30-31.

OHLSSON, STELLAN. 1986. "Some Principles of Intelligent Tutoring." *Instructional Science* 14, no. 3/4 (May): 293-326.

OLSEN, JAMES B., DENNIS B. MAYNES, DEAN SLAWSON, AND KEVIN HO. 1986. "Comparison and Equating of Paper-Administered, Computer-Administered, and Computerized Adaptive Tests of Achievement." Paper presented at American Educational Research Association, San Francisco, April.

OLSON, RICHARD, GREGORY FOLTZ, AND BARBARA WISE. 1986. "Reading Instruction and Remediation with the Aid of Computer Speech." *Behavior Research Methods, Instruments, and Computers* 18, no. 2 (April): 93-99.

OWINGS, RICHARD A., GAIL A. PETERSEN, JOHN D. BRANSFORD, C. DONALD MORRIS, AND BARRY S. STEIN. 1980. "Spontaneous Monitoring and Regulation of Learning: A

Comparison of Successful and Less Successful Fifth Graders." *Journal of Educational Psychology* 72, no. 2 (April): 250-256.

PALMER, DENNIS K. 1979. "STRIDE Reading: An Evaluation." Research report. Hanover, NH: Time Share Corporation.

PAPERT, SEYMOUR. 1980. *Mindstorms: Children, Computers, and Powerful Ideas.* New York: Basic Books.

PARK, OK-CHOON, AND ROBERT D. TENNYSON. 1986. "Computer-Based Response-Sensitive Design Strategies for Selecting Presentation Form and Sequence of Examples in Learning of Coordinate Concepts." *Journal of Educational Psychology* 78, no. 2 (April): 153-158.

PASCAL, BLAISE. 1938. *Pascal's Thoughts.* Translated by W. F. Trotter. New York: P. F. Collier and Son.

PATTISON, LINDA. 1985. "Software Writing Made Easy." *Electronic Learning* 4, no. 6 (March): 30-36.

PAUK, WALTER. 1974. *How to Study in College.* Boston: Houghton Mifflin.

PEA, ROY D., AND D. MIDIAN KURLAND. 1984. "On the Cognitive Effects of Learning Computer Programming." *New Ideas in Psychology* 2, no. 2 (Winter): 137-168.

PETERSON, PENELOPE L., AND ELIZABETH FENNEMA. 1985. "Effective Teaching, Student Engagement and Classroom Activities, and Sex-Related Differences in Learning Mathematics." *American Educational Research Journal* 22, no. 3 (Fall): 309-335.

PETKOVICH, MICHAEL D., AND ROBERT D. TENNYSON. 1984. "Clark's 'Learning from Media': A Critique." *ECTJ: Educational Communications and Technology Journal* 30, no. 4 (Winter): 240-250.

PETRICK, S. R. 1976. "On Natural Language Based Computer System." *IBM Journal of Research and Development* 20, no. 4 (July): 314-325.

PETROSKY, ANTHONY R. 1982. "From Story to Essay: Reading and Writing." *College Composition and Communication* 33, no. 1 (February): 19-36.

PFAEHLER, BRENDA. 1985. "Electronic Text: The University of Wisconsin Experience." *T.H.E. Journal* 13, no. 1 (August): 67-70.

PFAEHLER, BRENDA, AND JOHN CAREY. 1985. "Electronic Text: A New Path for Higher Education." *TechTrends* 30, no. 5 (July-August): 12-16.

PICHERT, JAMES W., AND RICHARD C. ANDERSON. 1977. "Taking Different Pespectives on a Story." *Journal of Educational Psychology* 69, no. 4 (August): 309-315.

PIKULSKI, JOHN J. 1985. "Questions and Answers." *The Reading Teacher* 39, no. 1 (October): 127-128.

PIPER, KAREN. 1983. "Word Processing in the Classroom: Using Microcomputer-Delivered Sentence Combining Exercises with Elementary Students." Paper presented at National Educational Computing Conference, Baltimore, June.

PISONI, DAVID, HOWARD C. NUSBAUM, AND BETH G. GREENE. 1985. "Perception of Synthetic Speech Generated by Rule." *Proceedings of the IEEE* 73, no. 11 (November): 1665-1676.

POLANYI, MICHAEL. 1962. *Personal Knowledge: Towards a Post-Critical Philosophy.* London: Routledge and Kegan Paul.

POSNER, MICHAEL I., AND PETER MCLEOD. 1982. "Information Processing Models: In Search of Elementary Operations." In *Annual Review of Psychology,* vol. 33, ed. Mark R. Rosenzweig and Lyman W. Porter, pp. 477-514. Palo Alto, CA: Annual Reviews.

PRESSEY, S. L. 1950. "Development and Appraisal of Devices Providing Immediate Automatic Scoring of Objective Tests and Concomitant Self-Instruction." *Journal of Psychology* 29, no. 2 (April): 417-447.

PRINCE, AMBER T. 1986. "Educational Computing: A Course Outline." In *Preparation of Teachers for Microcomputer Instruction in Reading and Language Arts,* ed. Ernest Balajthy, pp. 71-72. Newark, DE: Special Interest Group on Microcomputers in Reading, International Reading Association.

PROVENZO, EUGENE F. 1986. *Beyond the Gutenberg Galaxy.* New York: Teachers College Press.

QUEST PROMPTLINES. 1986. "QUEST Users—Higher Education: Project VIDALL." *QUEST Promptlines* 1, no. 1: 4-5. [Advertising newsletter published by Allen Communications, 5225 Wiley Post Way, Salt Lake City, UT 84116]

RANKIN, EARL F., AND JOSEPH W. CULHANE. 1970. "One Picture Equals 1,000 Words?" *Reading Improvement* 7, no. 2 (Fall): 37-40.

RANKIN, R. J., AND TERRY TREPPER. 1978. "Retention and Delay of Feedback in a Computer-Assisted Instructional Task." *Journal of Experimental Education* 46, no. 4 (Summer): 67-70.

REINECKER, LYNN. 1985. "Computerized Clinical Simulations." *Computers in Education* 9, no. 1: 57-66.

REINHOLD, FRAN. 1986. "Buying a Hardware Software System." *Electronic Learning* 5, no. 4 (February): 42-47, 67.

REINKING, D. P., M. KLING, AND M. K. HARPER. 1985. "Characteristics of Computer Software in Reading: An Empirical Investigation." Unpublished paper, New Brunswick, NJ: Graduate School of Education, Rutgers University.

REINKING, DAVID. 1984. "Reading Software: Current Limitations and Future Potential." Unpublished paper. New Brunswick, NJ: Rutgers University.

REINKING, DAVID. 1986a. "Computer Applications in Reading: A Course Description." In *Preparation of Teachers for Microcomputer Instruction in Reading and Language Arts*, ed. Ernest Balajthy, pp. 42-48. Newark, DE: Special Interest Group on Microcomputers in Reading, International Reading Association.

REINKING, DAVID. 1986b. "Using Computers to Enhance Readers' Metacognitive Skills." In *Preparation of Teachers for Microcomputer Instruction in Reading and Language Arts*, ed. Ernest Balajthy, pp. 8-13. Newark, DE: Special Interest Group on Microcomputers in Reading, International Reading Association.

REINKING, DAVID. 1987. "What Does the Reading Field Have to Say to Software Publishers?" Paper presented at the International Reading Association, Anaheim, CA, May.

REINKING, DAVID. In press. "Computer-Mediated Text." In *Computers and Reading: Issues for Theory and Practice*, ed. David Reinking. New York: Teachers College Press.

REINKING, DAVID, AND ROBERT SCHREINER. 1985. "The Effects of Computer-Mediated Text on Measures of Reading Comprehension and Reading Behavior." *Reading Research Quarterly* 20, no. 5 (Fall): 536-552.

RESTA, PAUL E., AND PAUL ROSS. 1986. "CAI: A Model for the Comparison and Selection of Integrated Learning Systems in Large School Districts." Paper presented at the American Educational Research Association, San Francisco, April.

RICHARDS, MEREDITH. 1984. *Word Processing Activities for Kids*. Reston, VA: Reston Publishing.

RICHARDSON, RICHARD C., JR., ELIZABETH C. FISK, AND MORRIS A. OKUN. 1985. *Literacy in the Open-Access College*. San Francisco: Jossey-Bass.

RICKARDS, JOHN P. 1976. "Interaction of Position and Conceptual Level of Adjunct Questions on Immediate and Delayed Retention of Text." *Journal of Educational Psychology* 68, no. 2 (April): 210-217.

RICKELMAN, ROBERT J. 1986. "Computers in Reading: A Proposed Course Outline." In *Preparation of Teachers for Microcomputer Instruction in Reading and Language Arts*, ed. Ernest Balajthy, pp. 49-52. Newark, DE: Special Interest Group on Microcomputers in Reading, International Reading Association.

RIEL, MARGARET. 1985. "The Computer Chronicles Newswire: A Functional Learning Environment for Acquiring Literacy Skills." *Journal of Educational Computing Research* 1, no. 3: 317-337.

RIESBECK, CHRISTOPHER K., AND ROGER C. SCHANK. 1976. "Comprehension by Computer: Expectation-Based Analysis of Sentences in Context." Research Report no. 78. New Haven, CT: Computer Science Department, Yale University.

ROBERSON, E. WAYNE, AND DEBRA J. GLOWINSKI. 1986. "Computer Assisted Diagnostic Prescriptive Program in Reading and Mathematics." Washington, DC: US Department of Education. [ERIC Document Reproduction no. ED 272 148]

ROBIN, ARTHUR L. 1978. "The Timing of Feedback in Personalized Instruction." *Journal of Personalized Instruction* 3, no. 2 (March): 81-88.

ROBINSON, E. J., AND W. P. ROBINSON. 1984. "Realizing You Don't Understand: A Further Study." *Journal of Child Psychology and Psychiatry and Allied Disciplines* 25, no. 4 (October): 621-627.

ROBINSON, FRANK P. 1961. *Effective Study*. Rev. ed. New York: Harper & Row.

ROBLYER, M. D. 1985a. "The Greening of Educational Computing: A Proposal for a More Research-Based Approach to Computers in Instruction." *Educational Technology* 15, no. 1 (January): 40-44.

ROBLYER, M. D. 1985b. *Measuring the Impact of Computers in Instruction.* Washington, DC: Association for Educational Data Systems.

ROBLYER, M. D., AND F. J. KING. 1983. "Reasonable Expectations for Computer-Based Instruction in Basic Reading Skills." Paper presented at the Association for Educational Communication and Technology, New Orleans.

RODRIGUEZ, DAWN. 1984. "Sounding the Depths: Computers and Basic Writers." Paper presented at the Conference on College Composition and Communication, New York, March. [ERIC Document Reproduction no. ED 248 505]

ROID, GALE H. 1986. "Computer Technology in Testing." In *The Future of Testing*, ed. Barbara S. Plake and Joseph C. Witt, pp. 29-69. Hillsdale, NJ: Lawrence Erlbaum.

ROPER, W. J. 1977. "Feedback in Computer-Assisted Instruction." *Programmed Learning and Educational Technology* 14, no. 1 (February): 43-49.

ROSE, FRANK. 1984. *Into the Heart of the Mind.* New York: Harper & Row.

ROSEGRANT, TERESA J. 1986. "It Doesn't Sound Right: The Role of Speech Output as a Primary Form of Feedback for Beginning Text Revision." Paper presented at the American Educational Research Association, San Francisco, April.

ROSENSHINE, BARAK V. 1979. "Content, Time, and Direct Instruction." In *Research on Teaching*, ed. Penelope L. Peterson and Herbert J. Walberg, pp. 28-56. Berkeley, CA: McCutchan Publishing.

ROTENBERG, LESLI. 1984. "Booting up for Reading." *Teaching and Computers* 1, no. 8 (May/June): 16-19.

ROTH, JUDITH PARIS. 1986. *Essential Guide to CD-ROM.* Westport, CT: Meckler Publishing.

RUBIN, ANDEE. 1983. "The Computer Confronts the Language Arts: Cans and Shoulds for Education." In *Classroom Computers and Cognitive Science*, ed. Alex Cherry Wilkinson, pp. 201-218. New York: Academic Press.

RUBIN, ANDEE, AND BERTRAM BRUCE. 1984. *Quill: Reading and Writing with a Microcomputer.* Reading Education Report no. 48, Urbana: Center for the Study of Reading, University of Illinois.

RUBINCAM, IRVIN, AND WILLIAM P. OLIVIER. 1985. "An Investigation of Limited Learner-Control Options in a CAI Mathematics Course." *AEDS Journal* 18, no. 4 (Summer): pp. 211-218.

RUDE, ROBERT. 1986. *Teaching Reading Using Microcomputers.* Englewood Cliffs, NJ: Prentice Hall.

RUMELHART, DAVID E. 1977. *Introduction to Human Information Processing.* New York: John Wiley.

RUMELHART, DAVID E., JAMES L. MCCLELLAND, AND THE PDP RESEARCH GROUP. 1986. *Parallel Distributed Processing: Explorations in the Microstructure of Cognition.* Vol. 1: *Foundations.* Cambridge, MA: MIT Press.

RUSSELL, ROBERT JOHN. 1983. "Computers: Altering the Human Image and Society: Edited Transcripts." *Computers & Society* 13, no. 1 (Winter): 2-9.

SAGAN, CARL. 1977. *The Dragons of Eden.* New York: Random House.

SALOMON, GAVRIEL, AND HOWARD GARDNER. 1986. "The Computer as Educator: Lessons from Television Research." *Educational Researcher* 15, no. 1 (January): 13-19.

SAMUELS. S. JAY. 1967. "Attentional Process in Reading: The Effect of Pictures on the Acquisition of Reading Responses." *Journal of Educational Psychology* 58, no. 6 (December): 337-342.

SCANDURA, JOSEPH M. 1981. "Microcomputer Systems for Authoring, Diagnosis, and Instruction in Rule-Based Subject Matter." *Educational Technology* 21, no. 1 (January): 13-19.

SCANLAN, CRAIG L. 1978. "Patient Management Problems: Simulations in Clinical Evaluation." *Respiratory Care* 23, no. 4 (April): 397-406.

SCHAFFER, LEMUEL C., AND MICHAEL J. HANNAFIN. 1986. "The Effects of Progressive Interactivity on Learning from Interactive Video." *ECTJ: Educational Communications and Technology Journal* 34, no. 2 (Summer): 89-96.

SCHANK, ROGER C. 1980. "Language and Memory." *Cognitive Science* 4, no. 3 (July-September): 243-284.

SCHANK, ROGER C. 1982a. *Dynamic Memory: A Theory of Language in People and Computers.* Cambridge: Cambridge University Press.

SCHANK, ROGER C. 1982b. *Reading and Understanding.* Hillsdale, NJ: Lawrence Erlbaum.

SCHANK, ROGER C. 1984. *The Cognitive Computer*. Reading, MA: Addison-Wesley.

SCHANK, ROGER C., AND ROBERT P. ABELSON. 1977. *Scripts, Plans, Goals, and Understanding*. Hillsdale, NJ: Lawrence Erlbaum.

SCHANK, ROGER C., N. GOLDMAN, C. RIEGER, AND C. RIESBECK. 1973. "MARGIE: Memory, Analysis, Response Generation and Inference in English." In *Proceedings of the Second International Joint Conference on Artificial Intelligence*, pp. 255-262. Stanford, CA: Stanford University Press.

SCHANK, ROGER, AND LARRY HUNTER. 1985. "The Quest to Understand Thinking." *Byte* 10, no. 4 (April): 143-158.

SCHIMMEL, BARRY J. 1983. "A Meta-Analysis of Feedback to Learners in Computerized and Programmed Instruction." Paper presented at the American Educational Research Association, Montreal, April.

SCHNECK, MARJORIE A. 1984. "PLATO Implementations and Evaluations: New Behaviors and Objectives for Education." In *Proceedings of EdCompCon 84*, pp. 91-103. Silver Spring, MD: IEEE Computer Society Press.

SCHNEIDERMAN, BEN. 1980. *Software Psychology: Human Factors in Computer and Information Systems*. Cambridge, MA: Winthrop.

SCHOFIELD, HILLARY L. 1981. "Reading Attitude and Achievement: Teacher-Pupil Relations." *Journal of Educational Psychology* 74, no. 2 (November/December): 462-471.

SCHOLASTIC, INC. 1984. *Activity Book for the Bank Street Writer*. Jefferson City, MO: Scholastic, Inc.

SCHOLES, ROBERT, AND NANCY COMLEY. 1981. *The Practice of Writing*. New York: St. Martin's Press.

SCHROCK, SHARON, MARGARET MATTHIAS, CYNDI VENSEL, AND JULIANA ANASTOFF. 1985. "Microcomputers and Peer Interaction: A Naturalistic Study of an Elementary Classroom." Paper presented at American Educational Research Association, Chicago, April.

SCHWARTZ, ED. 1985. *The Educators' Handbook to Interactive Videodisc*. Washington, DC: Association for Educational Communications and Technology.

SCHWARTZ, HELEN J. 1984. "Teaching Writing with Computer Aids." *College English* 46, no. 3 (March): 239-247.

SEARLE, JOHN R. 1984. *Minds, Brains, and Science*. Cambridge, MA: Harvard University Press.

SELFE, CYNTHIA L. 1984. "Software for Hardnoses: CAI for College Composition." *Educational Technology* 14, no. 9 (September): 25-29.

SELTZER, ROBERT A. 1971. "Computer-Assisted Instruction—What It Can and Cannot Do." *American Psychologist* 26, no. 4 (April): 373-377.

SHEINGOLD, KAREN, JAN HAWKINS, AND C. CHAN. 1984. "'I'm the Thinkist, You're the Typist': The Interaction of Technology and the Social Life of Classrooms." Technical Report no. 27. New York: Center for Children and Technology, Bank Street College of Education.

SHEINGOLD, KAREN, JANET H. KANE, AND MARI E. ENDREWEIT. 1983. "Microcomputer Use in Schools: Developing a Research Agenda." *Harvard Educational Review* 53, no. 4 (November): 412-432.

SHIFFRIN, RICHARD M. 1976. "Capacity Limitations in Information Processing, Attention and Memory." In *Handbook of Learning and Cognitive Processes*, vol. 4, ed. W. K. Estes, pp. 177-236. Hillsdale, NJ: Lawrence Erlbaum.

SIMON, JACQUELINE. 1984. "Teaching Writing on a Word Processor: Relationship of Self-Management and Locus of Control." Doctoral dissertation, Boston University. [*Dissertation Abstracts*, 45, no. 3, (1984), p. 729-A. Order no. DA 84-14 703]

SINGER, HARRY. 1978. "Active Comprehension: From Answering to Asking Questions." *The Reading Teacher* 30, no. 8 (May): 901-908.

SINGER, HARRY, AND DAN DONLAN. 1982. "Active Comprehension: Problem-Solving Schema with Question Generation for Comprehension of Complex Short Stories." *Reading Research Quarterly* 15, no. 2: 166-186.

SINGER, HARRY, MARIAM JEAN DREHER, AND MICHAEL KAMIL. 1982. "Computer Literacy." In *Secondary School Reading*, ed. Allen Berger and H. Alan Robinson, pp. 173-192. Urbana, IL: National Council of Teachers of English.

SINGER, HARRY, AND ROBERT B. RUDDELL. 1985. *Theoretical Models and Processes of Reading*, 3rd ed. Newark, DE: International Reading Association.

SLAVIN, ROBERT E. 1984. "Meta-Analysis in Education: How Has It Been Used?" *Educational Researcher* 13, no. 8 (October): 6-15, 24-27.

SLEEMAN, D., AND J. S. BROWN. (EDS.) 1982. *Intelligent Tutoring Systems.* New York: Academic Press.

SLEEMAN, D. H., AND M. J. SMITH. 1981. "Modelling Student's Problem Solving." *Artificial Intelligence* 16, no. 2 (May): 171-188.

SLOAN, DOUGLAS. 1984. "On Raising Critical Questions About the Computer in Education." *Teachers College Record* 85, no. 4 (Summer): 539-548.

SLOAN, DOUGLAS. (ED.) 1985. *The Computer in Education: A Critical Perspective.* New York: Teachers College Press.

SMITH, DAVID E., AND JAN E. CLAYTON. 1984. "Another Look at Frames." In *Rule-Based Expert Systems,* ed. Bruce G. Buchanan and Edward H. Shortliffe, pp. 441-454. Los Altos, CA: William Kaufmann.

SMITH, FRANK. 1975. "The Relation Between Spoken and Written Language." In *Foundations of Language Development: A Multidisciplinary Approach,* vol. 2, ed. Eric H. Lenneberg and Elizabeth Lenneberg, pp. 347-360. New York: Academic Press.

SMITH, FRANK. 1978. *Reading Without Nonsense.* New York: Teachers College Press.

SMITH, LANA, AND DEBBE DAVIS. 1986. "Micro vs. Mini Computer Reading Instruction." Paper presented at the College Reading Association, Knoxville, TN, October.

SOLL, LILA. 1984. "Introduction." In *Microcomputers and Teaching Reading in College,* ed. Clara Alexander, pp. 1-3. New York: Instructional Resource Center, City University of New York.

SOLOWAY, ELLIOT M., BEVERLY WOOLF, ERIC RUBIN, AND PAUL BARTH. 1981. "Meno-II: An Intelligent Tutoring System for Novice Programmers." *Proceedings of the Seventh International Joint Conference in Artificial Intelligence* vol. 2, ed. Ann Drinan, pp. 975-977. Vancouver, BC: International Joint Conference on Artificial Intelligence.

SOUTHWELL, MICHAEL G. 1984. "Computer Assistance for Teaching Writing: A Review of Existing Programs." *Collegiate Microcomputer* 2, no. 3 (August): 193-206.

SPACHE, GEORGE D. 1967. "A Reaction to Computer-Assisted Instruction in Initial Reading: The Stanford Project." *Reading Research Quarterly* 3, no. 1 (Fall): 101-110.

SPROUL, R. C. 1986. "Battle for Our Minds: World Views in Collision." Orlando, FL: Ligonier. [Cassette audiotape]

STASZ, CATHLEEN, AND RICHARD J. SHAVELSON. 1985. "Staff Development for Instructional Uses of Microcomputers." *AEDS Journal* 19, no. 1 (Fall): 1-19.

STAUFFER, RUSSELL G. 1969. *Directing Reading Maturity as a Cognitive Process.* New York; Harper & Row.

STEFFENSEN, MARGARET S., CHITRA JOAG-DEV, AND RICHARD C. ANDERSON. 1979. "A Cross-Cultural Perspective on Reading Comprehension." *Reading Research Quarterly* 15, no. 1: 10-29.

STEGMULLER, WOLFGANG. 1976. *The Structure and Dynamics of Theories.* New York: Springer.

STEINBERG, ESTHER R. 1977. "Review of Student Control in Computer-Assisted Instruction." *Journal of Computer-Based Instruction* 3, no. 3 (February): 84-90.

STEVENS, ALBERT, ALLAN COLLINS, AND SARAH E. GOLDIN. 1982. "Misconceptions in Students' Understanding." In *Intelligent Tutoring Systems,* ed. D. Sleeman and J. S. Brown, pp. 13-24. New York: Academic Press.

STOTSKY, SANDRA L. 1975. "Sentence-Combining as a Curricular Activity: Its Effect on Written Language Development and Reading Comprehension." *Research in the Teaching of English* 9, no. 1 (Spring): 30-71.

STURGES, PERIS T. 1972. "Information Delay and Retention: Effect of Information in Feedback and Tests." *Journal of Educational Psychology* 63, no. 1 (February): 32-43.

SWIGGER, KATHLEEN M. 1985. "Intelligent Tutoring Systems: A Tutorial." *AEDS Monitor* 23, no. 9, 10 (March/April): 6-9.

SWINTON, SPENCER S., MARIANNE AMAREL, AND JUDITH A. MORGAN. 1978. "PLATO Elementary Demonstration Educational Outcome Evaluation. Final Report: Summary and Conclusions." Urbana: Computer-Based Education Laboratory, University of Illinois, [ERIC Document Reproduction no. ED 86 020]

SZOLOVITS, PETER, AND STEPHEN G. PAUKER. 1978. "Categorical and Probabilistic Reasoning in Medical Diagnosis." *Artificial Intelligence* 11, no. 1 (August): 115-144.

TAYLOR, ROBERT. (ED.) 1980. *The Computer in the School: Tutor, Tool, Tutee.* New York: Teachers College Press.

TENNYSON, CAROL L., ROBERT D. TENNYSON, AND WOLFGANG ROTHEN. 1980. "Content Structure and Instructional Control Strategies as Design Variables in Concept Acquisition." *Journal of Educational Psychology* 72, no. 4 (August): 499-505.

TENNYSON, ROBERT D., AND DEAN L. CHRISTENSEN. 1986. "Memory Theory and Design of Intelligent Learning Systems." Paper presented at the American Educational Research Association, San Francisco, April.

TENNYSON, ROBERT D., AND OK-CHOON PARK. 1980. "The Teaching of Concepts: A Review of Instructional Design Research Literature." *Review of Educational Research* 50, no. 1 (Spring): 55-70.

THELEN, HERBER A. 1977. "Profit for the Private Sector." *Phi Delta Kappan* 58, no. 6 (February): 458-459.

THOMPSON, BARBARA J. 1980. "Computers in Reading: A Review of Applications and Implications." *Educational Technology*, 20, no. 8 (August): 38-41.

TIERNEY, ROBERT J., AND P. DAVID PEARSON. 1983. "Toward a Composing Model of Reading." *Language Arts* 60, no. 5 (May): 568-580.

TINKER, MILES ALBERT. 1963. *The Legibility of Print*. Ames: Iowa State University Press.

TROLLOP, STANLEY R., AND GREGORY SALES. 1986. "Readability of Computer-Generated Full-Justified Text." *Human Factors* 28, no. 2 (April): 159-163.

TURING, A. M. 1950. "Computing Machinery and Intelligence." *Mind* 59, no. 236 (October): 433-460.

TURNER, JON A., MATTHIAS JARKE, EDWARD A. STOHR, YANNIS VASSILIOU, AND NORMAN WHITE. 1984. "Using Restricted Natural Language for Data Retrieval: A Plan for Field Evaluation." In *Human Factors and Interactive Computer Systems*, ed. Yannis Vassiliou, pp. 163-190. Norwood, NJ: Ablex.

VAN DIJK, TEUN A. 1979. "Relevance Assignment in Discourse Comprehension." *Discourse Processes* 2, no. 2 (October): 113-126.

VAN DIJK, TEUN A. 1985. "Levels and Dimensions of Discourse Analysis." In *Handbook of Discourse Analysis*, vol. 2: *Dimensions of Discourse*, ed. Teun A. van Dijk, pp. 1-11. London: Academic Press.

VAN MELLE, WILLIAM, EDWARD H. SHORTLIFFE, AND BRUCE G. BUCHANAN. 1984. "EMYCIN: A Knowledge Engineer's Tool for Constructing Rule-Based Expert Systems." In *Rule-Based Expert Systems*, ed. Bruce G. Buchanan and Edward H. Shortliffe, pp. 302-313. Los Altos, CA: William Kaufmann.

VARGAS, JULIE S. 1986. "Instructional Design Flaws in Computer-Assisted Instruction." *Phi Delta Kappa* 67, no. 10 (June): pp. 738-744.

VICINO, FRANK L., AND SUSAN B. HARDWICKE. 1984. "An Evaluation of the Utility of Computerized Adaptive Testing." Paper presented at American Educational Research Association, New Orleans, April.

VINSONHALER, JOHN F., AND RONALD K. BASS. 1972. "A Summary of Ten Major Studies on CAI Drill and Practice." *Educational Technology* 12, no. 7 (July): 29-32.

VINSONHALER, JOHN F., ANNETTE B. WEINSHANK, RUTH M. POLIN, AND CHRISTIAN C. WAGNER. In press. "Computers, Simulated Cases, and the Training of Reading Diagnosticians." In *Computers and Reading: Issues for Theory and Practice*, ed. David Reinking. New York: Teachers College Press.

VINSONHALER, JOHN F., ANNETTE B. WEINSHANK, CHRISTIAN C. WAGNER, AND RUTH M. POLIN. 1983. "Diagnosing Children with Educational Problems: Characteristics of Reading and Learning Disabilities Specialists, and Classroom Teachers." *Reading Research Quarterly* 18, no. 2 (Winter): 134-164.

VOGT, KATHLEEN H. 1984. "Networking: To Do nor Not To Do!!!" In *Microcomputers in Education Conference: Literacy Plus*, ed. Ruth A. Camuse, pp. 425-428. Rockville, MD: Computer Science Press.

VON NEUMANN, JOHN. 1958. *The Computer and the Brain*. New Haven, CT: Yale University Press.

VYGOTSKII, LEV SEMENOVICH. 1978. *Mind in Society*. Cambridge, MA: Harvard University Press.

WAGNER, CHRISTIAN C. 1983. "The Trilog System: Supporting Clinical/Epidemiological Research in Reading." Paper presented at the National Reading Conference, Austin, TX, December.

WAGNER, CHRISTIAN C. 1984. "The TRILOG Computer System: Improving Reading Diagnosis Through Automated Experience Capturing." In *Changing Perspectives on Research in Reading/Language Processing and Instruction*, ed. Jerome A. Niles and Larry A. Harris, pp. 158-161. Rochester, NY: National Reading Conference.

WAGNER, WILLIAM G., WILLIAM M. O'TOOLE, AND RICHARD KAZELSKIS. 1985. "Learning Word Processing Skills with Limited Instruction: An Exploratory Study with College Students." *Educational Technology* 25, no. 2 (February): 26-28.

WALTZ, DAVID L. 1982. "The State of the Art in Natural Language Understanding." In *Strategies for Natural Language Processing*, ed. Wendy G. Lehnert and Martin H. Ringle, pp. 3-32. Hillsdale, NJ: Lawrence Erlbaum.

WALTZ, DAVID L., AND JORDAN B. POLLACK. 1985. "Massively Parallel Parsing: A Strongly Interactive Model of Natural Language Interpretation." *Cognitive Science* 9, no. 1 (January-March): 51-74.

WATERMAN, DONALD A. 1986. *A Guide to Expert Systems*. Reading, MA: Addison-Wesley.

WATERWORTH, J., AND A. LO. 1984. "Example of an Experiment: Evaluating Some Speech Synthesizers for Public Announcements." In *Fundamentals of Human-Computer Interaction*, ed. A. Monk. London: Academic.

WATTS, LYNNE, AND JOHN NISBET. 1974. *Legibility in Children's Books: A Review of Research*. Windsor, England: NFER Publishers.

WEBSTER, JONATHAN. 1984. "Software: Does It Make the Grade?" *Family Computing* 2, no. 9 (September): 57-61.

WEISBERG, RENEE K. 1984. "How Consistent Is the Clinical Diagnosis of Reading Specialists?" *Reading Teacher* 38, no. 2 (November): 205-212.

WEISS, DAVID J. 1979. "Computerized Adaptive Achievement Testing." In *Procedures for Instructional Systems Development*, ed. Harold F. O'Neil, Jr., pp. 129-164. New York: Academic Press.

WEISS, DAVID J. 1985. *New Horizons in Testing: Latent Trait Theory and Computerized Adaptive Testing*. New York: Academic Press.

WEISS, SHOLOM M., CASIMIR A. KULKOWSKI, SAUL AMAREL, AND ARAN SAFIR. 1978. "A Model-Based Method for Computer-Aided Medical Decision-Making." *Artificial Intelligence* 11, no. 1, 2 (August): 145-172.

WEIZENBAUM, JOSEPH. 1967. "Contextual Understanding by Computers." *Communications of the ACM* 10, no. 8 (August): 474-480.

WEIZENBAUM, JOSEPH. 1976. *Computer Power and Human Reason*. San Francisco: W. H. Freeman.

WELSH, JACK R., AND BRENT G. WILSON. 1986. "Expert System Shells: Tools to Aid Human Performance." Paper presented at American Educational Research Association, San Francisco, April.

WEPNER, SHELLEY B., JOAN T. FEELEY, AND DOROTHY S. STRICKLAND. 1987. "Action for Equity: Beginning with Awareness." *The Computing Teacher* 14, no. 6 (March): 54-56.

WEYER, STEVE A. 1982. "The Design of a Dynamic Book for Information Search." *International Journal of Man-Machine Studies* 17, no. 1 (July): 87-107.

WILHITE, STEPHEN C. 1986. "The Relationship of Headings, Questions, and Locus of Control to Multiple-Choice Test Performance." *Journal of Reading Behavior* 18, no. 1: 23-40.

WILSON, BRENT G., AND JACK R. WELSH. 1986. "Small Knowledge-Based Systems in Education and Training: Something New Under the Sun." *Educational Technology* 26, no. 11 (November): 7-13.

WILSON, H. A., AND NORINNE H. FITZGIBBON. 1970. "Practice and Perfection: A Preliminary Analysis of Achievement Data from the CAI Elementary English Program." *Elementary English* 47, no. 4 (April): 576-579.

WINKLER, JOHN D., AND RICHARD J. SHAVELSON. 1982. "'Successful' Use of Computers in Classroom Instruction." Paper presented at the National Educational Computing Conference, Austin, TX, June.

WINOGRAD, TERRY. 1972. *Understanding Natural Language*. New York: Academic Press.

WINOGRAD, TERRY. 1984. "Computer Software for Working with Language." *Scientific American* 251, no. 3 (September): 130-145.

WISELY, FORREST G., AND C. EDWARD STREETER. 1985. "Toward Defining the Function of Visuals Used to Support a Verbal Narrative." *Educational Technology* 25, no. 11 (November): 24-26.

WITHROW, FRANK B. 1985-1986. "The Videodisc: An Educational Challenge." *Journal of Educational Technology Systems* 14, no. 2: 91-99.

WITTROCK, M. C. 1974. "Learning as a Generative Process." *Educational Psychologist* 11, no. 2: 87-95.

WONG, BERNICE Y. L. 1985. "Self-Questioning Instructional Research: A Review." *Review of Educational Research* 55, no. 2 (Summer): 227-268.

WOOLF, BEVERLY, AND DAVID D. McDONALD. 1984. "Context-Discourse Transitions in Tutoring Discourse." *Proceedings of the American Association for Artificial Intelligence.* Los Altos, CA: William Kaufmann.

WOOLF, BEVERLY, AND DAVID D. McDONALD. 1985. "Building a Computer Tutor: Design Issues." *AEDS Monitor* 23, no. 9-10. (March/April): 10-18.

YANKELOVICH, NICOLE, NORMAN MEYROWITZ, AND ANDRIES VAN DAM. 1985. "Reading and Writing the Electronic Book." *Computer* 18, no. 10 (October): 15-30.

YU, VICTOR L., BRUCE G. BUCHANAN, EDWARD H. SHORTLIFFE, SHARON M. WRAITH, RANDALL DAVIS, A. CARLISLE SCOTT, AND STANLEY N. COHEN. 1979a. "Evaluating the Performance of a Computer-Based Consultant." *Computer Programs in Biomedicine* 9, no. 1 (January): 95-102.

YU, VICTOR L., LAWRENCE M. FAGAN, SHARON M. WRAITH, WILLIAM J. CLANCEY, A. CARLISLE SCOTT, JOHN HANNIGAN, ROBERT L. BLUM, BRUCE G. BUCHANAN, AND STANLEY N. COHEN. 1979b. "Antimicrobial Selection by a Computer: A Blinded Evaluation by Infectious Disease Experts." *Journal of the American Medical Association* 242, no. 12 (September 21): 1279-1282.

ZAHARIS JANE A. 1983. "Microcomputers in the Language Arts Classroom: Promises and Pitfalls." *Language Arts* 60, no. 8 (November): 990-998.

ZAJONC, ARTHUR G. 1985. "Computer Pedagogy? Questions Concerning the New Educational Technology." In *The Computer in Education: A Critical Perspective*, ed. Douglas Sloan, pp. 31-39. New York: Teachers College Press.

ZELMAN, SUSAN. 1986. "Motivational Differences in Learning About Computer Hardware and Software: Implications of Students' Ideas About Intelligence." *Educational Technology* 26, no. 8 (August): 15-19.

INDEX